THE COMPLETE LIFE

The Complete Life

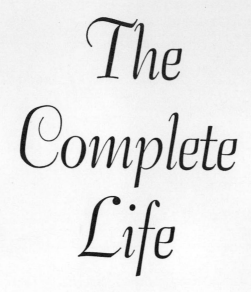

BY JOHN ERSKINE, 1879-1951

Essay Index Reprint Series

BOOKS FOR LIBRARIES PRESS

FREEPORT, NEW YORK

Copyright 1943 by John Erskine

Copyright © renewed 1970 by Helen Erskine

Reprinted 1971 by arrangement with
Julian Messner, a division of Simon & Schuster, Inc.

INTERNATIONAL STANDARD BOOK NUMBER:
0-8369-2153-4

LIBRARY OF CONGRESS CATALOG CARD NUMBER:
74-134073

PRINTED IN THE UNITED STATES OF AMERICA

Contents

THE COMPLETE LIFE

CHAPTER I

A Man's Portion

1.

WE DESIRE HAPPINESS, but more often than not we say we have missed it. We complain of frustration, by which we mean that the good fortune or the talent or the peace of mind which rightfully belongs to us, has been by some external bad luck withheld. We don't blame ourselves. But if we wanted a complete life, we could do something about it.

Do you really want a complete life?

If you don't, stop complaining and read no further. Many of us prefer to drift along comfortably, exercising only a few of our talents, making only an occasional and awkward use of our brain. If you're that kind of person, don't let me detain you.

This book is for those who want their share of life, and who believe that their share is defined only by their natural capacities when developed to the full. Yet even if you look for a complete life, this book may not be quite what you want. It will direct you to no magical formula for happiness or wisdom or wealth. It ventures no guess as to the age at which the ideal life should begin nor when it should end. I offer here merely an outline of such completeness as seems possible for an average life, and suggest steps by which each of us may grow to his proper stature.

I have not tried to conceal my own tastes and inclinations. Life, I believe, should be lived rather than watched from the sidelines. I know that wise and good men have defined culture as a knowledge of the best that has been said and thought in the world, and most earnestly I believe that we cannot afford to ignore ancient achievements and heroisms. But I believe also that merely to sit by the roadside and smile at the enthusiasms or applaud the conduct of others, is an occupation for ghosts.

Let me confess at once the stubbornness with which I hold this point of view. The ancients spoke of the difference between the active and the contemplative life, a contrast which seems to oppose the soldier in battle and the monk in the cell. But the most modern of us almost daily must choose between experience and the sideline attitude toward experience. I believe we should try hard to lead our own life, not only because those who don't lead their own life are in danger of leading someone else's, but also because many influences push us toward the sidelines.

For one thing, we may be afraid of life; in that case we probably say we are modest. Or we may be plain lazy; perhaps we pretend that we are sensitive. Or we may have a sincere talent for philosophy, for criticizing experience, for sorting it out, meditating upon it. Yet unless we've had experience ourselves, our meditations can hardly be free of error. Even if it's our own experience, we shan't always analyze it correctly, but at least we begin with life at first hand, whereas if we try to grow wise by contemplating what our neighbor is doing, we are guessing all along the way.

I'd be sorry if you understood me to say that mere action without thought and forethought is enough for the complete life. Experience is of little value until sublimated by the mind and the spirit. A successful life, even on a low plane, is possible only through the training and use of intelligence. But if this is the end of wisdom, the beginning is a willingness to keep our feet on the ground, to deal with experience as destiny flings it at us, and to be aware of all that is around us. We that have eyes and ears should see and hear, and we should see and hear for ourselves.

2.

Knowledge is more easily acquired if we intend to use it. Every high-brow subject is in the beginning a low-brow subject. Our ignorance is very low-brow, and we might as well start to cure ourselves where our ignorance hurts. Anything studied for use expands outward until it touches many aspects of society and human nature. Whatever is studied merely from the appreciative or contemplative point of view, develops inward. Through mere appreciation and contemplation you are more likely to discover something about yourself than about the rest of the universe.

The outward expansion is more important. Automobiles carry us around, but someone must drive them. If our attitude toward an automobile is the passive one of freight, we may appreciate the comfortable springs and cushions, the speed, the smooth running of the machine, or we may think of our own affairs and not notice the machine nor the landscape we are jammed through. The driver, however, will have his mind on the road and on all the vehicles he meets. He's likely to carry the map in his head. He takes a lively interest in gasoline and oil—in the amount he has, and in the places where he can conveniently get more, in the price of it, and where he can get a bargain. Through his contacts with the attendants at gas stations he is aware of the general social movement of the country, with theories as to why people go riding on certain days or during certain hours. Still closer at home, the person in your house who cooks the food will know more precisely the economic life of the neighborhood than the person who merely eats the food, even though the eater pays the bill.

Study done from the active rather than the contemplative point of view is likely to be complete, even though its quality is not of the highest. There is no subject which is not well within the intellectual powers of most human beings provided we take all the steps, but one theorem incompletely mastered will spoil our grasp of geometry, and in general it may be said that inefficiency is less often caused by total ignorance than by gaps in our knowledge.

In most schools and colleges courses are "passed" and degrees are earned by work which is incomplete. The passing mark is seldom higher than seventy-five per cent. In kindergarten or the first grades, where education is from the active point of view, such an absurdity as this would be obvious. If a child tries to draw a four-wheeled wagon, or to make one, he knows there must be four wheels. On three wheels, or seventy-five per cent, the wagon won't run. The child will continue to respect completeness so long as his point of view is active. If he grows up to be a lawyer, he will make sure that his brief covers all the points in the case, not seventy-five per cent of them. But meanwhile we have permitted him to think that incomplete work is not a disgrace.

If our contemplative studies are incomplete, and if our active moments are untrained and inefficient, as when the amateur types or drives a car, we shall feel the conviction of incompetence, but we'll get used to it; our condition at last won't worry us.

Don't think it frivolous to illustrate our portion of life, our human inheritance, by the typewriter and the motor car. The illustration is just, however it may seem out of scale. You and I invented neither the writing machine nor the automobile; they are, as it were, a potential inheritance; we take possession only if we know how to use them. But human speech is likewise a potential inheritance, and so is history, and so is philosophy. We may be content to recognize their existence and to leave them alone, we may flatter ourselves that we do better by contemplating them appreciatively, or we may make them actively ours, as instruments for living.

In school we studied other languages than our own, but we probably use none of them. We may have translated piecemeal and laboriously a bit of Goethe, or Molière, or Dante, and for the wretched results we may have acquired credits which added up to a diploma, but the day comes when we'd like to speak to a foreigner in his own tongue, and if we can't, we feel like throwing our diploma into the stove.

Here again I must protect myself against misunderstanding. I don't mean that the whole purpose of studying a foreign language is, as Matthew Arnold put it, to fight the battle of life with waiters in foreign hotels. I do mean, however, that if we have studied Dante and yet cannot speak or understand the Italian language when we meet it in the flesh, our acquaintance with Dante must be remote. By all means let the aims of our self-improvement be the highest, but we can't have the roof without a foundation under it, and if we sneer at the foundation as ignoble or insignificant, we aren't for that reason cultured; I'm afraid we're more than a little foolish.

For purposes of speaking and reading, any language can be mastered in a few months—not mastered completely and never mastered so far as accent is concerned, but at least sufficiently for use. An adult can edge into a foreign tongue exactly as infants invade their native speech, or as immigrants learn to talk in a strange country. For correct speech we of course need grammar, but a child or an immigrant begins with the vocabulary. We can imitate the method. We can learn to read and pronounce twenty words a day. We can try them out on anyone who speaks that language. I once heard Henri Bergson say a language must be taken not by siege but by frontal assault.

To master the grammar quickly, we have only to follow the method which men and women in the European Renaissance adopted four hundred years ago, when the gentry spoke Latin and Greek, French, Italian, and Spanish, in some cases German, and even the merchants who traveled to the ends of the earth, if we believe their reports of their own progress in Hakluyt's Voyages, picked up for practical purposes the language of any country they came to, Russian perhaps, or Chinese.

Their method was recommended to me by a great scholar when I was a student at the University. He asked me to report on an Italian book, and I said I knew no Italian. "Learn it, then," said he. "You can learn enough Italian in six weeks." "How?" said I. "Get yourself a small grammar and a dictionary," said he. "Learn the noun forms and the verb forms, the declensions and the conjugations. After that dig the words out of the dictionary. Of course," he added, "you'll get on faster if you use the words on someone who knows the language and will correct your pronunciation."

I won't pretend that the results in my case were brilliant, but the following year I enrolled in a Dante course, where the teacher was apparently satisfied with my work. He was a delightful gentleman, too human to be careful about academic routine, and I rather counted on him not to ask about my previous Italian studies. If he had known I was equipped with but six weeks of self-teaching, he would have been obliged by University regulations to bar me from the course.

3.

It's easy to see how language can be used, but you may hesitate about history. You may doubt whether in your portion of life you expect or wish to be a historian. I would answer that in no portion of life should a man be overcredulous, an easy mark. What we call history is sometimes only a chronicle, a body of information about the past, but it may be more than this. History as an instrument for living is half an art and half a science, and its usefulness is in criticizing the past and all reports of the past. Don't be hasty and say you're no critic, don't say any report by a well-known authority is good enough for you. If we are content to consult a book on our shelves and believe uncritically anything it says, we're as gullible as the small child who accepts the historical statement that little sister came out of a cabbage.

In school the so-called history taught to me was nothing but information, accessible in printed books and rather feebly commented on by the teacher, who having adopted those books for a text wasn't going to contradict them. Of course I could have done the reading by myself, but I suppose the authorities suspected correctly that I was as indolent as other boys, and the teacher was there to see I got the reading done.

But when we're grown up we want to be sure that what the book says has a large proportion of truth in it, and we wish to measure that proportion. The first step is to understand the problem of recapturing the past. Do you realize how hard it is to record accurately even the present? Make this experiment: Write an account, at least two pages in length, of some important thing that happened to you not earlier than yesterday. Put the record away for a month. Before you look at it again, try to write out the same statement you made before. You'll find you have two accounts which don't quite correspond, and you'll probably be baffled to say which version is truer. The first was written immediately after the event while it was still fresh in your memory, but on the other hand you have meanwhile picked up additional information about it. Are you not nearer the truth about the past the further you get away from it? There's no clear answer. With time the interpretation of the past becomes richer, but the memory of what we are interpreting becomes dimmer.

To make the best use of any historical book, we must distinguish between an account made at the time by someone involved and an account made later or at a distance by someone who came at his facts indirectly. Or we may find conflicting testimony from the same writer, even from one active in the original event. The account which Thomas Jefferson in his earlier years gave of Patrick Henry is quite different from the account he gave when he was old. Which was nearer the truth?

We should ask how the historian came at his facts. If he doesn't tell us his sources, he's a very careless historian indeed. If he does tell, we can go over the same ground, check him up and see whether we agree with his conclusions. We needn't be scared off by the amount of reading this will involve. Most history is based on slimmer material than we suppose.

4.

Just as history may be presented as a mere record of dates and events, so philosophy is often written and willingly accepted as a compendium of other men's ideas. We study Plato to learn what Plato thought, and later philosophers from Aristotle to Bergson to see what ideas they had and how they differed from each other. This, however, is not philosophy but history, and a poor kind of history at that. To know that Plato had a certain idea and stated it in a certain dialogue, the text of which has been edited by a certain scholar, is the same thing as to know that Columbus had a new geographical theory, made a long voyage to verify it, and bumped into an island off the western mainland. The record of ideas or actions may be valued as information, but to store our mind with facts is not the same thing as understanding history, and certainly it is not the same thing as knowing philosophy. I insist on the active point of view. Knowing philosophy is like knowing cooking. It is not simply the ability to recognize a stove when you see it; it's the ability to cook. Philosophy is the art of thinking. If from Plato we learn how to think, we have something more valuable than a memory of his ideas. We may have ideas of our own.

Nowadays the study of logic has been largely abandoned and true philosophy, the art of thinking, is rarely taught. The scientist, of course, preserves for us the mathematical art of thinking, and the lawyer follows his judicial logic, which compromises, as the mathematician's logic does not, with other kinds of experience. In the Middle Ages the theologians carried the art of thinking further than any other group of men, unless it was the small cluster of immortals in ancient Athens, but theology of any kind is now somewhat neglected, and the Church is not primarily concerned with teaching mankind to think. Unless we are a lawyer or a scientist we develop our heart and neglect our mind. Our heart is considered fully developed when our emotions are so strong that intellectual processes are for us impossible.

Yet the mind remains part of our inheritance. We cannot safely take the active attitude toward life unless we know how to think. The world at present suffers from programs which cannot be justified philosophically, and which are supported by large groups of people in whom hysterical emotions have been cultivated and the mind atrophied. Dictators are not the only examples. Many private persons like you and me are in our own limited way quite as bad. Even if the dictators obligingly withdrew and left us all in peace, we should not for that reason become at once rational creatures. Thinking is an active exercise, an art. We can learn the technique of it quite as easily as the technique of swimming or driving a car, but only on the same condition, that we learn by practice.

5.

I have suggested that we prepare ourselves for our portion of life by recognizing the difference between action and contemplation, and by taking first the active attitude. It may aid us before we consider a more specific program to make some further definitions, this time distinguishing not so much between possible attitudes as between different kinds of subject matter.

Man may acquire opinions, or information, or knowledge. Opinions of some sort are inevitable; information, whether correct or not, comes easily; knowledge seems to be unnatural and is achieved with pain. Yet knowledge is what we need. Information is wealth of a sort, an inferior but plentiful currency, a baser metal which may be transmuted into knowledge. It is our business to transmute it, not to collect it. It almost collects itself. No scholar ever collects so much of it, or so fast, as the village gossip. Opinion is that exercise of the human will which helps us to make a decision without information. The totally ignorant are full of opinion.

I must be careful not to give opinion too black a name. It is a proper instrument for dealing with the future. In spite of all that experience or science may prophesy, about the future we have no knowledge and no information—only opinion, which in its earnest and noble aspects we call faith. Opinion about the future should be encouraged, if we would enlist our will to make the future better than the present, and strengthen our trust in that part of experience which is as yet unseen.

Opinion becomes objectionable, however, when we rely upon it to deal with the present, where information is available. If we are asked about the state of the world five years from now, we express our hopes and fears, and as Thomas Hobbes said, the best guesser is the best prophet. But if we are asked what is the population of this or that city, we need not guess, our opinion is not welcome; the information is within reach.

Information rests more closely on knowledge than opinion does, but still it is knowledge at second hand. If I give you the information that our public library is at 42nd Street and Fifth Avenue, and if you are willing to believe me, you will acquire a kind of knowledge, but you could have a better kind by looking up the building yourself.

That is why we like to travel. Far-off things must be taken on hearsay, daily news must be accepted for what it seems worth, our imagination must eke out the very small amount of solid knowledge which we can prove or vouch for. But the obligation to increase that knowledge cannot be shirked. To be content with hearsay when we could know for ourselves, is as bad as to cling to mere opinion when we could have the benefit of information.

If opinion is valid for the future and if the present is full of information, perhaps you expect me to say next that knowledge is our mastery of the past. I'd rather repeat Bacon's remark, that knowledge is power. Our athletic sports are perhaps the best public demonstration we make of the acquisition of knowledge. In sports and to a large measure in science the difference is clear between looking on and doing the thing ourselves. In science and in athletics study ends in performance. By way of contrast the so-called cultural subjects, as usually taught, end in information and opinion.

When I urge you to acquire the knowledge which is power, I contradict our traditional idea of culture. Athletics and science should be practical, say our institutions, but to be cultural a subject shouldn't be usable. If a student will listen to lectures on Beethoven, if he will put down in his notes what we tell him about the opinions he should have of Beethoven's music in case he should hear it, and if from mechanical reproductions of enough of that music he will learn to hang these predigested opinions on the pieces to which they belong, we'll give him credit toward his degree. But if he wants to play a Beethoven sonata, we explain that practical music is an outside activity, and doesn't count toward a degree.

Many young people wish to dance, to paint, to model, to work in wood or in iron. In the arts and crafts they wish knowledge. More often than not they don't get it from us. We'll give them lectures on the history of the esthetics of dancing—ourselves not being able to dance a step—but we won't have them practicing the art on academic premises. I am not so stupid as to suggest that our schools should devote themselves to the training of professional artists, but I do believe that a man's portion should include knowledge of all subjects, arts as well as sciences, and that our knowledge should really be knowledge, not information or opinion.

I had my introduction to scholarship from Thomas Randolph Price, now long since gone to his rest, a superb gentleman, vastly learned. When I was an undergraduate at Columbia I asked permission to take his course in Middle English. It seemed honest to confess that I knew no Anglo-Saxon. "Well," said Professor Price, "in the Middle English period a number of children were born and learned to talk without Anglo-Saxon."

When the class met he told us we were to do the work. He

would not lecture. Each one of us was assigned a problem to report on. He asked me to report on all the subjunctive forms on the first ten pages of our text.

I waited that day till the class was gone, and asked him for the title of some Middle English Grammar which would show me how to recognize a subjunctive when I saw one. "But that's the whole point!" he exclaimed. "How do you think the man got on who compiled the first Grammar?"

6.

I've probably made it clear enough that I would ask for my portion in life the equipment to live actively. As actors rather than onlookers we are entitled to the use of at least one language besides our own, to a method for sound thinking, to an acquaintance with the history of our country and of our profession or trade, and to a working knowledge of those sciences which touch us every day. This would be only the beginning, and some of the things to which I attach the greatest importance are not yet mentioned, but to know one language which is not our own, and the history of our environment, and the techniques of control in the humblest matters which concern us, is the practical equipment to start with.

Many people will say that to know our own language is enough. They remind us that the unforgotten Greeks who left us extraordinary dramas, poems, histories, and philosophies, the noblest achievements in art, and the bases of all the sciences, were in most cases entirely ignorant of any tongue but the one they were born to. They will remind us of cases in our own day where men living close to the soil have produced very good literature indeed, without any special language training.

All this is true as a record of the past, but I doubt if it provides guidance for our day. We could do very well without other languages if no other language affected our life or influenced our thought. We may leave it to those who love argument to decide whether it was an advantage or a disadvantage to the Greeks to care little about other places and other times than their own. They built walls around their city and looked upon the outsiders as barbarians. They were poor in what we call the historical sense.

The past survived with them in religion, in poetry, in works of art, which were closely associated with religion. They had no Chaucer to read in an early and already strange form of their own tongue, no Vergil, nothing which had the relation to them which Homer, Plato, and Aristotle have to us. Whether or not it is to our advantage, the fact cannot now be ignored that we remember books and consult them after hundreds of years, nor the further fact that any language after five hundred years is changed beyond easy recognition, and that therefore an old book long survives only through some degree of translation.

One other and even more important fact is inescapable, that civilization can no longer be walled in and confined to a population of a few thousand, that the business of our world is carried on by the world as a whole, sometimes quarreling, sometimes cooperating, but always in close contact. We live in the Tower of Babel. We cannot hope to master all the tongues we hear, but by learning one language in addition to our own we approach an understanding of what language is in general, what thought is, no matter in what tongue it is expressed; what human nature is, no matter how differently it speaks.

Let me illustrate by a famous verse in the Bible. As a child, encouraged to memorize the Beatitudes, I thought I knew what was meant by saying, "Blessed are the meek, for they shall inherit the earth." I thought the doctrine was that mild and inoffensive people, meek as lambs, would ultimately be rewarded for their gentleness. Later I heard the usual gibes at this interpretation. The meek might indeed inherit the earth, but perhaps only when everybody else was tired of it. As I grew older I lost my enthusiasm for meekness, or at least I lost confidence in the promise that it would be rewarded. It was a revelation and a relief to come on the French translation of the New Testament, and to find the beatitude rendered, *Heureux les débonnaires,* "Blessed are the debonair." The debonair are gentle and polite and so are the meek, but there's an immense difference; the lamb-like kind of meekness is passive, long-suffering; the gentleness which is debonair is active, able to take possession of the earth through a highly developed technique of courtesy, of diplomatic good manners.

I rushed to the Greek dictionary to see which translation is right. They both are. The Greek word in the text could be applied to a lamb in the pasture or to Chesterfield in the House of Lords. But the Greek word is a translation of the speech Jesus used. How, then, do we know what he actually said?

I believe we do know, but not from sentences which may be quoted separately. When we understand, through acquaintance with at least two languages, the problem of human expression, we see that the Bible is to be found not exclusively in Hebrew, Greek, Latin, or any modern tongue, but in all of them together. We get a clear idea of the personality of Jesus and the essentials of his doctrine. We imagine what his earliest followers believed of him, even though their reports contradict each other in certain details. There is a reality in every great book which persists independently of the tongue into which it is translated, and even the original text is in a sense a translation. "A perfect user of words," as Walt Whitman said, "uses things."

It is not by accident that the books which have the widest appeal contain experiences, ideas, images, which are easy to recognize no matter in what tongue they are recorded. "Blessed are the meek" is perplexing because we are not agreed as to the definition of meekness, but nobody has trouble with "The sower went forth to sow." Wheat and bread are more widely distributed in the world than meekness, however defined.

7.

To know how to think, the study of formal logic is not necessary, though it would be helpful. Many a man and woman has thought clearly without other instruction than experience. Any skill in thinking which I can claim, probably came to me from the study of geometry. But the logic of geometry is not essentially different from the continuity which we demand of a book, and still more, of a play. Compared with life, geometry offers a field for disembodied logic, logic uninfluenced by emotion, undeflected by likes and dislikes, but whether we study logic in geometry or in everyday experience, the principles are the same. Ernest Dimnet a few years ago discussed them at length in a charming and popular book, *The Art of Thinking*.

The essential rule is to stick to your subject—and include all of the subject. The first part of the rule is easier to follow than the second. When a child pleads for candy or soda water, skill is usually displayed in sticking to the subject, but rarely or never are all sides of the subject included. We begin to be accomplished thinkers when we know what to do with the bothersome contradictions, with the exceptions to a true statement which would be only half true if the exceptions were left out.

Our thoughts rise from our emotions, and our emotions are sometimes precipitated by our sensations. A sensation is merely a physical experience which we may like or dislike in any degree. Our likes and dislikes are decided first in an emotion, which differs from mere sensation precisely in this, that it pronounces judgment. But we can be emotional without thought. By thought we analyze our emotions and explain them to ourselves or to others. St. Thomas Aquinas developed his marvelous logical skill, not to convert men to Christian doctrine, but to explain that doctrine rationally to those who already believed it emotionally. Sound thinking, as has often been said, begins in the heart.

We remember today at least one rule in the medieval art of thinking; divide each question into all its parts, and then define the terms in each separate part. When the thinker has accomplished this, his work is almost finished. Most human debates are a confusion of knowledge, information, and opinion. It's a great advantage to separate the three elements, to give knowledge the respect which is its due, and to leave opinion alone, since mere opinion is beyond rational persuasion. If you and I argue about war and I tell you that the defense of other countries, though an obligation, is not our first obligation, and that we haven't enough battleships anyway, you, if you are typical of the race, will perhaps answer that I am defeatist, unpatriotic, ignoble. In that exchange neither of us scores very high as a thinker. Just how many battleships we have is a matter of ascertainable fact, and whether the number is sufficient is a question for expert knowledge, but our interest in another country is emotion or opinion. On the other hand, for you to dismiss me as defeatist, as unpatriotic, as ignoble, means that though my opinions seem to you worthless, you allow them to distract you from the truly debatable matters which I, with no great credit to myself, at least touched on.

8.

The advantage of knowing the history of our own country is obvious, so long as history is for us more than information, a memorizing of dates and events. What is told us when we are young about the progress of the American Revolution is useful so far as it goes, but life in America during that long war was as full and complicated as at any other time. The issues of the conflict were not so clear as the text books make them, the opposition of the two sides not so absolute. From year to troubled year Colonists and Loyalists lived in certain conditions, ate certain kinds of food, cooked in certain ways, built houses in a certain style, made themselves furniture of a certain design, wore clothes of a certain cut. There was as always the drama of friendship and animosity between individuals, families, and neighborhoods, there were parents kind or unkind, sons ambitious or otherwise, industrious or lazy. Our history is the whole picture, not frozen at any one moment, but as it changed from decade to decade. The modern reader, alert to social and economic problems, is often offended by the silence of old books or old letters about the problems of the working class or of social betterment. A growing alertness to such questions is itself a historical fact of importance, perhaps of more importance as a sign of human progress than most of the dates and incidents which can be located and remembered more readily.

To learn the history, therefore, even of our own country we need to fill in the gaps in the mere chronicle. We do so by continued and perhaps endless reading. We have the rest of our lives before us, and each year ought to see us much wiser and better read than the year before. We shall read biographies, volumes of letters, or more formal histories as they appear and come within our reach. Once having started correctly to explore this field, we shall find it easy to put any additional information in the niche where it belongs.

What is the right start for the study of history? A teacher of mine long ago suggested the simple method which in one form

or another is followed by all scholars. He said we could begin
with any one event or any one man, and it made little difference,
except for the advantage of starting with something we were
interested in, so that curiosity might be our motive rather than
a sense of duty. Suppose we wish to know about the battle of
Bunker Hill. First we look up Bunker Hill in the most available
encyclopedia, all the better if it's a fairly compact encyclopedia
with short articles. We learn where Bunker Hill is, who fought
in the battle which is called by its name, the date of the battle,
how it has come about that Bunker Hill gets the fame though
the actual fighting was done on Breed's Hill near by. At the end
of the article the encyclopedia lists the books and documents on
which the account is based. We then read those authorities so
far as they are available, and finding references to still more books
or documents, we pursue our reading in all directions until we
reach the original sources. In the process we learn most of American history before the famous battle, and a good deal after it.

This program may seem staggering. Only a professional scholar,
you may say, could look forward to so much study. As a matter
of fact, however, we all do an enormous amount of reading without purpose or plan. We read without intending to remember.
We read for entertainment of the most ephemeral kind, merely
to kill time. A little of that time might as well be left unkilled
and devoted to our improvement, which will not be completed
in a year, nor even in three or four.

Some of the best-equipped men I know got their education by
exploring the history and the social relations of the craft or profession they follow. Why should curiosity of this kind be so rare?
The grocery store in a modern town has in it, at least by implication, as much romance and as wide a sweep for the mind as
the public library. When we buy our coffee and tea, our sugar,
salt, and pepper, our rice and our spices, perhaps we don't stop
to speculate in what part of the world these familiar luxuries
are produced, by what human beings under what conditions, nor
by what complicated system of exchange they are brought to our
table. Perhaps we don't even know by what procedure they arrive
on the grocery counter. The people who sell these things can
probably answer a few of these questions, but perhaps they have

not asked about the human beings far away who produce the goods and start them toward the consumer. Perhaps the grocer has never wondered how food is supplied to the ultimate purchaser in other countries, or how it was supplied in other times. When did Europeans first drink tea? When did they first use coffee? At what date was sugar introduced? When did it become a commodity within reach of the common purse? And how did people sweeten their food before they had sugar? The grocer who knew the answers to all the questions which his store suggests would not only be extremely well educated, he would also realize that he inherits an ancient tradition and is himself as it were a link in one of the most important of social chains.

The sciences, as they touch our daily life, I shall speak of at length in later pages, but here I conclude this preliminary sketch of the active life, the portion of us all, by reminding you that even men and women who never think of themselves as scientists, nevertheless drive automobiles, use typewriters, occasionally do emergency carpentering or plumbing, plant vegetables or flowers, cook, use electric light, and speak over the telephone. The conveniences at our disposal should be intelligently used. You may boast that though you know little about gas engines or electricity, you can drive a car. I am not so sure about that car-driving. Until you learn a thing or two about the motor and the battery—which is which, for example—I'd rather not be your passenger.

CHAPTER II

Reading and Writing

1.

WHY WE SHOULD read at all, is a question worth asking. We want life, to be sure, as complete a life as possible, but to come at experience through a book is to approach life indirectly, and few of us, if we could get at the real thing, would stop over second-hand accounts of it. Isn't it true, we ask ourselves, that certain famous men, like Napoleon, going straight to the source, have talked to the authors instead of consulting their pages?

It is true. In the United States today, moreover, we like to hear lectures by popular writers and afterwards to read their works if, decidedly if, they prove interesting in person. I suspect that this instinct of ours has soundness in it, though it asks much of an author, and may lead us to a disappointment, since not every writer is a good speaker, and some spellbinders are poor writers.

But a book has its place even in the most impatient zest for living. To take possession of our share of life we must first know what we are, and though there is a promise that in another world we shall see ourselves face to face, at present the vision is possible only in a mirror. There's little sense in refusing to look in the glass, and none at all in looking instead at the man who manufactured it. A book is a mirror. Conversing with an author we may indeed learn something of his character, his mind, or his heart, but we read his book to study our own.

We usually say that we read either for a serious purpose or for pleasure, but perhaps we fail to ask what gives us pleasure, or where the pleasure differs from the serious purpose. Perhaps we haven't observed that our reading satisfies always one of two cravings—for information, to acquire new experience, or for recognition, to enjoy again what is already ours.

To read for information, we need neither instruction nor other inducement beyond natural curiosity. If we wish to catch a train, the timetable will tell us when it leaves. If we would locate a city or verify a date, the geography or the history book are within reach. About questions more urgent, involving peril or death, we are supplied by nature with curiosity of a deeper sort. Few of us need preliminary coaching before we can fix our attention on a murder case or a detective story.

But only with difficulty can we be persuaded to look in the mirror and recognize what we see there. We are not interested in ourselves, nor in any aspect of normal life. Here our curiosity gives out. Because an experience is ours, we think we already know it. Reading for recognition, for clearer sight of our too familiar selves and for a definition of our particular share of life, presents itself too often not as a pleasure but as a task, undertaken if at all from a sense of duty.

To master the art of reading we must recover our childhood delight in the mirror. When we were at the nursery stage we enjoyed the literature of recognition, the literature which enables us to repeat experience and to study it anew. We liked to have our parents hand out as fiction what we could identify as a piece of ourselves. "Once upon a time there was a very peculiar child who loved candy but didn't care for oatmeal." We recognized ourselves, even if the mirror were turned upside down. "Once there was a nice child who ate candy every day in order to humor the parents, but who really preferred spinach." At a later age, if we were boys, having played baseball all afternoon we probably read a baseball story in the evening, filling out in imagination the experience of which in time and space we couldn't have enough. Still later we read love stories, probably because we had become aware of girls, perhaps because we noticed one girl, and ancient poets, to our amazement, had accurately portrayed her.

When grown people neglect books, their excuse sometimes is that they find life all-absorbing. They deceive themselves. If their interest in life were really strong, they would want more of it than our brief days yield, they would feed on all convincing reminders of it, they would study it from all sides, they would gladly see it through the eyes of others. If a traveler visits our town and writes an account of it, his intention may be to enlighten the folks in the place he came from, but we shall be his best audience, it is to us that he will say most. We may disagree with his verdicts, but right or wrong they will enable us to see ourselves in a new light. If a poet imagines a hero or heroine with whom we can identify ourselves, or in whom we at least recognize the kind of person we'd like to be, the fortunes of our double, as they unfold, will challenge us, or encourage, or warn. Or we may think the poet doesn't understand the character. But whatever he says will hold our attention.

In all cases a book is to be measured, not by other books but by what we know of life, not by its author's private experience but by our own. This I think is the first principle of sound criticism. Reading is important because it helps us to more life; if it helped us only to more books, we could do without it. To know books without finding or even looking for the vital experience which produced them, is to be a pedant. Why retire crablike into the past, as is the sad habit of misguided dust-connoisseurs, as though life couldn't be studied here and now? The meaning of life is contemporary with life. Who really lives must find the meaning quickly before the moment is gone, instead of waiting to dig it up afterwards.

The habit of reading is important. What impressed us deeply at one time may have become less vital—or more so. We look in the mirror, from day to day, to observe the changes which have taken place, not in the mirror but in life. Those changes in life will affect our opinion of the mirror.

If you have read Wordsworth's "Lines composed a few miles above Tintern Abbey," you recall how the poet goes back to nature exactly as I am advising a habitual return to books. After five years, he says, he is revisiting a famous landscape, and much as he loves the scene spread before his eyes, he is more interested in the change which the interval of time has made in himself.

The landscape is the same, but looking in the mirror he sees a new reflection.

The habit of reading and rereading is important, not only for our enjoyment of imaginative literature but for our study of history. Perhaps the principle can be explained most easily in the field of recorded fact—or what we hope is fact. If we allow life to revise our opinion of books, some books will remain as highly esteemed as ever, or may grow in value, while others will drop away. Those which remain least changed, evidently reflect what is most permanent in experience. Those that seem true only for a brief moment, were mirrors only of a passing phase. If we could, we'd like to read the books which will last longest.

But if we recognize the changing values of books, we must admit also that an author may be very great indeed even though one of his works is out of date, just as a character in history may remain admirable even though his actions were wiser in his own day than they seem in ours. We can be flexible enough to admire the author and the historical figure without endorsing everything they wrote or did.

For example, George Washington located the capital of the United States where it is now. The northern states would have been content with New York, but the southerners in those days of slow travel found it too remote, and not even Philadelphia was satisfactory. In July, 1790, Congress passed what is known as the Residence bill, authorizing the President to choose ten square miles for the site of a federal town in the region of the Potomac, the Potomac being approximately in the center of the thirteen original states.

Of course the capital is now badly off-center. Even during the Civil War, Walt Whitman, much as he loved the city, could write in his notes that perhaps Washington would some day be moved to Illinois or Indiana. His prophecy isn't likely to come true, nor is the central location a matter of such importance since the airplane has speeded up travel, but in the second half of the nineteenth century Congressmen from the West and Middle West grumbled about the advantage possessed by those from the Atlantic states. The western agricultural states complained that the federal government was far from them and near to Wall Street. Even at the present moment the criticism can be heard that our leaders are too close to Europe, too remote from the heart of the country.

By all this, however, Washington's greatness as a man is not lessened any more than Homer's greatness in poetry is modified by his failure to foresee some of our modern improvements. On first reading *The Iliad* we may be disturbed to find there no concern for modern ideals of liberty, or social justice, or sanitation, or public hygiene. Even Shakespeare is silent on much that stirs our emotions today. If these two men deliberately shut their eyes to wrongs they were well aware of, we should have a right to be disappointed, but to call them less great because they said nothing about public health or social justice is as absurd as to blame them for not having mentioned electricity or gasoline. The part of their work which even after centuries still mirrors us, is the part which gives them importance.

I don't blame early American historians for having misled me into the faith that our country was explored and settled only by the English. Doubtless the American historians got that impression from English historians, and doubtless both were sincere, knowing no better. The English settlers monopolized attention along the Atlantic seaboard, particularly in Virginia and Massachusetts. Few of us when we were in school thought to ask what was happening in the rest of the continent, in the North or the South. My own youthful conviction, I must confess, was that our West was entirely given over to the Indians, that Central America was occupied by volcanoes and Aztecs, and that South America grouped itself around the Amazon River on the banks of which naked Indians waved a salute to passing steamboats. I got this last impression from an imaginative woodcut in an old book of travels in my father's library. What the steamboat was doing down there, the picture didn't explain. When I first traveled as far west as Colorado, I learned vividly along the way the part the French played in the discovery and development of the lands along the Mississippi, and I realized from the place names of Colorado and adjacent states how active the Spanish explorers must have been in that region. If our school histories are not already rewritten, they soon will be, and our children's children, while giving just admiration to the English colonists, will know also what our country from the very first owed to the Spanish and the French, to the Dutch and the Swedes, to the Italians and the Portuguese.

And I hope they will be taught the truth which I am stressing here, that all books, whether historical or imaginative, are mirrors, that we who look into them constantly change, yet that even with the alteration in our features which time insists on making, there is a constant remainder by which we recognize ourselves.

2.

If I could select the authors for you to begin with, I'd choose Plutarch and Montaigne. Since they are so famous, you may be reluctant to look into them. It is therefore wise to tell you at once that in a sense their reputation is not primarily literary. They are valued for their substance rather than for their manner, and they impress us even in translations which reproduce little of their style. From their own time to our day both have been read by an extraordinary number of men in practical affairs, and between them they have supplied our modern world with a fantastically large proportion of its historical knowledge and its philosophical ideas.

Perhaps Plutarch owes his peculiar appeal, it has been suggested, to the country and the times in which he lived. He was born at Chaeroneia in northern Boeotia about 50 A.D. He was always prosperous, he had an excellent education, and though he was by temperament a philosopher, he was far from a dreamer. During his long life he took part in local politics, he served his native land on political missions and in posts of honor under the Roman Governor, and he traveled widely in Asia Minor, in Egypt, and in Italy. His visits to Rome and perhaps these other voyages were occasioned by public duty. Whenever he was free to do so he returned to his study in his quiet home at Chaeroneia. There in the latter part of his life, out of full experience and wide reading, he wrote his *Parallel Lives of Greeks and Romans*.

These biographies, some fifty in all, cover the history of the two nations up to his day. They are masterpieces of dramatic portraiture, the admiration and the envy of all later writers, and a source book for later imitators. They were translated gorgeously into French by Jacques Amyot in 1559, and with almost equal success into English by Sir Thomas North in 1579, North being more familiar with Amyot's French text than with the original Greek. From North, Shakespeare got the material which went into his *Julius Caesar, Coriolanus,* and *Antony and Cleopatra.* When you read Plutarch you'll be surprised at the amount he lifted from Shakespeare!

But though the *Parallel Lives* were written by a philosopher in leisurely retirement, their most striking trait is that they focus always on the active side of life. This explains their appeal to all sorts of readers, and this is the lucky slant which Plutarch received from the pressure of his time. After Greece succumbed to the Roman power and was incorporated in the Empire, she naturally set great value on those intellectual and artistic accomplishments in which the Romans could not rival her. Rome was the center of the political, economic, and military world, but Athens remained the center of culture, the city of the mind. It became the tendency among the Greeks not only to make this point, but to exaggerate it by minimizing their own talents for practical affairs. They neglected the memory of Pericles, of Themistocles, of Timoleon. Plutarch restored the balance. In his *Parallel Lives* he included none of the Greek philosophers, poets, or sculptors, and where he compares orators, as in the case of Demosthenes and Cicero, he offers no estimate of their style nor of their speeches as art; he compares them as practical statesmen.

In his life of Demosthenes he gives another reason for this neglect of the orations as such. He had, he says, but an indifferent command of the Latin tongue, since his visits to Rome had been on business, with no opportunity for literary study. The passage in which he makes this confession is a famous sample of his common sense and of his genius for portraiture—in this case, for self-portraiture.

"If any man undertake to write a history that has to be collected from materials gathered by observation and the reading of works not easy to be got in all places, nor written always in his own language, but many of them foreign and dispersed in other hands, for him, undoubtedly, it is in the first place and above all things most necessary to reside in some city of good note, addicted to liberal arts, and populous; where he may have plenty of all sorts of books, and upon inquiry may hear and inform himself of such particulars as, having escaped the pens of writers, are more faithfully preserved in the memories of men, lest his work be deficient in many things, even those which it can least dispense with.

"But for me, I live in a little town, where I am willing to continue, lest it should grow less; and having had no leisure, while I was in Rome and other parts of Italy, to exercise myself in the Roman language, on account of public business and of those who came to be instructed by me in philosophy, it was very late, and in the decline of my age, before I applied myself to the reading of Latin authors. Upon which that which happened to me may seem strange, though it be true; for it was not so much by the knowledge of words that I came to the understanding of things, as by my experience of things I was enabled to follow the meaning of words. But to appreciate the graceful and ready pronunciation of the Roman tongue, to understand the various figures and connection of words, and such other ornaments, in which the beauty of speaking consists, is, I doubt not, an admirable and delightful accomplishment; but it requires a degree of practice and study which is not easy, and will better suit those who have more leisure, and time enough yet before them for the occupation.

"And so in this fifth book of my *Parallel Lives,* in giving an account of Demosthenes and Cicero, my comparison of their natural dispositions and their characters will be formed upon their actions and their lives as statesmen, and I shall not pretend to criticize their orations one against the other, to show which was the more charming or the more powerful speaker."

Notice the sentence in which Plutarch says it was not so much by the knowledge of words that he came to the understanding of things as by the experience of things that he was able to follow the meaning of words. If you've studied a foreign language you will agree with him. Going still further, we may add that a foreign language is not completely mastered until we have lived in the country and know the life which finds expression in the words.

The study of language, like the study of literature, begins with the study of life.

Men of different times have found in Plutarch's work a mirror of contemporary problems and experiences. I am advising you to read one of the most up-to-date of writers. To every country the threat of war comes, sooner or later, and with the threat come conflicting kinds of advice, as familiar to Plutarch as to us. One patriot believes that if there must be a war, it is best to get into it quickly; another prefers to stay out as long as possible. One believes in preparedness; another fears that a strong armament may provoke attack. One believes in a federation with the neighbors; another, seeing the advantage of a unified command, would rather go it alone. A long and hard war suggests the advantage of a federation of some kind to preserve peace, a federation to which all the members contribute equally; but in such a partnership not all the partners will perhaps show an equal readiness to assume their share of the burden. Would you expect from Plutarch a comment on all this confused and conflicting advice? In the life of Cimon he tells us of an association of peoples long ago, and how one small city, Athens, schemed successfully to control the others.

"The allies of the Athenians began now to be weary of war and military service, willing to have repose, and to look after their husbandry and traffic. For they saw their enemies driven out of the country, and did not fear any new vexations from them. They still paid the tax they were assessed at, but did not send men and galleys, as they had done before. This the other Athenian generals wished to constrain them to, and by judicial proceedings against defaulters, and penalties which they inflicted on them, made the government uneasy, and even odious. But Cimon practised a contrary method; he forced no man to go that was not willing, but of those that desired to be excused from service he took money and vessels unmanned, and let them yield to the temptation of staying at home, to attend to their private business. Thus they lost their military habits and luxury, and their own folly quickly changed them into unwarlike husbandmen and traders; while Cimon, continually embarking large numbers of Athenians on board his galleys, thoroughly disciplined them in his expeditions, and ere long made them the lords of their own paymasters. The allies, whose indolence maintained them, while they thus went sailing about everywhere, and incessantly bearing arms and acquiring skill, began to fear and flatter them, and found themselves after a while allies no longer, but unwittingly become tributaries and slaves."

In a quite different field Plutarch sets us thinking again when he tells us in the life of Pericles about the ram which had one horn. When Pericles was born, a queer-looking animal was discovered on the family estate, a ram with a single horn growing out of his forehead. A local soothsayer named Lampon interpreted this phenomenon as meaning that the new-born child would some day head the government. But a scientific gentleman named Anaxagoras asked permission to split the ram's skull, and in a few minutes showed the bystanders that the bony structure was peculiar, the brain had not filled up its natural place, but being oblong like an egg, had collected in a point to that place from which the root of the horn rose. This display of science caused the soothsayer to be laughed at. But his reputation was restored years afterwards when Pericles did indeed become head of the state.

Plutarch's comment is that both the soothsayer and the scientist may have been correct, except that the scientist thought he was contradicting the soothsayer, whereas they were talking about two very different things. The soothsayer told what the single horn meant; the scientist showed what caused it. Reading this passage long ago in my youth I had Plutarch to thank for elementary instruction in the art of thinking. Whenever we ask "Why?" there are two possible answers, one assigning the meaning or purpose, the other giving the cause. In my classroom the bell rings at the end of the hour. Why? Well, the purpose is to let the students know the hour is up and to stop me from talking. But if the bell fails to ring, the students will ask why it doesn't, and the janitor will probably say the battery is out of order.

As a biographer Plutarch is remarkably objective; both the good and the bad are in the picture, and the man is allowed, as far as possible, to speak for himself. Had famous men done much letter-writing in those days, Plutarch would doubtless have quoted from the correspondence, and his biographical technique would have been completely modern. But unconsciously and inevitably he passes judgment on all his characters, and we soon become aware of his philosophy. We can find it plainly set forth in his collection of essays called *Moralia,* but it is even clearer in the *Parallel Lives.* For almost two thousand years his readers found in this philosophy little they could wish otherwise. Christians and non-Christians, men of the Church and men of the world, soldiers and scholars, agree that he understood human passions and aspirations, that he observed well the inexorable results of moral choices, and that his profound awareness of universal law brought him close both to those who feel the mystery of life and to those who, as they say, like to keep their feet on the ground.

3.

Plutarch had no more ardent admirer than Michel Eyquem Seigneur de Montaigne. There's hardly a chapter of the Essays but pays tribute to the famous Greek. Yet except for their common study of human nature and their common preference for a wisdom that is practical, the two men differed widely as two men well can.

In the first place Plutarch wrote always in a serious mood. Though he was familiar with the whole range of human character, he preferred to write about those who had done good or evil on a large scale. His philosophy of life was clear, and he chose as subjects for biography, as other Greeks would have chosen for the persons in a tragedy, only famous men.

Montaigne, in contrast, was not at all sure of his own philosophy, but he had an enormous interest in all life and in all sorts of people, including Plutarch. He knew that a preference for great folk would always be natural, and he realized that his inclusive and wholesale zest for humanity would strike the reader as highly original. He apologized for it frequently, as for other peculiarities of his which we now reckon among his great merits. What he could not have foreseen was that the generosity underlying his wide sympathy would become more and more a democratic ideal.

His rambling style he liked to explain by saying his memory was

poor, and his education had been if not defective, at least eccentric. But when he offered this apology, perhaps he smiled. He will
regret his lack of memory in an essay packed with quotations and
references to ancient literature and history, and he will insist on
his poor education while he is dazzling us with the range of his
experience and his reading. He was a wit and something of a
tease, and whether or not his self-depreciation should be taken
with a grain of salt, he was extraordinarily garrulous. Was he
unable to stick to the subject? All that we know is, that he never
did. For a paragraph or so he will tell a story as vividly as Plutarch, and into a few lines or a sentence pack wisdom, but further
than that his gift or taste for organization does not go. He tells
us he liked to walk up and down his small library in the remotest
tower of his house, pausing to glance at a book or to write another
paragraph. It wasn't necessary that successive paragraphs should
be on the same subject. Yet his Essays, taken together, have a
unity, a single attitude, a complete philosophy, and they convey
a portrait of the author's heart and mind, of his appearance and
conduct, more vivid and more convincing than anything in
Plutarch.

He says he was himself the subject of his book, and so far as
memory served he must have left nothing of himself untold. "I
will as near as I can prevent," said he, "that my death reveal or
utter anything my life hath not first publicly spoken."

He was born at his father's château in the midst of the family
vineyards at St. Michel de Montaigne, not far from Bordeaux.
The plain old castle in which his father before him had been
born still stands, and though one side of its quadrangle was
destroyed by fire and has been restored, Montaigne's favorite
tower by good luck remains, much as it was when he spent his
happiest hours in it. He chose that particular tower, he says,
because it was the least accessible part of the building, and a man
should always reserve one spot where his family can't get at him
On the ground floor of the tower is a small chapel to which he
and his questioning spirit went to mass. On the second floor is
his bedroom. His wife and his daughter had their apartments
more than a hundred feet away, but we gather that he slept alone
only in summer; in winter he found the tower too chilly. On the

top floor was his library. The thousand books of which he liked
to speak, are now preserved at the University of Bordeaux, and
the bookcases have long been removed, but we can still read the
quotations from great authors which by his order were traced
on the rafters.

He adored his father, from whom he inherited his boldness of
thought. To spare him in childhood the usual drudgery of language study, Pierre Eyquem engaged a tutor who could speak
Latin. For years, we are told, parents and servants mastered sufficient Latin phrases to converse with the boy, who, thanks to
this prodigious experiment, spoke Latin before he knew any
French. Later, he says, when he went to college, his Latin deteriorated, yet in moments of sudden emotion, as once when he feared
his father was dying, the speech he had used in childhood sprang
to his lips.

The elder Montaigne had a theory which his more famous son
developed at length, that education should be for children a
happy experience. He disapproved of corporal punishment. He
saw no disciplinary value in pushing the young into subjects for
which they are not ready or for which they have no bent. Perhaps
he pressed his attractive theories too far. The mind of his son,
though it has charmed the world, seems not very well disciplined.
Whether the charm results from lack of discipline, we may argue
as we please.

Montaigne went to school early, studied law, practiced in
Bordeaux, became, like his father, a magistrate, retired in 1571
at the age of thirty-eight to his château, intending to devote the
rest of his life to his books and his writing, incidentally managing
the family wine business, which yielded a more than comfortable
income. Although twice recalled from his quiet to be Mayor of
Bordeaux, he was able to publish the first and second books of
his Essays in 1580, and a third book in 1588. To satisfy his abound-
ing curiosity he made an elaborate tour of Europe, but it may
be doubted if he learned anything elsewhere which he hadn't
already observed at home. He died in 1592 at the age of fifty-nine.

His writings are cast in a form of his own invention. He calls
them essays or trial pieces, because he intended nothing final,
nothing which he might not on other pages change or contradict.

We now give the name of essay to any exposition or narrative which is less than a full book, but Montaigne's essays have never been imitated, nor could they be except by a mind like his own.

In matters of taste he knew his own mind, and in most of his preferences he anticipated us. Though his age expected men like himself to drink out of metal goblets, he preferred clear glass, so that he could see what he was drinking, and in the case of wine so that the color of it could delight the eye. He was opposed to all the legal cruelties of his age. If a criminal must be executed, he said, let it be as painlessly as possible. All torture he thought infamous, and the use of the rack the worst of all ways to get at truth.

But in broader and deeper regions of philosophy he was less sure, and he has been called a great skeptic. His motto, now blazoned on the restored part of his house, was *"Que scais-je?"* —What do I know? Just how you understand this question depends somewhat on your temperament. If you are the sort of person who wants truth laid down in undebatable propositions, relegating to the realm of error all those who disagree, then the skepticism of Montaigne will seem a great fault. But if you are willing to admit the possibility of error even in yourself, and can hold your faith sincerely because it *is* your faith, even while admitting the possibility of truth in other faiths, then Montaigne will seem to you one of the wisest and most honest of men. He was born a Catholic, and the account of his last moments, left us by a friend who was at his bedside, shows that he died a good Catholic, yet he says that his faith came to him, like his French citizenship, by the circumstance of his birth. Had he been born elsewhere he would have belonged to another nation, and perhaps to a different church. Does this seem skeptical? Isn't it as true of us as of him? Those who choose their faith are few indeed.

Montaigne's tolerance has often been explained by the religious history of his family. A grandfather of his mother's was a Jew, a number of relatives on his father's side were Protestant. It was like him to remember that in another time and place he might have held the Jewish faith, and that in another part of France he might have been a Protestant, but because he was born in his father's house he was a Catholic. Just how a wise and loving God would sort out his children in a final accounting, Michel de Montaigne didn't know, but he accepted the ideals and ideas which were his inheritance, and by honest thought he tried to understand them.

Montaigne says he wrote about himself because that was the subject he knew best. There is a curious resemblance in effect but none at all in intention between his frequent use of the personal pronoun and Walt Whitman's. Whitman assumed that anything he said of himself would be true of us; when he says "I" he hopes that we, with his book in our hands, will feel that we ourselves are the speaker. Montaigne intended nothing so philosophical or subtle. He really spoke of himself and he enjoyed emphasizing his peculiarities, but having looked honestly into his heart and mind, he produces the same effect as Whitman.

No writer illustrates better the truth that a book is judged not by other books but by the experience of the reader, nor has anyone stated the truth better. In the long essay on the education of children he distinguishes between the learning which can be gathered from books and the knowledge which can be acquired only from life. He would have a child learn his own nature, his own conditions, the conduct proper to himself, before studying the orbits and behavior of the stars. He wishes the child to be acquainted with men, and on guard against those who live only by the memory of printed pages. He would introduce the child by history to the worthiest minds that were in the best ages, and of course he would look for those worthiest minds first of all in Plutarch. But the study of history, he adds, is profitable only if the child is taught what history is and how to use it, to acquire not so much the knowledge of dates and events as of the actors in the events, their manners and morals. Read histories, he says, less to know them than to judge them.

4.

No man in my judgment had his share of good things if he doesn't know Plutarch and Montaigne, but many other writers are too important to pass by. Which of them, by a minimum standard of completeness, should we know? Since some were voluminous, which of their works should we look at first?

In a moment I shall suggest a list of books, representative examples of all western literature, a list not too formidable for any reader. But I can't tell you which books would be ideal for you to begin with. We usually study literature chronologically, but the authors who mean most to us appeal at odd times, quite out of sequence. Each of us develops at a different pace; the mirror in which you see yourself in your twenties or thirties may reflect me in a condition less mature or more so. Use a reading list in any way that suits your temperament, dipping into the various authors, postponing those for whom you are not ready, exploring at once those that appeal.

Since I presume to guide your reading, perhaps I ought to confess how far I have practiced my own theories, and what on the whole is the result. In my childhood I had no guidance in my reading, none at least of the sort which I am suggesting here, but I was influenced by our family library, which represented the taste of my parents, both of whom were great readers; and though no one prepared for me a list of books, I found for myself, on the household shelves, a bulky volume called *Cassell's Illustrated Readings,* edited by Tom Hood, and published in London and New York by Cassell, Petter, and Galpin. I have the book, now somewhat dilapidated, in my own library today, and the sight of its Victorian title page in black and red ink and its none too well engraved illustrations, revives old emotions. It was for its time, and still remains, a remarkable anthology drawn from English and American authors. Its table of contents begins with the names of Washington Irving, Miss E. B. Barrett, George Coleman, Edgar A. Poe, Charles Dickens, Oliver Goldsmith, H. W. Longfellow, Laurence Sterne.

In that volume I sampled Tennyson, Dickens, and Scott, and promptly dug into their complete works. A passage from *The Deerslayer* made me an early devotee of Fenimore Cooper. I still think him a very great writer in spite of the changes of fashion which on the surface have out-dated him. "The Pit and the Pendulum," by Edgar A. Poe, was included entire. I still admire Poe's stories, in which I can readily grant his genius, even the poetic aspects of his genius, but his verse never appealed to me, and the famous "Raven" has always seemed dreadful clap-trap.

Dickens and Scott I still regard with my boyhood admiration. Both I think supreme masters. Most of my life I have ranked Scott above Dickens, having in mind his enormous influence on world literature, but there is a tendency today to find in Dickens sociological implications which escaped me when I was young, and are not entirely clear to me even now. Much is made today of his influence upon Dostoyevsky and other Russians. However that may be, and for whatever reason he is read, no one who reads at all in our time can afford to neglect him.

Among my early enthusiasms Alfred Tennyson stood very high, and even now, when a reaction has set in against him, I think him a great poet. Perhaps he is temporarily handicapped by his unusual ability to say what he means. Browning is thought more profound, perhaps, because he makes such heavy going of the language. But English literature would be poorer without Tennyson's shorter lyrics, without that astounding *tour de force,* "Maud," to me finer than any of Browning's monologues, or without the best passages in *The Idylls,* my favorite for sheer drama being "Lancelot and Elaine," or without *In Memoriam.* This great modern elegy is I think much misunderstood. It raises dark questions about life and the human soul, questions which the poet does not answer, yet which are concluded in a mood of tranquillity and hope. Critics have said that the poem is philosophically a failure, or they have tried to inject into it brave arguments from Christian theology which I am sure have nothing to do with Tennyson's immediate purpose. He was recording the moods of grief for a dead friend over a period of years. The record is realistically true to general experience; the hard doubts which bereavement suggests are more often outlived than solved.

If my experiences with great books had followed chronology, my enthusiasms would next have gone to more modern authors, or if they had been confined to English literature, they might have flamed up at once for earlier masters like Wordsworth, Milton, Shakespeare, or Chaucer. But understanding of these writers came much later, and though the four I have just mentioned are perhaps more important in some ways than all their successors put together, yet I can't yet read them without a reservation.

To Wordsworth I owe much. At one time in my life I knew the "Prelude" almost by heart, as I still know the "Lucy" poems, and the verses called "Expostulation and Reply." But there is in the English temperament a tendency now and then to exalt character at the expense of intelligence and imagination, and Wordsworth is at times very English. Even his most enthusiastic admirers try to soft-pedal his "Ecclesiastical Sonnets" and to ignore altogether his shocking praise or defense of capital punishment in the "Sonnets Upon the Punishment of Death."

The wonder of Milton's verse does not lessen for me as I grow older, but I appreciate more and more the qualities of his early poems, "Comus," "Lycidas," "L'Allegro," "Il Penseroso," and the austere beauty of "Samson Agonistes." In *Paradise Lost* the descriptions of heaven and hell now seem less majestic than once they did; on the other hand the pathos, the humor, and the human psychology of Milton's Adam and Eve grow upon me. It may be that Milton will be remembered longest for his eloquence in the cause of liberty, in such prose pamphlets, for example, as *The Tenure of Kings and Magistrates.* He was not in the American sense a democrat, but he was a pronounced individualist, so much so that I'm not sure now, after years of reading him, whether he would have preferred complete anarchy or complete dictatorship. Theoretically he admired Oliver Cromwell, but even under the Protector he seems to have gone his own way.

My favorite reading in Shakespeare used to be *Love's Labours Lost,* which always seemed to me an ideal libretto for a Mozart, *Twelfth Night, Romeo and Juliet, Much Ado, Midsummer Night's Dream,* and *The Winter's Tale.* The plays which I now prefer, or at least the ones which I read most often, are *Macbeth,* my favorite, *Measure for Measure,* which seems to me a much under-rated masterpiece of irony, *The Tempest,* and those scenes from *Henry IV* and *Henry V* in which Falstaff and Dame Quickly appear. I think Falstaff is perhaps the greatest of Shakespeare's tragic creations. But I don't enjoy Shakespeare on the stage. Everybody talks too much.

Chaucer is difficult for us because of his language, but even so, it's not hard to fall in love with the combined Anglo-Saxon and Latin elements in his work. I suppose he gives the most intelligent account of life to be found in English literature, frank, honest, complete and sane, and I suppose he owes his sanity chiefly to the French culture of his day, which included much Italian culture. When I haven't his poems at hand I praise him extravagantly, but if I turn all his pages, I find there, let me confess, much that is of no interest at all, whether human or literary. He was a universal poet but also a man of his own time, and the temporary part of him is large.

Perhaps I shouldn't qualify to this extent my love of great English writers if I hadn't encountered while I was very young some Greek masterpieces, and soon afterward some French. At school I had a rare teacher of Greek, Dr. Francis Bacon, whose regard for the ancient language was little short of an obsession. He taught us to speak it, at least in a lame and halting fashion. Every day at the end of the recitation he asked each of us a question or two, taking the words from the page we had just studied, and we picked our answer from the same handy reservoir. Of course the ability to converse in ancient Greek would have done us no good even if we had acquired it, since there are no ancient Greeks left, and we may seriously doubt if scholars have guessed correctly the pronunciation which the ancient Greeks used. But at least our tongues became accustomed to the words, the text came alive to the ear, and we read Greek with a measure of fluency. Thanks to Dr. Bacon I elected Greek through my college years as a snap course, and when I was a senior I happened to read, not for the class but for pleasure, Plato's *Symposium*.

I have had few experiences so moving as the discovery of Plato's fables and parables, the noblest achievement, I think, of the poetic faculty. The contrast between the vision of heavenly love as unfolded by Socrates and of earthly friendship as depicted by the drunken eloquence of Alcibiades, struck me with an impact which I had never supposed a book could make. I read the great dialogue in the Low Library at Columbia University. For fully an hour afterwards, as I remember, I walked around and around the corridor outside the reading room, intending to go home but too dazed to notice the staircase when I came to it. Later I read *Phaedrus* and the other dialogues. Nowadays, though my gratitude is still lively, I set little store by the endless questioning which Plato ascribes to Socrates; I prize rather the insights by the way, and the surprises of intelligence and poetry. I'm sorry for anyone who has not read the *Republic,* source book of later theorizing about justice and a planned society. As I grow older I find myself reading again and again, to my surprise, the volume called *The Laws,* which at first seems but a poor re-hash of the *Republic,* but which has special merits of its own.

To praise Shakespeare fanatically I find hard after reading Aeschylus, Sophocles, and Euripides. The Greek dramatists have, to be sure, enjoyed a special advantage; all but their best works were probably lost to the world in the burning of the library at Alexandria. We have not much more than ten per cent. of their product, but we believe we have the plays which the ancient world valued most highly and distributed, therefore, in many copies. Perhaps Shakespeare's reputation would gain if only his eight or nine best plays remained.

But even then the Greek dramatists would show to advantage. They probed life deep, and though we miss in them some of Shakespeare's companionableness, their opinion of mankind and their understanding of human destiny was nobler than his.

They had, for example, a more philosophical idea of tragedy. To Shakespeare, tragedy is caused by weakness of mind or character; Macbeth and his wife are murderers, King Lear is senile, Iago is a devil. Out of such material the Greeks would not have drawn an important drama. They would have said that for a murderer nothing is more logical or natural than to commit a murder; from a criminal, crime is to be expected, and weakness from a weakling. The real tragedy of life should be looked for in strong and good characters, in a high intelligence which even at its best is inadequate for the problems of life. To a Greek, Benedict Arnold would have been simply a traitor, but Robert E. Lee would have been a tragic hero. When a noble spirit is compelled to choose between two courses, both of which present themselves as duty, his plight, on the frontier of intelligence, is what the Greeks called tragedy. Anything he does will be right, and anything he does will be wrong. This is essentially the theme of the *Antigone* of Sophocles, to my mind the finest drama ever written. Antigone was compelled by her religion to give her brother proper burial. He had turned traitor to his city, he had been slain, and according to law his body was exposed to the ravens. Capital punishment was decreed to anyone who should cover the corpse ever so slightly. Antigone was a patriot, and she thought her brother a criminal, but she buried him and went to her death. What else could she do?

Herodotus and Thucydides, the Greek historians, I studied in college, but I didn't appreciate them until years later, perhaps for that reason. With ten or a dozen classmates I read Herodotus in my senior year. Sydnor Harrison, the novelist, was one of the group. For each recitation we tried to think up sparkling translations of the marvelous stories with which Herodotus has fascinated young men and old for more than two thousand years. Our teacher was a specialist in archaeology. He listened to us courteously, but aside from an occasional emendation or a question about grammatical constructions, he made no comment. In fact, he was as responsive as an icicle, and we invited him to dine with us at Martin's hoping to thaw him out, but he declined with thanks, looking scared. I never saw a class try so hard to interest a professor in his own course.

Twenty years later I learned for myself the importance of both Herodotus and Thucydides. Herodotus illustrates for all time the historian's difficulty and the historian's skill in recovering a distant past. He visited the places he wrote about, talked with people on the spot, gathered legends and whatever other evidence remained, sifted this miscellaneous testimony, reported the result, and told us just how far he thought the information was dependable. Modern historians have more evidence to work on, but they are not likely to surpass Herodotus in the historical spirit, nor in common sense, nor in ability to tell a story.

Thucydides wrote an account of the Peloponnesian War while it was going on, beginning, he says, at the moment it broke out. It may seem easier to write contemporary history as it happens than to dig up a dead past, but the historian of his own day is not likely to have perspective, nor to come at any fact without prejudice, nor to have all the facts. Yet Thucydides wrote of his times with the clarity of a great judge unravelling complicated and contradictory evidence. He wrote also with eloquence, since the story he told was tragic for the civilization he loved. How unique he is among historians you can measure by a parallel. Imagine a German historian in the first World War, undertaking a month to month record of what happened until the signing of the Armistice. Imagine an account so inclusive and so unprejudiced that neither Germans nor the victorious Allies could find anything to correct in it. That kind of historian has occurred only once.

At the University I read rather widely in Latin literature, but with the exception of Vergil and to a less extent Lucretius, the Roman writers have not meant much to me. As in every other case where I am unappreciative, I know it's probably my fault. The austereness and the integrity of Lucretius must be admired; but I never care much for those who try to prove a negative point, least of all for those who attack religion or any kind of faith. Superstition is another matter. If you say that superstition and religious faith are one and the same thing, you'll have no credit with me for straight thinking. Faith is creative hope and trust in the future; superstition is the embodiment, not of hope and trust, but of negative fears. It closes the mind in the past instead of opening it on the future. At one time in my early thirties I studied Lucretius thoroughly, reading and rereading his stately lines, but though he tells me it's natural to die and death ought to be as agreeable as life, I still would rather be alive than not, and though he tells me not to worry about the hereafter, since all consciousness ceases with death, I am not touched by his argument, never having believed that a future life would necessarily be less worthwhile than the present one.

Lucretius seems to me the climax of an era, a commentator on a faith that had slipped away. In Vergil I find a question which from his time to ours has troubled civilization—the problem of national and racial rivalries, of imperial expansion. The problem was always present but it caused no worry until it was faced with a broad, human sympathy. All very well for the stronger nation to oust or enslave or annihilate the weaker, all very well so long as the stronger nation has no heart, but once a humane imagination is aroused, how can the country which has the most soldiers be assured that it has also the most brains or the greatest gifts to

confer on posterity? Vergil wrote *The Aeneid* at the supreme
moment of the Roman Empire, and his intention was to glorify
the long building up of that world-wide structure, but in the first
lines he stresses the terrible cost both to conquerors and to conquered, the heartbreak and the misery which attended every step
of the way. From no modern poet could we quote so many verses
applicable to the present world agony.

With Vergil I associate Dante, not because Vergil appears as
a character in Dante's poem, but because in complementary ways
they mark the passage from the ancient world to a new and more
troubled era. Vergil had no philosophy to deal with the vast
pageant of imperial Rome. Dante, on the other hand, applied a
universal philosophy to the quarrels of a small city. The greatness
of Dante's philosophy gives to Florentine politics an unlooked-for
dignity. The inadequacy of Vergil's philosophy does nothing for
the city of Rome, but perhaps it does a good deal for Vergil himself and for the appeal of his epic; it shows him as helpless, contemplating the march of Rome, as were the victims of that impe-
rialism. He seems brother to all the baffled, whereas Dante was
and remains a solitary figure.

A writer whom I associate with Dante in my admiration, a poet
of vastly inferior character and far less universal genius, yet still
a poet of the first order, is François Villon. I made his acquaintance
first in Dante Gabriel Rossetti's translation of "The Ballade of
Dead Ladies," and in a university course in old French, but it was
not till middle life that I felt the power of his concrete imagery—
here he makes me think of Dante—or the large humor and tender-
ness of his unhappy spirit. The usual opinion of him forty years
ago was expressed by Robert Louis Stevenson in his short story,
"A Lodging for the Night," and in his biographical and critical
essay on the poet, a performance which now seems too ungenerous
and too nearly hypocritical to have emanated from the pen of
R.L.S. But in Stevenson's time Villon's own account of his
shames and frailties was accepted. Nowadays we check his story
by the evidence contained in his long poem, "The Testament,"
and we conclude that he had good blood in him, that if he
hobnobbed with rascals he was also on familiar terms with
the respectable, and that much of his self-accusing was exagger-

ated. He spoke so often of the gallows that earlier biographers argued too hastily that he was hanged; now we ask how he could be hanged and write so well of it afterwards. There is testimony, if not evidence, that he died in prosperity at a ripe age.

In certain respects he is for me the greatest poet of France, and it's a pity he wrote so long ago that he's not easily read, still more a pity that he has never been completely translated by a first rate poet. We admire him now for his love of his country, for his affection for his mother, for the humility with which he confessed his misdeeds, for his sincerity, and for his sympathy for human misery. To these last traits, sincerity and sympathy, I would add his passion for life, the high flavor he extracted from all experiences, physical, intellectual, or emotional. I have never been able to understand how anyone in this exciting world could be bored. François Villon was the least bored person I have met among great authors. If he really came to old age, I'm sure he was alive to the last minute.

Some of his zest is in a later French writer, Voltaire. I'm particularly grateful for his *Philosophical Dictionary*. Critics still echo the pronouncement of those who feared him, that he was over-rational, over-skeptical, heartless, destructive, but having read what he wrote, I hold no such mean opinion of him. He hated humbug, hypocrisy, cruelty, and intolerance; with equal fervor he loved the virtues without which a civilized society is impossible. Liberty and justice have had no more effective champion. I think he was essentially religious, though he lived in a period when the Church was perhaps displaying more of its earthly than of its divine character, and against all institutional dry-rot, fanaticism, and persecution, he waged tireless battle. For me he illustrates the good uses to which intelligence at its human best can be put.

His moral greatness, that passion in him which I think obvious, many readers cannot recognize. Perhaps they would be helped by a comparison of him with Anatole France. This master of irony, this superb stylist, this discriminating connoisseur of all beautiful things, has for most of my days been for me a model of good writing, not only in his great stories such as the *Rotisserie de la Reine Pédauque* (The Queen Pédauque Cookshop), or *Les Dieux ont Soif* (The Gods are Thirsty), but even more in the four volumes of criticism which he published under the title *La Vie Littéraire*.

But he lacks Voltaire's faith, his vigorous pulse, his crusading spirit. It is true that he took Zola's part in the Dreyfus matter, and at other moments also he roused himself to defend what he believed in, but for the most part his extraordinary gifts were employed to no important end. He lacked a cause. With each return to his pages I am once more amazed at his talents, and baffled by the uncertain use he made of them.

About the time I first discovered Anatole France I met also two very great Spanish writers, Calderon de la Barca and Miguel de Cervantes. My college teacher, the poet George Edward Woodberry, introduced me to both, and continuous reading of them has deepened my conviction that they belong with the great writers of all time. Since they both, in slightly different ways, are very Spanish, and since their qualities are not usually found in Anglo-Saxon character, they receive less than justice from English readers, and small attention from American professors of literature who revere the limitations of English taste. We know Cervantes by name, and some of us have read *Don Quixote,* at least as far as the windmills, but who Calderon was or what he wrote, we'd rather not be asked.

Less important than Cervantes, he was still a great Spaniard and a noble poet, and his works preserve for us a kind of idealism which belongs to his country and which is rarely found in other parts of the world. I hope the tradition of it in South and Central America may ultimately enrich the spiritual life of the United States. The mark of Greek literature is a lofty intelligence; the chief quality of French literature is intelligence in a less exalted sphere, with an eye on the soil and the ways of nature and the facts of life; the strength of English literature is character. These statements are too sweeping, but in a rough way they state recognizable truths. There is a logic of intelligence, and there is also a logic of conduct. There is still another kind of logic related to these other two yet distinct, the logic of emotion. This emotional logic distinguishes Spanish literature. To a certain temperament, love, hate, faith, or fear, involve, as consequences, obligations of loyalty, or at least of consistency. Let the mind say what it will, a Spaniard is not a Spaniard unless he obeys to the last his heart and his soul. His capacity for devotion, for fidelity and for sacrifice, is very great.

Calderon was a gentleman of distinguished family, a brave soldier and a successful diplomat, but in middle life he retired from his bright world and took Orders, not because he had only then found religion, but because he sought leisure to study, meditate, and write. He left us many *autos,* or miracle plays, and even more secular dramas, my favorite among them being *La Vida es Sueño*. It's one of the few literary masterpieces which deal with the theme of aristocracy—of true aristocracy, let me add, the aristocracy of the soul. The story is of a king's son who at birth is exiled and brought up in a savage condition. He is returned to civilization, proves unfit for society and is sent back to his forest jail. He believes his brief freedom was a happy dream from which his own rudeness and violence woke him. Restored at last to his throne, he wants revenge, but resolves, when his conquered enemies are brought before him, not to break the dream a second time. For revenge he substitutes magnanimity. He behaves, in fact, like a perfect Spanish gentleman.

Since children in the United States usually are taught history with an English bias, I grew up in the opinion that Queen Elizabeth was a model of justice, that her realm was in its time the most advanced in culture, particularly in literature, that Spain, on the other hand, was benighted and decadent and rather stupid not to acknowledge the supremacy of England, instead of making that futile sally with the Armada. Since the Armada was destroyed as much by a storm as by the English fleet, I accepted readily the doctrine which my text book implied, that God did not approve of the Spanish, and I understood that their empire, after this severe rebuke, folded up and disappeared.

Calderon and Cervantes drove this nonsense out of my head. They were contemporaries of Shakespeare, products of the richest and most broadminded civilization in their time; they write with knowledge of the world, as men of the world, but always with a spiritual scale of values, putting man above possessions or the lack of them, and the condition of the soul above other kinds of fortune.

Don Quixote is out of his wits, a poverty-stricken gentleman who has read so many romances of chivalry that he takes them seriously, gets himself some dilapidated armor and an old horse, and rides down the road to rescue ladies and others in distress. His squire, Sancho Panza, is the embodiment of common sense, an earthly realism, but he has the Spanish talent for loyalty; he follows the mad old gentleman as devotedly as Don Quixote follows his ideal.

Before we reach the end of the book we are not at all sure that the Don is mad, nor that we who, like Sancho, pride ourselves on good sense are really sane. Cervantes even more than Calderon disturbs us by asking what we sincerely believe. In the famous incident of the windmills we smile of course at the lunacy which mistakes mills for villainous enemies. Yet the assault displayed immense courage against great odds. Would it really have been braver or saner to fight human beings? Is any fighting sane? We laugh at the Don because he puts on antique armor in order to redress wrong, but if he really was trying to redress wrong, should the costume make much difference to us? Or if we are authorities on costume, in what costume do you and I redress wrong? If we have tender consciences we may be bothered by the thought that on his errand of mercy the Don has the road all to himself.

Don Quixote is in my opinion the greatest novel yet written. I am not unmindful of Honoré de Balzac with his *Human Comedy* and his other remarkable pictures of a varied world, nor do I blind myself to his influence; he set the fashion for social panoramas in one continuous or interlocked story, and the various cycles in which our contemporary world is portrayed follow him rather than Cervantes. But in art as elsewhere I'd rather have quality than quantity, and I rank very high indeed a novel which in short space gives me a picture of the world as complete as though it took a dozen or twenty volumes. On the highway, in the mountains, at the roadside inns, the Don meets every aspect of life, life with a very Spanish flavor yet recognizable by us all.

Of German literature I have never been able to frame an opinion satisfactory to myself, probably because I don't know the country. German music I love, and the Germans whom I have met in the western world or in Europe have, as it happened, all been men of culture, admirable and likeable in character. Outside of music, however, I don't understand German taste. This, by way of confessing my limitations. Goethe I studied of course in the University, and though I have never appreciated *Faust* as I suppose I should, I have a particular fondness for *Wilhelm Meister,* partly because Schubert put the incidental songs to lovely music. Goethe's lyrics on the whole seem to me his supreme achievement. I like German literature best in its lyrical moments. For that reason I have read much in Heine, in Richard Dehmel and in Rainer Maria Rilke.

My difficulty with German literature is a matter of temperament. The western civilization which I care for began in Greece and Palestine and traveled westward along the shores of the Mediterranean—the great legacy of Aristotle, be it remembered, coming by way of the southern shore, transmitted to us by Arab scholars. On the northern shore the tradition of Graeco-Roman-Hebraic culture, having spread till it reached the Atlantic, was carried by the Romans northward into Britain. Germany was not touched by the tradition until late in her history, and having already a northern culture of her own, she has never been entirely at ease with the Mediterranean heritage. Goethe is unique, a gigantic and universal figure, but his German readers, so far as I have observed, pick out of him only what they can recognize as the northern or Germanic element in his work. Other German writers, exactly in proportion as they are at home in the Graeco-Latin tradition, seem to me dislocated from their own country.

Of South American literature I, like most northerners, know altogether too little, though in recent years I have made up some lost time. When I was a student, José Enrique Rodó, the famous Uruguayan man of letters, published his *Ariel,* a protest against the materialistic and mechanical civilization which he feared might take possession of the United States and spread over the rest of the continent. When *Ariel* appeared, George Edward Woodberry, the poet, was teaching literature at my university, a man not unlike Rodó in temperament and devoted to the same

ideals. Some years later he called my attention to Rodó's book.
I was immediately impressed by the coincidence that the Uruguayan had published *Ariel* the same year that Woodberry had
brought out his *Heart of Man,* one of the very noble books in
American literature, a collection of studies in human ideals. The
chapter on Poetry gives Rodó's own protest against materialism
and against all civilization based on the worship of force. But
Woodberry, I think, put the matter in a better way, less as criticism than as advocacy of an ideal.

My knowledge of South American writers began with Rodó and
his *Ariel.* Only recently have I made the acquaintance of another
and later Uruguayan poet-philosopher, Juan Zorilla de San
Martin, who died but a few years ago after a career of great honor,
and who is remembered now in Montevideo with veneration. In
his book of essays called *Detalles de Historia* he has a chapter of
comment on *Ariel.* For Rodó, Ariel was the symbol of the soul.
He represented the Latin countries. Caliban represented the
United States. Zorilla de San Martin made the more generous
point, that North America as well as South had its spiritual
civilization, and that the menace of Caliban was present in Latin
as well as Anglo-Saxon civilization. I admire Rodó's essay as a
sincere warning against a genuine peril. South Americans know
the book well; it articulates their distrust of us. I hold Zorilla de
San Martin's essay in admiration and in gratitude; it is one of
the important utterances which have prepared North and South
America for a better knowledge of each other.

All the countries of South America are at this moment producing writers we cannot afford to ignore. In Argentina, Enriqué
Larreta and Ricardo Rojas have acquired even in their lifetime
the position almost of classics. Brazil, Chile, Ecuador, Colombia,
and the rest are in a ferment of literary creation, most of it I
believe now turning toward economic, social, or political themes.
Northern readers, I fancy, will be busy, as I shall be.

North American authors I read while I was very young, admiring Hawthorne and Mark Twain at that time without quite understanding either, and finding difficulty with Emerson, Thoreau
and Whitman. These five I still read constantly, though the value
I set on each has changed. I still think Hawthorne's *Scarlet Letter*

a wonderful book, as remarkable for its thoughtfulness as for its drama. I now attach less importance to Thoreau's journals and much more to his few essays, notably the one called "Civil Disobedience." In Mark Twain I find the out-and-out fun wearing a little thin, but the vein of satire much richer. *Huckleberry Finn* and *The Man That Corrupted Hadleyburg* I'd put at the very top. Emerson's poems I care less for than his essays, though from time to time I come on some isolated lines of his or a separate stanza which startles by its incisive truth or by its absolute beauty. Of his books I like best *The Conduct of Life* and that early slender volume called *Nature,* but here in the prose, as in the verse, separate chapters or paragraphs are precious indeed. I can't count the number of times I have felt grateful to the Phi Beta Kappa address, *The American Scholar,* or to passages in the two series of Essays. The quality of Emerson's mind being what it was, his letters and journals are almost or quite as important as his finished work. Many pages from the journals, of course, were transferred bodily to lectures which later were developed into essays.

Anyone who is indebted to Emerson for aid toward a richer life usually acknowledges a similar debt to Walt Whitman. You may prefer one or the other, but you are not likely to deny that they are among the most American of writers. To me Walt Whitman is not only the great American poet, but one of the chief forces in modern, even in contemporary, literature. Some of his admirers praise him as a seer and prophet but deny that he is a poet; the frame of his verse, the studied casualness of his manner, throw them off. For me he is in every respect a supreme poet, not to be understood perhaps nor to be completely appreciated as artist until we have read all that he left us, the poems which he rejected from later editions as well as those he kept, the prose notes and prefaces, the garrulous-seeming memorabilia, which tell us more about ourselves than about him. To rate him as many Americans still do on a par with local poets, no matter how individual, poets like Emily Dickinson, for example, is I think an obvious error. One at least of the measures by which a poet must be judged is the size and range of his audience. *Leaves of Grass* is known and closely studied wherever books of western civilization are read at all.

Emily Dickinson, whose reputation in the United States at present rides high, is on occasion very poignant, and she has an uncanny felicity of phrase, but the range of her thought and feeling seems to me extremely narrow. I doubt if a poet should be considered necessarily universal or epoch-making just because his or her verses make constant mention of God, nature, heaven, hell, death and the grave.

Of contemporary English writers I admire greatly Somerset Maugham, and for quite different reasons, the late John Galsworthy. Maugham's novel *Of Human Bondage* is a masterpiece, and his short stories give a wonderful picture, not of England, but of some aspects of society in outlying parts of the British Empire's distant places where Englishmen and Americans meet. As a craftsman he writes superbly, and by nature he has that objective, ironic sight which we usually expect of the French rather than of the English. Perhaps I like him chiefly for this reason, that his English mind has in it much of the French spirit.

John Galsworthy was in some ways far less able as artist and craftsman. He had none of Maugham's irony, but I think him important just because he seems thoroughly English, and his books, whether or not otherwise the result of great inspiration, give a rare picture of English life. Perhaps I should say of English life in a state of transition. My favorite among his novels is *One More River,* full of nostalgia for the England which ended in 1914. To have left such a record of such a moment is enough to make any writer remembered.

In the last few years the books which have interested me most have been those appearing in my own country. All my life I have read widely in as many literatures as I could, and I can't now think of any art in a narrow nationalistic way, but the tragedy of Europe brings to the United States a host of writers, good, bad, and indifferent, stirred by grief, indignation, or anger, all eager to speak their minds. When or where has there ever before been such a migration or exodus of civilized men and women, all articulate by nature or endowed by sorrow with touching eloquence?

Of those who now publish books in the United States, many have acquired the English language late. Yet for the moment we are not bothered if the literary quality of our current books is somewhat low. What they say is important no matter how they say it.

I still believe that writing is an art. My guess is that a book won't last unless it is well written. Yet I think that American literature at this moment is making a great advance, and I hope the progress will continue a while even at the temporary sacrifice of art. The American writer and his audience, as no one knows better than the writers themselves, have always been a little afraid of life. We have asked books to supply us with relaxation, with sentiment, with amusement. The exceptions are not few but they are all the more prized because they were indeed exceptions. The welcome growth today is in the subject matter. Life insists at last on being noticed. Our current books on agonized or perplexing conditions or events may be all the better for our purposes when they are artless. Mankind is thinking and feeling out loud. We ask only that thought and emotion should be sincere.

5.

This sketch of my own adventures in reading is offered, not as a pattern to follow, but as an example of growth and change in taste over many years. Complete lists of famous classics are easily available. I once prepared a reading list for students in Columbia College. About fifty authors were selected, and so much of their best work chosen that by reading a book a week for two years a student could survey the whole field. That list in its original form was published by the Columbia University Press under the title, *Outline of Readings in Important Books.* The authors chosen began with Homer and ended with Karl Marx, Nietzsche, and William James. Writers in all fields were included, but some of the best known Americans were omitted simply because they were indeed well known and must have been studied in school.

This list, somewhat enlarged, was republished by the American Library Association in Chicago under the title, *Classics of the Western World.* Later the same list with further expansions became the basis of the course around which St. John's College in Annapolis builds its curriculum. Most recently Professor Mortimer J. Adler, in *How to Read a Book,* gives the list again with a few changes and additions which seem to me excellent. Dr. Adler was a student of mine at Columbia when this reading list was first devised. *How to Read a Book* is a masterly development of what I here can only sketch, and I refer you to it.

For young students in college and for maturer readers I believe the initial attitude toward literature is of the utmost importance. Here I go with Montaigne rather than with Dr. Adler. My former pupil says that though the reading course made him at home with books, he soon realized that his enjoyment of them was superficial, and that the art of reading involved much that so far he had over-looked. He is quite right, of course, and he has taught thousands of people, already fond of reading, how to read more intelligently and more thoroughly. Yet I gladly leave to others all such deepening and refining of the love of books, if only I can aid my fellows in the first place to acquire that love.

My point of view, which I dare say I learned long ago from Montaigne, was illustrated in the origin of the Columbia College reading list. My fellow teachers habitually lamented the fact that our students did not know the great books. The lament implied that in this respect the students differed from their elders. It implied also that no cure was possible, and the world of culture would continue to go to the dogs.

I challenged that pessimism. At this late date I'm not sure whether I had already formulated my ideas, or whether I was merely irritated by so much complaining, but I said it was far from clear that the elder generation had themselves done the reading which they expected of the youngsters, and if they still wished to do it, they and the youngsters, by running through a book a week, could cover a large proportion of the great authors in two years. Great books, however, should be read now as they were before they gained the reputation of greatness. Our attitude toward the *Iliad,* for example, should be that of a conscientious reviewer toward a new novel. Homer like the novelist told his story for the entertainment of the audience. Enormous fame, however, has now brought on him such an embarrassment of scholarship that his own beautiful book lies, as it were, at the bottom of the pile, hard to get at, and even if we can reach it, we hesitate to enjoy the doings of Achilles and Odysseus, Hector and Andromache, Paris and immortal Helen, unless we hold a scholar's commentary in the other hand. I proposed that great books, which gained their reputation when they were new and extremely up-to-date, should be read now as if they were just out today. The necessary commentary or scholarship should be supplied by the students, discussing the book with their teachers exactly as they would discuss a new novel or a new work on politics or economics.

This method of coming to know great books has been followed by so many generations of students at Columbia College and elsewhere that the effect, even of first and single readings, is well known. The study of an art, as Ezra Pound once told us, is a study of masterpieces. In literature, scholarship, criticism and commentary are all a small matter compared with the great book itself. Great books, read in succession, gradually form the best of commentaries on each other. You judge them by your own experience, but each great book widens your experiences, teaches you to observe more, gives you keener insight.

Don't misunderstand me; I honor scholarship as much as anyone. But here I consider how large a share of the world's treasures in this particular year of grace a human being may reasonably hope for. There is only so much time, no more for the scholar than for the general reader. If the life of the scholar is the kind of life you want, you must specialize, you must sacrifice to your subject the time necessary for an acquaintance with some other things. I write here not for the specialist but for those who, like Plutarch and Montaigne, ask how to live most nobly and most richly, in those active experiences which are the heritage of us all.

6.

To understand the art of writing is, I am sure, essential to a complete life. We probably don't know how to read until we have learned to write. The two processes may appear different, and reading may seem easier—we speak of a writer as having a special gift—but reading and writing are opposite approaches to the art of communication, and unless both are understood we are not likely to solve the greatest human problem, the problem of speaking to each other.

In conversation the dialogue proceeds by instinctive addition; each speaker modifies what has been said by contributing further ideas or facts. When nothing more is added, there is a break.

Addition is the method of writing as well as of talk. Of course when your listener is before your eyes and you have heard him speak, you know just where he stopped and just where you must continue; you can count also on the expression of your face to help out your words; you may have won his good will in advance by appearing interested while he was doing the talking. The writer, on the other hand, has to start cold, with strangers. His readers, more often than not, never see his face nor hear the sound of his voice. He must be acquainted with them prophetically. No matter what he wishes to communicate, he knows that they will understand him in terms of their own experience. He must know what their experience is. He knows by instinct the truth of Whitman's saying, "The proof of a poet shall be sternly deferr'd, till his country absorbs him as affectionately as he has absorb'd it."

Though you have no intention of becoming a novelist, essayist, a poet or a dramatist, at least you write letters. A good letter begins with the person to whom it is addressed, with a reference to some interest which the writer is sure of. By natural sequence the letter then adds whatever the writer wants to say. The process is no different in a novel or a drama. The audience is caught and held by the title and the first words, which must strike, as we say, a responsive chord, an interest which is already keen. Yet the audience must not control the writer's message; if he has integrity and knows his business, he will say what he likes. The reader merely determines the point at which the book should begin. The writer determines the point at which it should end.

The process of addition shapes the form of our sentences and the structure of our grammar. To sharpen a point in human discourse we whittle nothing away, as in the case of a lead pencil, but rather add and build up, as though we were constructing an architectural pinnacle. Since writers are usually well educated, they know and respect traditional grammar, but they are conscious that it has been bequeathed to us, not by writers, but by philosophers. Our traditional grammar was promulgated by the English and the French during the seventeenth century, and refined and over-refined by German scholars in the eighteenth. Grammar in the Germanic condition interested Samuel Taylor Coleridge, as you can see for yourself by glancing at the famous *Table Talk*, recorded by his son Hartley. All this early grammar dealt not with problems of writing but with abstractions, closely related to theology. On March 18, 1827, in some light conversation, Coleridge had this to say:

"There are seven parts of speech, and they agree with the five grand and universal divisions into which all things finite, by which I mean to exclude the idea of God, will be found to fall:

Prothesis
1.

Thesis   Mesothesis   Antithesis
2.   4.   3.

Synthesis
5.

"Conceive it thus:

1. Prothesis, the noun-verb, or verb-substantive, *I am,* which is the previous form, and implies identity of being and act.

2. Thesis, the noun.

3. Antithesis, the verb.

{ Note, each of these may be converted; that is, they are only opposed to each other.

4. Mesothesis, the infinitive mood, or the indifference of the verb and noun, it being either the one or the other, or both at the same time, in different relations.

5. Synthesis, the participle, or the community of verb and noun, being an acting at once.

Now, modify the noun by the verb, that is, by an act, and you have—

6. The adnoun, or adjective.

Modify the verb by the noun, that is, by being, and you have—

7. The adverb.

Interjections are parts of sound, not of speech. Conjunctions are the same as prepositions; but they are prefixed to a sentence, or to a member of a sentence, instead of to a single word.

The inflexions of nouns are modifications as to place; the inflexions of verbs, as to time.

The genitive case denotes dependence; the dative, transmission. It is absurd to talk of verbs governing."

Though Coleridge was himself a writer, he obviously thought of grammar as something for a philosopher to analyze, not for a writer to use. Modern grammar, fortunately, has come out of the clouds, but not even today do the schools quite abandon the philosophical approach. We do not yet teach grammar as we use it.

When Adam named the animals he got at the heart of all communication. Speaking or writing we name things, persons, or ideas which we and our audience have already met. The name of a person or a thing we call a noun, the name of an action we call a verb, but nouns and verbs remain names. To designate a person more accurately we add another name, which grammar calls an adjective or a relative clause. So-called adjectives or relative clauses, even according to the grammarians, may be used interchangeably as nouns. The same is true of adverbs and subordinate clauses. If you say, "The man," you have used a name which isn't very precise unless it follows some previous question or discussion. If you begin in cold blood with, "The man," I'll probably ask you, "Which man?" But if you and I have been watching a man and a woman in an argument, and I ask which you think is getting the best of it, and if you reply, "The man," you are using a name as an addition. The grammarians would say that your noun is becoming an adjective.

The grammar books still give the impression that a noun is more important than an adjective, an adverb more important than a verb, a subordinate clause more important than a main clause. Nouns, verbs and main clauses are said to be important because they can stand alone. But a writer knows that a name which stands alone means nothing. If you have never heard the name before, it is well at least to have before your eyes, as Adam had, the thing which goes with the name. Pedants sometimes advise you to strengthen your style by omitting adjectives and adverbs, and they sometimes suggest tombstone inscriptions for a model. The famous inscriptions which the Greeks carved in marble do indeed avoid adjectives and adverbs; the powerful understatement which results is called the lapidary or the stone-cutter's style. Greek writers were not stone-cutters, but they understood the two excellent reasons why their monumental inscriptions were economical and severe. In the first place, a piece of marble is hard to cut, and there's never much room on it, if you use letters large enough to be read at a distance. In the second place, Athens put up monuments and cut inscriptions only for people who were well known. The inscriptions were brief reminders, not bulletins of information. If you and I, walking through a cemetery, see a name unadorned, without even a date, we ask, "Who was he?" In that case the deceased gentleman, so far as we are concerned, is not sufficiently named. If we recognize, however, a famous citizen, the simple name is enough. With time, however, all names tend to be forgotten. The lapidary or tombstone style, therefore, has but a temporary usefulness. You might find on an old stone in Athens the name of one of Plutarch's men, but unless you knew Plutarch, the name would say no more to you than a bare John Smith in the cemetery at home.

For the writer the first essential is to connect with the reader's interest; the second is to speak clearly. In the process of making definite points the writer learns that a name by itself, a noun or a verb or a clause, is only a base upon which the meaning will rise. The meaning lies always in the additions. The grammarian may say if he wishes that the main clause is more important than the subordinate clause; the writer by experience knows better. If he is dealing with two ideas, one universal and majestic, the other personal and trivial, he puts the big idea in the subordinate clause, and throws the little stuff into that part of the sentence which, as the grammarians tell us, can stand alone. Would you say, "When the sun rose, I got up?" or "When I got up, the sun rose?"

7.

Far be it from me to make a novelist or a dramatist out of you. Yet I am convinced that unless we know the process by which life is re-created in words, and character portrayed, and ideas dramatized, we don't know how to write. What is worse, we are in some degree blind or deaf to life.

No doubt you have often felt the power of a story teller who makes the character come alive on the page, but I should be astonished if you noticed the process which produced this effect. It is not a literary trick; it is merely an accurate observation of life. Merely? What could be more important! Yet most of us observe just enough of life to serve our needs at the moment. We form the habit of insensitiveness. A poet-teacher told me long ago, "Don't look for the waters of Lethe in another world; that river runs at our feet." Those who have eyes to see and ears to hear must be warned now as in old days to make sure they do hear and do see.

A simple experiment will show what I mean. On one side of a sheet of paper write a line or two describing the characters A and B. Say, if you will, that A is lazy but good-natured, talented but unambitious. Give a different account of B; say he is energetic and forceful, but he jumps at conclusions, his mind is untidy, and he probably isn't reliable. These preliminary annotations will serve later to check results.

Now turn the paper over and on the other side write a minute or two of conversation between A and B. Let them talk on any subject, long enough for each to speak three or four times. Remember the character of each, and let each speak on the given subject as such a character would.

Now show the dialogue to a friend who hasn't seen the preliminary annotations, and ask for a summary of A's character and B's. If the friend receives from the conversation such clear impressions that he will describe A as lazy but good-natured, talented but unambitious, and B as energetic and forceful, but he jumps at conclusions, his mind is untidy and he probably isn't reliable, then you may congratulate yourself. You are equipped to be a novelist or a dramatist, so far as character portrayal goes, but what is more important, your powers of observation go very deep.

But in all probability your friend won't learn much from your dialogue, and will miss by a wide margin the portraits you intended. You foresee, I am sure, the same result. Even before you try the experiment, you think it far too difficult. Yet it merely calls for the commonest of human skills, used as it were in reverse. After you have talked with a stranger two minutes, you are ready to estimate his character and his personality, and in most cases you will be right. Of course you have examined his appearance as well as listened to what he said, but this advantage does not affect the sad truth, that although we judge character accurately, few of us notice the signs or symptoms upon which our estimate is based. If a single comment conveys unconsciously the impression of indolence or of some other trait, we might as well ask what kind of comment conveys that specific impression. Observe more closely when next you hear a stranger talk; you'll be amazed at the speed with which the secret discovers itself, once the ears are open and the attention awake.

Years ago I learned how rare is the habit of thorough observation. I was then a teacher. Among themselves teachers discuss their students, and around examination time you may hear, "He can answer all the questions, but he knows very little. He may come out near the top of the class by grace of his marks, but he won't be an educated man." Or by way of contrast, to restore faith in the universe, the conversation may turn to some other student, present or past, who frequently muffed the answers but who even in his mistakes showed an alert mind and gave evidence of a healthy intellectual life.

There is no reason why teachers should not read character; indeed, there might seem to be a reason why they, having done more study than the rest of us, should observe character more profoundly and should have the art of dramatizing it. But few teachers can exhibit in a dialogue the character of their pupils. That means that few teachers observe life thoroughly, and few know how to write.

I realized my own inability when I came on a famous passage in a famous book, in which a famous teacher, who was also a famous writer, composed fanciful dialogues to illustrate what kind of boy he would admit to college and what kind he would keep out. The writer was Cardinal John Henry Newman, the book was called *The Idea of a University*, and in the second part of it there is a chapter on grammar. A student may know how to parse a sentence correctly and yet remain profoundly ignorant of grammar. Or to put the matter another way, grammar when properly taught becomes a door to life and character and the world of the intellect. Cardinal Newman makes the point delightfully clear in a conversation between the teacher and a boy who can parse glibly but who doesn't know what it is all about, and in another conversation between the teacher and a boy whose parsing sometimes stumbles, but who has learned how to think, and who thinks hard.

To portray character in dialogue, we must first be able to observe through the ear. It is just as simple, and for most of us just as difficult, to observe through the eye. Hearing and seeing are the only senses we make much use of. Our sense of smell is keen, but more often than not we are ashamed of it, and when we do use it, it's probably for a silly purpose, to make sure that a rose is a rose, or that the perfume bottle contains what we paid for. At other moments we accept the rose scent as a fact of nature, and the perfume worn by a woman as one of the things women wear, and to beauty in this form, whether natural or artificial, we pay, for the most part, no attention at all.

It's hard to describe anything exactly as we see it, for the reason that we don't see it. In the use of the eye, as of the ear, we are satisfied with a superficial result and do not get down to essentials, and to observe life, even superficially, through all the senses at once, seems to most of us so difficult that we resist the flood of experiences which otherwise would enrich every moment of our days. Yet our senses are a gift of nature, and if we weaken them by neglect, we can restore them by use.

You can prove this for yourself. Walk half a dozen blocks anywhere in your city, and afterwards write down a list of all you saw, heard, smelled, or otherwise became conscious of. At the first attempt your list won't be very long but you will have noticed a few things which if you hadn't been making the experiment, you would have ignored. Ordinarily when we pass a grocery store or a drug store, our nose tries to tell us what is there, but since we are in a hurry—"going somewhere," as we say—we don't allow our mind to recognize what is along the road. On a warm day of early autumn we may almost notice a strong camphor or tar smell, but we're probably too occupied with our errand to recognize completely a suit which has just been taken out of the camphor closet or the moth bag. We come to a place where the sidewalk is being mended, and for a few yards we walk on ashes instead of cement. Our sense of touch would tell us the difference, but our callous habit tries to shut out the news, and usually succeeds.

If the walk is repeated daily for a fortnight, either in the same streets or elsewhere, the progress in sensitive observation will be great. A novelist couldn't get along without cultivating a receptive attitude through the senses to all the impacts of life; without such a channel for the constant inflow of experience he may write a few books, but then he will stop, having nothing more to say. Since life itself should come before any art, it's rather terrifying that those who don't write, even more than those who do, permit the inflow of experience to become choked. Unless we recover the use of our senses, we have less and less to be interested in, and we become less interesting. Instead of growing towards completeness, our life shrinks.

If writers, from indolence or from any other cause, lose the power of observation, they sometimes compensate or set up an excuse by reporting in their books what can't be seen or heard. Whether a report of the unseeable and the unhearable is correct, no one can say. The novelist is beyond challenge who tells us at length the thoughts or motives of a character, especially those thoughts and motives which the character himself is unaware of. But if we read to acquire experience, or a new way of gathering experience, then these psychological story tellers are baffling.

So to a minor extent are the novelists who give us, not what they have seen or heard, but what might be seen or heard if the story were produced on the stage. All novelists envy the play-wright his privilege of telling his story with living persons, with direct appeal to the eye and the ear. But the attempt to seize for the novel the advantages of a play, ends in absurdity. The mis-guided begin by adding to the dialogue what seems an innocent tag. They write:

"No," said Alice, in a pleasant voice.

If that little stage direction really meant anything, you should be able to illustrate in the privacy of your room by making your voice sound pleasant. Try it.

Growing bolder, the novelist makes the stage direction more subtle.

"No," said Alice, with difficulty suppressing her annoyance.

Try that in your room too. You could easily produce a sound to show you're annoyed, but if Alice has suppressed her annoyance, what kind of tone would she use?

Losing all sense of humor, the novelist may perpetrate this absurdity,

"No," said Mrs. Brown, in the tone of a woman resolved not to tell all she knows.

I came across that sentence a few years ago in a novel which was widely read. No critic showed amazement at Mrs. Brown and her miraculously revealing tone. I deduce from their forbearance a certain indifference, not only to literary technique, but to the facts of life.

Instead of burdening their text with directions which would be helpful only to one who is putting on a play, good story tellers assume that life is indeed a play, already produced, and that their business is not to furnish us with the prompter's copy or the stage manager's, but to report the action as it appeared to the ear and the eye—what was said and what was done. To tell a story thus simply is to tell it in terms of experience, and to read a story so told is to gain practice in reading life itself. It seems to me an obvious advantage that a story so told must be read between the lines, since by that method alone can life be read.

"Now Naaman, captain of the host of the king of Syria, was a great man with his master, and honorable, because by him the Lord had given deliverance unto Syria. He was also a mighty man in valor.

"But he was a leper.

"And the Syrians had gone out by companies, and had brought away captive out of the land of Israel a little maid, and she waited on Naaman's wife.

"And she said unto her mistress, Would God my Lord were with the prophet that is in Samaria! for he would recover him of his leprosy.

"And one went in and told the king of Syria, saying, thus and thus said the maid that is of the land of Israel.

"And the king of Syria said, Go to, go, and I will send a letter unto the king of Israel. And Naaman departed, and took with him ten talents of silver, and six thousand pieces of gold, and ten changes of raiment.

"And he brought the letter to the king of Israel, which read as follows: Now when this letter is come unto thee, behold I have therewith sent Naaman my servant unto thee, that thou mayst recover him of his leprosy.

"And it came to pass when the king of Israel had read the letter, that he rent his clothes, and said, Am I God, to kill and to make alive, that this man should send unto me to recover a man of his leprosy? Wherefore consider, I pray you, and see how he seeketh a quarrel against me."

I wish there were space here to quote the superb story, all of it, but these opening paragraphs will serve our purpose for the time being, and you can look up the rest of it in the fifth chapter of the second Book of Kings.

Don't you feel, from sentence to sentence, that you are standing by, watching, listening, reading the characters? Why did the little maid tell Naaman's wife how Naaman could be cured? The girl was Naaman's captive; he was the enemy of her people. Perhaps she had come to like his wife. Perhaps she liked him. Perhaps she wanted to show him the power of the God of Israel, even though that God had for a season permitted his people to suffer defeat.

Why didn't Naaman take the girl's advice until the king of Syria sent him? He probably had no faith in the prophet of a people he had just defeated. Throughout the story, until the miraculous cure, he was contemptuous of Israel. There's no evidence that the king of Syria, either, had much faith in the prophet, but his attitude probably was that in a desperate case it's wise to grasp at every straw.

How much is told us about the king of Israel! He had had a hard time with the king of Syria, and his first thought was that he was in for it again. His nerves must have been rather jumpy. He had far less faith than the little maid. He might never have thought of the prophet, if the prophet hadn't spoken up for himself, as the full account informs us.

If you want to see how a story shouldn't be told, dilute this

Biblical account of Naaman with my comments, or with comments of your own. Give the perfect text some unnecessary stage directions.

Even an unsuccessful attempt to report experience increases the power of observation. I suppose that is why a novelist, unless he chokes himself off by turning his eyes inward, will keep on giving us book after book till he drops, and we'll understand what he means when he says his best book is always his next one. The more he observes, the less he is satisfied with what he has done. He will try again.

The idea that reading and writing are two approaches to the same experience, I have developed at length in a volume called *The Delight of Great Books*. And no one in our day who wishes to write or who loves to read, can overlook Somerset Maugham's *Summing Up*, the autobiographical record of a master-writer and master-reader, who over and beyond his craftsmanship is a seeker of wisdom, a brooder on the mysteries of life.

CHAPTER III

Music and Dancing

1.

EITHER MUSIC OR dancing is the most natural of the arts. Primitive man, we are told, danced before he sang, and long before he told stories. This thesis, I believe, is based on the fact that it's easier to make a dog or bear dance than to sing. But I confess small interest in primitive man. If he didn't have a complete life, it's now too late to help him. Man today, in the condition which can still be improved, is well disposed toward music. Most of us like to hum a tune or whistle, and we don't mind if others do it too.

Through the radio and the motion pictures music has become the most widely used of all the arts. Dancers are, I believe, sometimes presented over the radio, but only as they might perform for the blind; all that we can enjoy is the rhythmic tap of their feet. Though the films are for the eye, music helps to keep the attention of the spectator on what he sees. Without sound the constant flicker would put him to sleep. Yet though we hear more music today than the world ever heard at any earlier moment, it's still a common impression among us that music—really good music—is hard to appreciate correctly and should be left to the specially gifted. This mistaken notion is combated nowadays by the theory that the specially gifted, who with training might become a virtuoso, is an expensive nuisance and should be suppressed, music being the domain of the strictly amateurish, in whom technical competence is replaced by faith, hope, and charity.

I hold with neither of these extreme views. Far too many touring performers have awed the public by exhibitions of temperament; their contribution to the happiness of mankind is now better made by phonograph recordings of masterpieces, performed by authentic genius. But I wouldn't set the amateur, as some enthusiasts do, above the great professional. The artist who is richly endowed and thoroughly trained, and the composer who puts into music what his fellows wish to say and can't, are more than ever important. The amateur also has his importance, if he doesn't exaggerate it, and for the completeness of his life some knowledge of music, in proportion to his talent, is essential.

In homes where there is a piano the children, unless their parents prevent, usually investigate the instrument out of curiosity, and as often as not the untrained fingers teach themselves to pick out a tune. In time both hands get to work and the child either plays by ear, or develops by experiment some slight, very slight, skill in improvising. If the parents themselves know something about music, not too much, they will probably warn the child against both tendencies. Playing by ear, they will say, is a dangerous habit because it keeps you from learning to read music. Improvising, they will say, teaches you nothing, it develops your conceit, it spoils your taste for music that is really good.

The parents have here got hold of a little truth, but it isn't what they think, and they don't appreciate the instincts which they discourage. Playing by ear is impossible unless the child has a pretty good ear. Improvising would be impossible if the child didn't naturally think in the language of music. The danger is not in doing these two things, but in doing nothing else. The impulse to play by ear and the impulse to improvise are evidence of musical talent, something not to suppress but to develop.

These aptitudes can still be developed even in the mature. Up to a certain point it is so easy to teach ourselves, that we have small excuse for remaining musically uneducated.

If we play by ear, why not learn at once what notes we are playing? Why not be sure we play the notes the composer intended? It may be that our taste for music isn't so good as our ear, but that can be attended to later. If we love music and try to learn something about it, our taste will improve. The first step is to understand the symbols by which the composer tells us, precisely and simply, the notes he wishes us to play or sing. Those who make music by ear are exactly in the position of medieval folk before our musical notation was invented. They could sing many tunes, they could even sing two melodies at once, but they could learn new music only by listening to others, and they had no way of correcting a slip of memory.

The musical notation they evolved was fairly practical and not too complicated. With time it has become simpler and more accurate. It undertakes to record only the essentials, leaving the rest to the performer's judgment. The essentials are four—pattern, pitch, tempo, and rhythm.

Notation probably began with a waving line to indicate the pattern of the tune, a line which went up or down with the melody. To represent a slight rise in the tune, the line would turn up ever so little; on a sudden high note the line would be lifted as by an explosion. This graphic method of recording a tune is still practical if all you want is something to jog your memory. Try the experiment yourself; make graphs of *Swanee River* and *Yankee Doodle*. Your friends will probably recognize each song, though portrayed only in this crude fashion.

But suppose they never heard the tunes before. The graphs, however helpful as general reminders, fail to convey at all accurately any new information. A waving line by itself wouldn't tell whether the tune started on a high note or a low, nor would it be easy for the eye to measure how far the melodic line rose or fell, even though the symbol were accurately drawn. The next improvement in musical notation was probably a straight line drawn horizontally across the pattern, with a letter or by some other symbol placed on the line to indicate the pitch. Measuring from the lettered line, the musician could tell with considerable accuracy how far up or how far down the waving line was supposed to go.

Since the musician could measure still more accurately if further lines were added, we're not surprised that some old manuscripts show the musical graph with two lines, and later manuscripts with as many as eight. As the number of lines increased, additional letters were needed as guide-posts to the pitch. Suppose, for example, the original letter indicated the note which we call Middle C. The next line above it would represent E. Anyone could figure out quickly the interval between C and E, but when a third line was added above, it was found helpful to mark it with the letter G. Similarly, reckoning down instead of up, if the first line represented Middle C, the next below would be A, and the one below that, F.

If the tune lay in the notes which clustered about G, only those guiding lines were drawn which were needed, not more than three, four, or five. This group of lines was in time referred to as the G clef. By the same process the C clef developed, and the F clef. Today in our piano music and vocal quartets, we use the G clef and the F clef. The letter G has been rounded into a graceful symbol which designates accurately the line next to the bottom. The letter F has been rounded into a symbol which designates the line next to the top. Each clef has now five lines. If the G clef needs a Middle C, the composer writes the note on a fragmentary line below E. This fragmentary line which appears only when it is needed is called a ledger line. If the F clef needs a Middle C, it makes use of a ledger line above A.

Of course we might print the Middle C line exactly like the lines of the G clef and the F clef, but then we should have one solid bank of lines, eleven in all. By using for Middle C's the intermittent or ledger lines, we keep the G and F clefs easily distinguishable at a glance.

In early musical notation the waving line of the tune was broken up into different lengths to indicate the duration of the sound, and from these fragments our system of whole notes, half notes, quarter notes, etc., was gradually evolved. This development is a fascinating study in itself, but it isn't necessary for a practical knowledge of music. It interests the musician perhaps less than the writer. The notes we use, rounded ovals, or solid black circles with a straight line for a tail, sometimes with a flourish at the end, were adaptations of the accents by which the literary folk in late classical times tried to convey the changing pitch of the voice, as well as to stress the accent. We still indicate long or short syllables by a straight line or by the lower segment of a circle. In French we are familiar with the acute accent, the grave, and the circumflex. These are but a few of the signs which directed the reader to raise or lower his voice, to read fast or slow. The writer today would be happy if he could print his words as he wishes us to read them. It is poor consolation for him to know that early attempts of this kind were diverted to the profit of music.

We may not know the importance of the pitch and the importance of the tempo, but once our attention is directed to the matter, we can enlighten ourselves by a few experiments. We can sing *Yankee Doodle,* for example, in the lower part of our voice or in the upper, and we can try it so fast that it seems a jig, or slow enough to be a funeral march. Every change in pitch or tempo makes a different tune out of it. How can the composer indicate the particular tune he had in mind?

He fixes the pitch by the system of notation which we have just glanced at. If he intends the melody to begin on G, then G is the first note he writes. But suppose you and I can't recognize the sound of G? We may find it on the piano if there is a piano in reach, but suppose there isn't? The music won't mean much to us unless the note which the composer wrote calls up in our imagination the right sound. Few of us have that kind of imagination, but if we have, we are said to possess absolute pitch. That is, we distinguish just as accurately between different notes as most people can between different colors, or as many people can between subtle shades.

If you enjoy any acquaintance among musicians, you probably have seen this faculty in action. Perhaps a friend, showing off a bit, has awed you by naming the key of an automobile horn in the street, and has proved he was right by playing the sound on the piano. Perhaps you felt that only those can have this ability who are born with it.

This is not true. I doubt if anyone develops an entirely accurate sense of pitch unless all his time is given to music, but anyone with a fair ear can acquire as much accuracy as he needs. The method is ridiculously simple. You can teach yourself with a piano or a pitch-pipe or any other instrument. The important thing is that the pitch should be constant, and that you should know which note it is.

Let's assume a piano in the house. Have you any idea what Middle C sounds like? You probably haven't, but do your best —sing or whistle what you think is Middle C, then open your piano and check up. If you are five or six notes too high or too low, don't waste time contemplating that disaster; put your attention hard on the piano's Middle C. No other note has the same number of vibrations, the same color. Fix in your memory every trait of Middle C which on that brief acquaintance you can notice. Then go about your business for the day, and when you are within reach of the piano again in the evening, repeat the exercise; sound what you think is the note, and ask the piano to correct you. Do this morning and night for a week. Your range of error will diminish steadily. At the end of a month you ought to sound Middle C with respectable accuracy. You will have increased your enjoyment of music. Having become more sensitive to what you hear, you will hear more.

The importance of pitch to the composer I learned in my college days at Columbia, where Edward MacDowell spent some of his great genius trying to teach us. The music department at the time I speak of was located on the lower floors of an old building. On the top floor were the rooms of the glee club. The Department of Buildings evidently thought there was some connection between music and the glee club of those days.

One afternoon I met in the glee club room a fellow student, a high tenor, who at sight of me was overtaken by a desire to sing. In particular, he wished to sing MacDowell's famous song, *Thy Beaming Eyes,* which is intended for a baritone and has no note higher than F. For my friend's convenience I transposed it up to the key of A♭. We had done the song once and were about to do it again by way of giving ourselves an encore, when Mac-Dowell mounted the stairs, two steps at a time, burst into the room and pounced on me. It was the only time I ever saw him angry. "What right have you," he demanded, "to change my song? You know what key it should be in!" I replied that I hadn't changed it, I had merely transposed it. He came back hard: "What right have you to transpose it? If I painted a canvas in a sombre gray, and if you came along with your paint box and made a light gray out of it, you'd be a vandal and I could have you arrested!"

Not till several hours afterwards did I think of the retort that he and other composers permitted the publication of their songs in several keys. I am glad my wits were so slow. Had I been quicker, I might have brought this inconsistency to his attention, and after all, he was right. No song should be published in several keys. I should not have transposed his work.

Tempo is just as important as pitch. The earliest notation made no attempt to designate the right speed, since one singer learned the piece from another, but for several centuries it has been the custom to describe the tempo by a word printed over the music at the beginning. These words, however—allegro, andante, largo, and the others—are only descriptions. To indicate the exact pace we now depend upon the metronome, an instrument containing a pendulum which can be lengthened or shortened for changes in velocity. The earliest metronome was described in 1698 by a Frenchman named Étienne Loulié. The metronome now in use was developed by Johan Nepomuk Maelzel, who put it on the market around 1816. It is usual now to place the metronome mark at the beginning of the piece. For example, in the Debussy edition of Chopin's *Mazurkas,* the pace of Mazurka No. 1 is indicated by a quarter note and the number 132, with an equation sign between them. This means that 132 quarter notes are to be played each minute.

There are various ways of indicating the rhythm, but the most important and the only one that need detain us, is the division of the music into measures, and the indication of the number of beats to the measure. The waltz rhythm calls for three beats, the march rhythm for four. In a waltz, at the end of each three beats, a heavy perpendicular line called a bar is drawn across the clef. The group of beats between bars is called a measure. The number of beats to a measure is given at the beginning. Four quarter notes to a measure, what is called common time, we indicate by the letter C printed on the clef. The other rhythms are indicated by Arabic numerals, three quarter notes to a measure by 3 over 4, two quarter notes by 2 over 4.

I have tried to describe musical notation in outline. I have said nothing about sharps and flats, nor about the theories abroad in the world today which would alter our way of writing music. Anyone who is interested can find good books on the elements of the subject in local libraries, or he can easily be directed to them by local music teachers. My purpose here is to suggest that there is no great difficulty in reading music, as there is none in training the ear to recognize pitch.

The next step toward an understanding of music would be to acquire at least a general idea of counterpoint and harmony. Harmony is the grammar of music, counterpoint is, so to speak, the rhetoric. The music student usually begins with harmony, but in the development of the art counterpoint came first. The earliest music in western Europe, so far as we know, consisted of a melody sung by one voice or by voices in unison. In the next stage there were two voices, or choirs, one singing the melody, another sustaining a fixed note against it, or singing a counter-melody. When two melodies are sung against each other, it is obvious that they can move in the same direction, up and down together, or in different directions, one going up while the other goes down. Three patterns are the basis of counterpoint—a melody sung against a sustained tone, two melodies in parallel motion, or two melodies in contrary motion.

Harmony, the grammar of music, has to do with the relation of a number of notes heard at the same time. A single chord involves harmony. In a limited way, therefore, harmony can exist without counterpoint. It is less evident but equally true, that counterpoint cannot exist without harmony. Any tone is composed of the sound which we are sure to hear, and of certain harmonics or sympathetic tones which the inexperienced ear may not at first detect. When we strike Middle C on the piano, we set a whole chord vibrating. The other notes of that chord are E and G. G, the fifth above C, is easily recognized, but E, the third, is there too. The basis of even the most modern harmonies is this chord which lurks in every note. It took musicians some time to find it.

The first gropings after something more than a single note seems to have led to the discovery of the octave, which is a

doubling of the harmonic chord. The next complication discovered by the primitive ear was probably an octave with the fifth
inserted, as though you played Middle C, G above it, and C above
that. I have no doubt at all that the wild fellow who stuck in the
fifth was damned for his ultra-modern tendencies. In time the
third was added, not without some protests with which, to a
degree, we still sympathize. The third belongs in the major triad,
the ordinary harmonic chord, but it is less essential than the fifth,
and it is a bit saccharine. Text books warn the harmony student
against doubling the third in a chord. We don't want too much
of the sweet mixture. On the other hand, we can stand any amount
of the sturdy fifth, as were reminded by Debussy and Ravel.

The development of harmony from the simple triad to the
chords used by Arnold Schoenberg or Charles Griffes and by still
later composers, follows the progress of growing sensitiveness in
the ear. Musicians did not at first hear the harmonics of the tone
C. When they at last used with C the accompanying E and G,
it was some time before they realized that E and G would also
have their harmonics. E played as the third of the chord on C
would sound the harmonics B and D. Disregarding for the
moment the harmonic thirds, we can trace the development of
harmony by playing first the chord on C—that is, C, E, G; then
adding the fifth above E, so that the total chord will be C, E, G,
B; then the fifth above the original G, so that the total chord
will be, C, E, G, B, D. Continuing this process we may add the
fifth above B, which is F sharp, and the fifth above D, which is
A. I use the fifth in this illustration because it is the harmonic
easiest to hear, and for that reason it has controlled the discovery
of new chords. As each new chord was put to use, it was greeted
by protest on the part of those who hadn't noticed it before. With
practice, however, they could hear the new harmonic, and when
they heard it they liked it.

To the composer the essence of harmony is a respect for harmonics. No chord really sounds well unless it obeys the order
of those ghostly tones which almost elude the ear, yet dictate
the terms on which it can be pleased. We can illustrate by building up a fairly extended chord on the natural harmonics, a chord
consisting, say, of the notes C, E, G, B, D, F sharp, A. Suppose

we play this chord two or three times, striking the notes firmly but not harshly, trying to find all the beauty in the combination; there's a good deal. Now let us play the same notes close together, moving the D, F sharp, and A down an octave. The chord will then read—I assume that we begin with Middle C—C, D, E, F sharp, G, A, B. Play this! We'd better play it soft. It's not a chord, it's a discord, a rather horrible noise.

Why should the same notes sound so differently in different positions? Why should the combination when extended be agreeable, and when condensed be atrocious? The answer is the key to the science of harmony. In the extended order each note emphasizes a harmonic which is already sounded by another note. The D above G has been sounded by the G. When we put the D an octave lower, it is no longer a harmonic; harmonics do not sound down hill.

Here again I attempt merely to sketch the outlines of an art into which the reader may care to go further. How much harmony and counterpoint you need is for you to say. But no man or woman who must listen to sounds at all times, if it's only the ringing of a bell or the call of a bird, can afford not to hear completely. There are innumerable text books on ear-training and harmony and counterpoint; any music teacher or publisher will suggest titles. Two admirable introductions to the whole subject are *The Layman's Music Book,* by Olga Samaroff Stokowski, and *The Gist of Music,* by George A. Wedge.

2.

To suggest what music you should hear or in what order you should hear it, is even more absurd than prescribing the approach to books, for music must be performed and even the best music is at the performer's mercy. If you have the opportunity, hear Toscanini or Heifetz or Josef Hofmann or Kreisler or Lhévinne, no matter what they are playing.

The histories of music, like the histories of literature, impress chronology so deeply upon us that the program of any concert you are likely to hear will begin with Bach and work on down toward modern times. This arrangement always annoys me; I want to argue about it, but the performer is busy on the platform and even if he weren't he'd probably be stubborn. Why not begin with modern music and end with Mozart, Haydn, or Bach, whose idiom is bold and clear and who, even when they are massive, remain beautifully serene? Or why not discard chronology altogether, and group the pieces by their inner relations, whether of resemblance or contrast?

Your study of music, like your concert-going, had best begin wherever the music is good. If you like modern composers, then begin with Stravinsky and Schoenberg, with Prokofieff and Shostakovich. If Chopin bewitches you, let him introduce you to the art. But be sure you move on from your first admiration to the composers of other ages and different styles. There is an enormous body of western music, and an equal amount of oriental music, and a practically inexhaustible store of primitive or folk music, all of it fascinating and much of it available now on phonograph records. Begin where you like and let your curiosity spread.

My own experience with music is not typical, since I grew up in a musical family, before the phonograph or the radio brought into the home great artists, even whole opera companies and symphonic orchestras. Whatever music was heard under your roof in those days, you had to make yourself, and most of it, to tell truth, was very bad. Even when I was a small child I knew I had unusual luck. In my grandfather's house, at 28 East 8oth Street, New York City, there was a piano, a two-manual organ, my grandfather's violin, Uncle Arthur's flute and Uncle Will's 'cello. When a good chance offered, I used to walk on the organ pedals, hoping always to touch the full two octaves of them before some sensitive elder called a halt. My grandmother would tell me of happy evenings when her family circle was still unbroken, and there were players for all the instruments, with a quartet of singers in addition.

My first instruction in music I had from my father, as gifted an amateur as I have known. His tenor voice was well trained, and though he didn't pretend to be a pianist, he could play better than most singers, and his interest in music didn't stop with the exhibition of his own voice. Two or three times a week an accompanist came to our house, and Father would spend the evening singing, going over his large repertoire, trying out new songs which he had practiced alone. His audience on those occasions would be the family. I tell myself I can remember the singing from my fourth year, or even my third, but I admit I may be exaggerating. At all events, when I was put to bed in early childhood I used to ask my mother to leave the door open so that I could listen. I liked particularly the way Father's voice carried when he sang pianissimo. He often had in some musical friends, professional as well as amateur, and the program on those occasions would be richly varied. I speak of all this not merely to record my great good fortune, but to suggest that nowadays with our phonograph we can enjoy even more music, more wonderfully performed, than my father and his friends brought into our home.

He was my earliest music teacher. He began by letting me share the music bench with him and rest my hands on his while he played. When I was four years old he taught me the notes, the scales, and the elements of harmony, major and minor triads, tonics, dominants, diminished sevenths. When I was twelve I began to play his accompaniments, and until I left home for my first job in the world, eleven years later, I should have felt cheated if anyone had taken my place. As a result, though the piano was my instrument, music for me is primarily song, the music of the human voice, and I know best the singer's repertoire. Father was devoted to Schubert, but he loved all great *lieder,* and he sang many beautiful things which I never hear now on public programs, and wonder why not. He admired MacDowell's songs, though he would say they were far too difficult to be popular. He thought highly of Anton Rubinstein's compositions, and I suppose it is his influence that makes me regret the neglect into which Rubinstein has fallen. When I was fourteen I had quite a time mastering the accompaniment of *Die Lerche* (The Lark), one of Father's favorites.

In middle life I had a pianistic house-cleaning and revivification under the magnificent coaching of my dear friend Ernest Hutcheson, but I speak now of my approach to music in youth. The first teacher, after my father, was a young man named Frank Fruttchey, a brilliant pianist who spent most of his short life playing church organs and drilling choirs, occupations which wouldn't have interfered with the development of his talents as pianist and composer, had he not indulged to excess his curiosity about all things musical. I must say he stimulated my mind, however costly to himself was the scattering of his energies. At one time, for example, he built a two-manual practice organ in his own house. Why he wanted to build it, I don't remember. The construction of the instrument at odd hours occupied him for about two years, and the final condition of his front parlor was deplorable, the temper of his family was on edge, and after all the commotion the bellows proved inadequate. So far as my childhood engagements permitted, I hung around and watched the slow growth of the wonder, and what knowledge I have of organs and of acoustic problems I date from Mr. Fruttchey's experimental extravagances.

As a pianist he had technique but a small repertoire. He specialized in Chopin, whom he played with little discrimination, admiring the earliest pieces quite as much as the great scherzos and ballades. He knew Mozart well, and played the sonatas acceptably, but he was first and last a romantic, and his soul craved endless Chopin, Liszt and Schumann—and his own improvising. His improvisations were serious and altogether remarkable. I have heard no pianist, and only certain French organists, who could equal him in this fast-disappearing branch of the musical art. I recall a concert program on which he had put down for one number the stark word *Improvisation*. Since he told me in advance what he intended, I knew he approached the piano with nothing but two themes in his head. Yet the piece came out a well rounded composition in three sections, both themes serving picturesquely upside down for the second movement, an *Andante*.

In him I first encountered absolute pitch. My father had an excellent ear but in accuracy he was miles away from Mr. Fruttchey, who could sound a picket on a fence and announce with confidence that it was tuned to B flat, a few vibrations above or below. He first demonstrated this power, as I remember, on an iron pipe in front of my father's house, where workmen dug a trench. I hurried back into the house to check him up by the piano. For some years thereafter I believed in miracles.

Mr. Fruttchey taught me harmony and counterpoint. He knew

—rare wisdom—that music is for the ear rather than the eye. I suppose it was my father who taught me in very early childhood to read music; I can't remember the time when I didn't know how. Mr. Fruttchey taught me what is called nowadays aural harmony. At the close of each piano lesson he reserved ten or fifteen minutes for theory. I would stand in the curve of the piano with my back to him; he would play a chord and ask me to identify it; he would repeat the chord in another position, and I would call out the notes, always beginning with the bass; he would then improvise, and whenever he stopped he expected me to name the key and again call out the notes of the chord. Nowadays we write books and give lectures on how to listen to music. Mr. Fruttchey's method is the simplest I've met.

My second piano teacher was Carl Walter, a lifelong friend of my father's who had come from Germany to Cincinnati, and afterwards to New York, looking toward a concert career. He was an original character, full of so much common sense that to many of his friends he seemed a humorist. He had superb technique and the repertoire of a virtuoso, but the New York of the 1870's was no paradise for even good pianists, and after two or three seasons Carl Walter decided to abandon the public platform altogether and play privately just for fun. Since he was an excellent teacher, he had many pupils and lived in comfort. Few pianists enjoy so pleasant a life. He was much sought for in the New York society of his day, but he never would accept a dinner invitation except where the host and hostess, in his own words, had brains and understood music. If he were asked to play he would gladly do so, but only on condition that the piano was a Steinway, that it was in tune, and that the keys were clean. I have heard him make cutting remarks about keyboards on which children did their after-lunch practicing without first washing their hands. He preferred Ivory soap.

Like Mr. Fruttchey he played much Chopin, but with a manliness which made the music noble. His admiration for Mozart and Haydn was not unusual in his time, but his attitude toward Bach was. I had heard the Bach organ fugues much played, always in a conscientious, rather mechanical style. Mr. Walter held the sound opinion, too seldom stated though most artists agree with

it, that between classical and romantic music the difference is not
in essential elements but in the proportion in which they are
mingled; that even romantic music, if it is good music, is intellectual to a high degree, and that even classical music is to the
same degree emotional. He insisted that Bach should be played
romantically. I remember his delight when Paderewski came to
our shores and first played to us the *Chromatic Fantasy.*

Most of Carl Walter's musical judgments would be generally
held today. Bach, Mozart, and Beethoven were his idols, with
Chopin following close. But he had eccentric ideas about even
the greatest composers. I'm not sure he was wrong. Richard
Wagner's music, as music, he valued as highly as anyone today,
but Richard Wagner as a dramatist and composer of operas, he
would say, was "one lengthy mistake." Mozart, he thought, was
the master for the stage. A dramatic situation, he believed,
whether or not music went with it, must move with speed, or the
attention, like an over-stretched rubber band, would have no life
left in it.

He said once—and this is a theory which I promptly made my
own and have held ever since—that those with a natural taste for
Italian music should study the German composers, and those who
have the German temperament should specialize in Italian music.
Unless we broaden our taste by such correctives, we remain or
become narrow, he thought, and in the large and rich world of
music undue specialization is a calamity.

But this theory of broad-mindedness Carl Walter carried so far
as to shock some of his musical friends. He had the courage to
like a piece even though by a second rate or old-fashioned composer; he enjoyed playing for example, some of the tinkling bril-
liancies of Louis Moreau Gottschalk, particularly the *Murmures
Eoliens,* a confection as lush as its title, under bungling fingers a
stupid piece but an entrancing series of tone effects when well
done. I once ventured the opinion that Gottschalk had no musical
subject matter, merely a fine rhetoric. He rebuked my youthful
dogmatism by saying that Gottschalk was no Beethoven, as Edgar
Allan Poe was no Shakespeare, but even Poe's verbal sound-poem,
The Bells, was in its kind a masterpiece when recited by a master.

The year I entered college Edward MacDowell came to Columbia University as Professor of Music, and I enrolled in his courses of composition and orchestration. He was an authentic genius, a sturdy and manly character with an excellent mind and broad interests. He was the first example I knew of the all-around professional musician who composes as well as plays, who is as much at home with the orchestra and the voice as with any particular instrument, who conducts as well as composes. I am indebted to him for many things, but chiefly for provocative ideas about art. One day in his composition class he scolded us for writing music imitative of other times and other lands. It was an interesting thing for him to say, considering his own long residence abroad and the extent to which European composers had influenced him, and no one saw this point more clearly than he.

"If your work were better," he said, "it might just as well have been written by Liszt or Schumann or Richard Wagner. It contains no evidence that you were born in America and now live in New York City. Around the campus, when you're not on musical dress parade, I catch you humming the tunes you like, and most of them are rag-time. (This was in the hey-day of Sousa.) If rag-time rhythms are your rhythms, why not write them? Music can be sincere only when it's written from what's inside of you."

He stopped and looked out the window a moment, then went on with a whimsical smile. "I tried a stretch of mild rag-time myself in the Scherzo of my *D minor Concerto,* but I've been too much away from America, and I haven't, like you, rag-time in my bones."

Years afterwards Charles Martin Loeffler, shortly before his death, told me that if he had his career to live over again, he would use in his symphonic compositions the instrumentation of the jazz orchestra. He dilated with enthusiasm on the rich effects secured with great economy by Ferde Groffe. I think MacDowell would have agreed with him.

When I asked MacDowell one day which composers one should study in order to understand what was called modern music, he replied that to get at modern music you should look into modern composers. But declining to be smiled off, I insisted that some contemporary composers, like his own pupils, were, as he had pointed out, too old-fashioned. He turned serious. "For harmony," he said, "study Palestrina. For modern harmony, study Bach." His understanding of these two composers was remarkable. I often wonder why his own writing shows so little of their influence.

I must set down here my love of his music. I hesitate to say I think him the greatest American composer; I can't forget Stephen Foster, supreme in his class, nor George Gershwin, whose work I rank very high indeed, nor many composers still living who write in all kinds for the concert hall, or the stage, or the radio, or the screen. Musical talent abounds, and some of it we may decide is genius. But MacDowell's four-piano sonatas and his second piano concerto, his *Indian Suite* for orchestra and his songs, are great music. His *Sea Pieces* and his *Woodland Sketches* are damaged by inadequate pianists who play to death the easy sections and never perform the series as a whole. Both groups of pieces when played straight through, emerge as impressive suites.

After my university studies I taught for six years at Amherst College, where William Pingry Bigelow was Professor of Music. It was not then a general custom in American colleges to organize student choruses and orchestras, but Mr. Bigelow had a group of ninety or a hundred voices who rehearsed several times a week, and Monday evenings they joined forces with the college orchestra. Girls and women from the local high school or church choirs supplied the contralto and soprano sections, and three or four times a year some large work was given. For the concerts Mr. Bigelow strengthened his orchestra by engaging the first desk players of the Boston Symphony.

I thank Mr. Bigelow and the Amherst singers for the opportunity to study works none too often performed, Mozart's *Requiem*, Haydn's *Seasons*, Mendelssohn's *Elijah*, *St. Paul* and *Hymn of Praise*, Handel's *Messiah*, *Acis and Galatea*, and many others. I am grateful also for the opportunity in Amherst years and earlier to serve as church organist and choir-master. In the United States we are as likely as not to encounter the art of music first in church or at dances, and it is to the interest of every serious musician, I think, to raise the standard of music wherever music is most frequently heard. For that reason George Gershwin was, I believe, very important to America in his songs and in his music for Broadway shows. Far more of us hear the songs and see the shows than can attend opera or symphonic concerts. And those of us who love music should join some singing group, a church choir or a choral society. If there is no such group in our neighborhood, we should organize one.

If our ambition is to be a professional musician, we must acquire as quickly as possible familiarity with all the best composers—those which musicians and our colleagues consider the best. But it would be a calamity if even the professional sacrified sincerity to conventional opinion and pretended to admire what he didn't really care for. Those of us who wish only such knowledge of music as belongs to a reasonably complete life, may resemble the good professional at least in this, that we are honest in our tastes. Let's hope that we don't prefer bad music to good, but let's hope also that we can suspend judgment about the great names which for us are not yet and perhaps never will be convincingly great. To occupy our time there are enough good composers who are within our range.

I learned early that Sebastian Bach ought to be admired by every well-bred musician, and in my youth I did my best, but it wasn't until very much later that I realized his importance, and not until later still that I loved his music. Even now I won't pretend to love all of it. *The Art of Fugue,* for example, I'm willing never to hear again. On the other hand, I believe that Handel is nowadays under-rated. So far as the decline of his once enormous reputation is a natural counter-swing, there's nothing to worry about; he will come to his own again. But there's no point in running Handel down merely, as it seems to me, to make a clearer case for Bach. Both composers wrote stupendous choruses, and in my opinion Handel's best choral work has this excellence, that he doesn't need to be lengthy in order to be stupendous. The choruses in *Messiah* and in *Israel in Egypt* keep a higher level of excitement than I find in any other composer, except on occasion Mozart. Handel's great arias seem to me unequalled, and if Bach's organ fugues seem unique, it is perhaps because Handel's are not played.

In contemporary criticism it is hardly good form to speak highly of Liszt, and having turned most of his pages, I know well that he had his thin moments; but whether I'm right or wrong, I believe he was one of the greatest in music, perhaps as creative a performer as Bach himself, and in his best compositions a dynamic influence, still vital. He invented much useful material, themes and harmonic sequences, which later composers patronizingly borrowed or filched; he evolved new forms for orchestral and piano music; he fixed the concert tradition both in the type of program and the manner of performing it; and he was the unselfish champion of other music than his own. Those critical biographers who would undermine his fame, and who incidentally disclose certain Freudian conditions in themselves by poking their nose into the details of his sex life, make me sick.

The piano sonata which I like best is Chopin's in B minor. Next I would put Liszt's great sonata. I know this is heresy. By most well-grounded musicians Beethoven is supposed to have written the supreme sonatas, but they don't give me the same intense pleasure as the two I've mentioned. If I live long enough I may change my mind. The *Appassionata* or the latest sonatas contain some of the most marvelous music I've heard, but the piano doesn't seem heroic enough to sustain such material; I hanker for an orchestral arrangement. On the other hand the later string quartets of Beethoven are for me altogether wonderful, with no impertinent reservations on my part.

With these exceptions my taste in music is fairly orthodox— unless it's unusual to enjoy modern music as well as classical. Mozart, Haydn, Schubert, Chopin, Schumann, Brahms—I have never found the slightest difficulty in loving them all. Mendelssohn in my lifetime has seemed under-rated, and popular though Schubert is, we probably don't yet appreciate his greatness. Wagner's best work I love as music, though I don't share the flattering opinion he had of his librettos. As a literary man, he's neither a poet nor a dramatist, simply a long-winded story teller. But the music of *Die Meistersinger,* which I consider his masterpiece, and the music of *Tristan und Isolde,* which I place second, is incomparably noble.

The great dramatist among the composers seems to me Mozart, and next to him—I am speaking of dramatic genius, remember —Verdi and Puccini. Some composers have left us a single theatrical triumph and no more—Bizet, for example, with his *Carmen*, Leoncavallo with *Pagliacci*, Debussy with *Pelleas and Melisande*. This last seems to me quite the most successful opera in modern times.

The art of music progresses today as always on two different planes. There are the producers of what we call modern music, Stravinsky, Schoenberg, Chavez and a host of others, who carry on the highbrow or academic tradition by extending the resources of harmony, rhythm, and tone-color. There are also the countless popular composers, the inhabitants of Tin Pan Alley, writers of songs and dances to supply an unfailing demand.

It's a great mistake to sniff at the modern composer with his new harmonies, and an equal error to patronize the makers of popular music. The best in each kind point to the music of tomorrow. George Gershwin was a great musician. I am sure the histories of music will say so. I have no doubt that Jerome Kern's *Show Boat* is in its kind a masterpiece, more likely to be remembered than most contemporary attempts at opera in the old style. As for what seems to the conventional the weird extravagance of modern music, I can only suggest this experiment: listen to it with as much openness of mind as you can improvise, and immediately afterwards listen to some famous music at least fifty years old. If you are frank I believe you'll admit that however raucous the modern idiom, it makes old styles by comparison pale. If this describes your experience, then the modern music you have listened to is pretty good. In the development of the art each advance adds color and intensity. Perhaps for that reason symphony and recital programs are usually arranged in chronological order, the older and tamer pieces first. Perhaps if we began with the latest things and worked backward, we'd put the old masters to a terrible disadvantage.

3.

It is hard to explain music without an illustration for the ear, and equally difficult to say anything helpful about the art of the dance unless there is an illustration for the eye. A fixed picture is not adequate. The drawings of dancers on old vases do not enlighten us as much as they seem to. Music and dancing, we are accustomed to say, are time arts; to be enjoyed they must be re-created. All that can be done on the printed page is to set down some general hints and reflections, in the hope of stimulating the reader to practical experiment.

It is often said, rather carelessly, that dancing is more closely associated with music than with the other arts. The fact is that all the arts are interrelated. Anatole France liked to say that there is but one Art, of which the various arts are diverse manifestations. When we investigate the history of music, we soon come on minuets, mazurkas, waltzes, and other dance patterns. If we go deeper into the past, we find primitive dances so bound up with primitive rhythms and primitive chants that we can't now say which came first, yet the dance has associations just as close with sculpture, with painting, and with the drama. For the purpose of this book we shall assume a knowledge of all these relations. Not only are there books in plenty on every phase of the subject, but better still, there is an instinctive recognition in us all that dancing is more than keeping time to the music and executing the correct steps. It is about that something more that I wish to speak here.

Whether dancing is the earliest and basic art interests me, I confess, very little. I never could get properly excited over any theories of creation, since the fact that the world is here now seems more vital than a description of its start given by some man who wasn't there. The importance of the dance is timeless. We can observe it at any gathering, public or private, where dancing is in progress. We have but to watch the dancers and the onlookers, and check carefully our own emotions and instincts.

You and I have seen fairly mature people, perhaps in a group, taking dancing lessons, trying to master the tango, the samba, or something still newer. Most beginners learn the rhythm quickly and soon do the right steps, but if their teacher, a professional, dances with them, they and the onlookers notice the contrast. In the beginning something is missing, some essential poise of the body, some necessary flow of motion.

The onlooker may have some critical thoughts which though he doesn't know it tell tales about himself. If he is good-tempered, he won't pass a direct verdict on the satisfactory cavortings of the imperfect dancers; he'll merely feel an impulse to get up and do it himself, an impulse which to some extent is an implied criticism. But the onlooker wishes to dance even if the dancing he watches is perfectly done. I shan't delay here over the reasons for this wish; it's enough to call attention to the fact that we do have this impulse, and also that we usually resist it. Much to our loss! The practice of any art is a normal and wholesome occupation. To hold back because of bashfulness or false pride is a bad mistake.

When we say we don't wish to make ourselves ridiculous, we are aware of something very important in all art—the audience. When our criticism of poor dancing is most severe, we perhaps marvel that anyone should make such an exhibition. Again we are conscious of the audience, which in this case is ourselves.

Every art must have its audience. Even the amateur when he dances should remember we are looking at him, otherwise he is not likely to dance well. Any man or woman who seeks complete self-development and self-fulfillment, should learn as soon as possible this consideration of the audience, without which no art is significant.

We come at an elementary understanding of the dance by considering the difference between the kind of enjoyment we have when we are circling the floor with our partner, and the kind we have while watching another couple. For the dancers there is excitement in the music and the rhythm, a satisfaction in keeping step, the pleasure that comes from any team work, but if there were nothing more we probably should not consider dancing an art. Apart from the audience, dancers would be merely isolated human beings engaged in private exercise. Some of us do our morning calisthenics to the sound of a phonograph; our evening evolutions on a dance floor, to the accompaniment of a band, are not more conducive to health nor, if we haven't an audience in mind, to art.

The onlooker may have his pulse quickened by the rhythm of the music, but his profit is not in exercise as such; what he enjoys in dancing is the flow of motion and the sculpturesque poise of the bodies. He is delighting in a paradox. Since the bodies move in strict time and by definite steps, the natural effect would be jerky, a little monotonous. Accomplished dancers, however, execute the steps correctly without drawing attention to them. They are conscious of their steps but they don't wish the onlooker to be. They wish to create an effect which is not natural, the illusion of unbroken movement.

It is a further paradox that though the dance exists only in motion, it suggests, by the correct carriage of the body, by poise and balance, the attitudes of sculpture. That this effect is an illusion is indicated by photographs of an actual dance, which usually seem anything but sculpturesque or poised or balanced.

The essence of the dancers' art is in these two illusions, the illusion of fluid motion, the illusion of sculpturesque poise. You and I should know how these illusions are created, even if we are not dancers. To be presentable at all to the eye of our neighbor we must to some degree contradict or correct the structure of our bodies. Our skeletons are angular, to put it mildly, and though we do round ourselves out by some muscle and more fat, we remain a jointed creature. There are schools of dancing which play up the joints, but I don't admire them, and what merit they may have you must learn from someone else. What seems to me important is that a very angular woman like Sarah Bernhardt, with ugly arms, could with those arms create the illusion of rounded waves of motion, or that an extremely thin woman like Pavlowa could persuade you with the rush-like grace of her legs that she had no kneecaps. The kneecap is the last infirmity which the human animal overcomes.

The problem of poise was attacked in former days by finishing schools for young ladies. The pupils walked, as you recall, with books on their heads, or they worked at their lessons sitting up uncomfortably straight, strapped to a plank. Boys received parallel instruction in certain sports and in military drill. Nowadays the technique once thought proper for a lady is taught in training schools for actresses, models, and dancers, to all of whom it is professionally profitable, but the rest of us also might as well know what is good for our physical and mental well-being.

I said I was little interested in theories of creation; whether mankind once moved on all fours, I neither know nor care. I am disturbed, however, to notice that though I can't walk on all fours, I have a tendency to walk as though I preferred all fours to two feet. This tendency, to my infinite embarrassment, accents itself when I try to dance. Or even when I try to stand up straight. If I moved on all fours, my elbows would bend toward my knees, and my knees would bend toward my elbows—the opposite of the angles in the legs of a horse, another creature which moves on all fours. The difference between the horse and the human quadruped—I mean the human who tries to go on all fours—is that the horse travels fast on flat surfaces but can't climb, whereas man is a great climber. The hind legs of a horse, therefore, bend backwards, and the front legs forward, to push and pull over the horizontal surface; a man's hind legs bend the other way for convenience in grasping a tree trunk.

These ideas of mine, I warn you, are without scientific value; I merely clear the ground for the essential point, that in our daily walk, and still more, in our dancing moments, it is well to avoid the impression that we are galloping in a paddock or climbing a tree. We remind ourselves that though the stomach has a right to hang down in those animals which go on all fours, we'd rather not have it stick out when we try to stand up. Similarly, though the hind quarters of a horse are permitted a certain prominence, are even admired for it, the upright creature need not make a specialty of this feature. We are in the way of grace so long as we hold the spine straight. It's all right for the spine of the horse to sag, but if we have round shoulders we'll have round something else, by way of compensation. It's hard enough to stand straight when we do nothing but stand. To move around without making our backbone into a corkscrew, is still harder. To keep the spine straight and all the joints camouflaged, yet move as freely as a flowing stream, is to dance.

For dancing which does not try to be an art I have little enthusiasm; most of us if we wished could dance well, and I can't see why we should be content either not to dance at all or to do less than our best at the one art which can be practiced with no other equipment than our bodies and our minds. Yet it is fair to add that dancing would belong in the complete life even though our performance were very modest. Rhythm is a mysterious source of health upon which we draw too seldom, and the most rudimentary kind of dancing, so long as the feet keep time, attunes us to vital forces. While we dance we ourselves are the language through which we speak, and the influence which keeps planets in their tracks and stars in their places has power also on us. How stupid and how sad for mature men and women, any more than stars, to surrender to bashfulness or vanity, and though they'd like to dance, let the moment go by.

4.

Here again I feel bound to confess what I myself have learned, since I presume to suggest the complete life for others. In practice I never got beyond drawing room dancing, and even there I didn't excel. As a child I was sent to dancing school, where the instruction and the society of extremely young females annoyed me. Not until I was seventeen or eighteen did I discover that dancing was fun. This tardiness indicates, I think, that I had little talent for the art. A natural dancer would have found himself earlier. Dancing of a more complicated type, group dancing, folk dances, ballet, I have neither studied nor attempted. I am old enough to remember quadrilles and other square dances, and I can believe that any form of dance which involves numbers and team play, must give to properly endowed folk a pleasure concealed from me.

As a spectator I have enjoyed most of the great dancers of my time. Nijinsky I missed, to my lasting regret. Pavlowa I saw a number of times, and her perfect art haunts me. I saw Isadora Duncan before I was equipped to appreciate her stimulating ideas. Between her own work and the instruction she imparted to her pupils, I noticed, unfortunately, the wide gulf, and the paradox blinded me a little to her really wonderful achievement. She was, as everyone knows, an instinctive artist, and though she had a keen and stimulating mind she was not very successful in rationalizing her inspirations. To remember her and Pavlowa is to carry around with you supreme examples of opposing types in art.

Nowadays I find myself deeply interested in folk dances, or rather in sophisticated solo developments of folk dances. For that reason I greatly admire Argentinita. Her development of Central and South American dances is always interesting and usually very beautiful. In general, though I have tried in the preceding pages to indicate the ideals of the abstract or pure dance, I derive most pleasure from the dancing which is close to drama. About popular dancing I feel as I do about popular music; when it is excellent only a conventional highbrow could esteem it lightly. Fred Astaire and the tap-dancer Bill Robinson are masters in their specialties, and though I may damn myself with the *cognoscenti* for saying so, I'd rather watch them than any ballet whatever.

5.

In what is here said about music and dancing, I have assumed our contacts with those arts would be largely through practice; that is, I have suggested certain experiments with our own hands on the piano and on the dance floor with our own feet. Anyone who cares at all for music or for dancing will of course seize every opportunity to hear and to watch the expert performers. In our time, however, the music lover has a remarkable aid in the phonograph, if he will take care to get the most out of the records. Merely to listen is not enough; if we don't use our mind actively or creatively, even while listening, we may tire at last of the music which once pleased and ought still to do so. With a little effort we can put ourselves in the position of the virtuoso, who finds new beauties in the playing of his colleagues just because he constantly studies his own interpretations.

When we listen to a phonograph record, we should have the music before our eyes, or we should study it in advance. Until we have followed a performance with the score in front of us, we'll probably doubt our ability to follow the notes or to learn much from them, but the experience will prove exciting and in various ways rewarding. The ability to read increases, and though we have heard the piece often, we discover lovely things in it which when we listened less attentively, we failed to hear. A professional, before he goes to a concert, is likely to glance over anything on the program on which his memory is vague. The humblest amateur gains by preparing himself the same way. If he has recordings of the same piece by different players or by different conductors, he soon learns to appreciate different interpretations.

We have as yet no convenience, parallel to the phonograph record, for studying the dance. We must see the dancers in person. Perhaps you wish to correct me here; in motion pictures you've been delighted with the dancing of Fred Astaire or Ginger Rogers or other experts. Well, so have I. But the difference between good dancing in a concert hall and good dancing on the screen is wide. Motion pictures present motion in many forms, but in my opinion they do not succeed in capturing the illusion of the dance. When I've watched Fred Astaire dance on the stage, I've been able to keep my attention on that flow of motion, on those glimpses of sculptural attitudes, which it is the purpose of the dancer's art to produce. But for some reason the camera brings me back to his feet and legs, and though I marvel at his agility, I wonder where the poetry has vanished. The screen demands of us, and gets, much greater attention in order to create an illusion in us. However that may be, I'd advise studying all good dancers on the stage or on the dance floor. The pleasure we get from dancers on the screen is of a different kind, far less likely to help us in our own mastery of the art.

The questions which I have here tried to define are beautifully illuminated in *The Dance of Life*, by Havelock Ellis. If you know this book, you'll probably be glad to read it again. It contains helpful ideas about literature—indeed, about all the arts.

If you don't know it already, you will find profit in Isadora Duncan's autobiography, *My Life*. A good popular survey of the modern ballet, illustrated by excellent photographs, is Arnold S. Haskell's *Balletomania*. Since satire and teasing can be instructive, I advise you not to overlook *Ballet Laughs*, a series of humorous drawings by Alex Gard, with an introduction by Walter Terry. For an insight into many aspects of the dance, as well as for a glimpse of one of the greatest dancers, you will wish to read *Nijinsky*, by Romola Nijinsky, his wife.

CHAPTER IV

Painting, Sculpture, and Architecture

1.

IN KINDERGARTEN AND the early school grades our children now are taught to draw, to paint, and to model, and through even a modest practice of these arts they gather some of the equipment which is necessary for a complete life. Perhaps we elders envy them, those parents especially who like myself went to school before the value of art studies was recognized. Musical education in my time was imparted at home, or at the teacher's studio, in private lessons. Drawing and painting and, to a less degree, modeling in clay, were also taught, or to some degree encouraged, at home, but not so well taught as music. I perpetrated myself a large number of watercolors and a smaller number of clay figures, all awkward, fantastic, and worse than useless. Happily these little monstrosities perished long ago, but I remember with considerable uneasiness the bad instruction which led to them.

I remember, for example, my lessons in perspective and in proportion. Drawing and painting, as my teacher believed, should emerge from inside of you, not from your imagination so much as from your memory. You should cram your memory with rules, you should then apply the rules remorselessly to whatever object you chose to portray, and the result would logically be art, even though to the eye it didn't seem so. I drew in a large book which carried on the upper third of each page geometrical figures, solids, for me to copy. These cubes and cones were to be "shaded." I suppose the shading was intended to indicate the third dimension as well as to fix the angle from which the light came. I was taught also to mix colors by certain rules. The hope was held out to me that when I became an expert mixer, like my teacher, I should be able to lay down a series of brush strokes which would give the whole range of the spectrum.

But never once was I advised to take a good look at the object I hoped to draw or paint. Never was I urged to draw or paint what I saw. The subject of a picture, apparently, was important only as an occasion to try out the rules. If my picture when finished failed to resemble what I had copied, I was told to follow the rules more conscientiously. Looking back now I can see no reason why this method should ever produce a recognizable portrait of anything; it would have been just as logical to expect the object I was working on to acquire obligingly some resemblance to my picture.

As for the color-mixing, my youth was devoid of ambition to paint a spectrum, and the accomplishment seemed to me then, and still seems, of uncertain value.

Later I was startled by the doctrine that painters and sculptors should use their eyes, that if we look at an object intently we have a fair chance of noticing its shape, even of observing what parts of it are in shadow. Light from a fixed point will theoretically cast shadows straight from that point, but shadows so logically projected have a trick of seeming unnatural or untrue. The eye helps us to modify our logic, as shadows are modified by reflected rays; if more than one object is in the picture, the neighboring surfaces cast either light or shadow, and we can't tell which until we look.

Of course a shadow is cast by light, but light is not white and what we call a shadow is not black, though in my early attempts at painting I worked on this theory, misled by childhood discipline in shading with a soft lead pencil. The mahogany table on which the lamp shines is light brown in one spot, darker brown in another, with specks of green or yellow or what-have-you, produced perhaps by reflection from a book or a paper cutter. It was a great advance in my knowledge of the world around me, the world which I thought I had seen, to discover that an honest attempt to set down what I saw exactly as I saw it would produce a result half of recognition and half of surprise.

If the arts were long neglected in our schools, the reason was that their educational value was not recognized. It is not yet entirely established among many of us who are middle-aged or older. We can see the benefit of reading and writing, of mathematics, of history, and of science, but why on earth should a grown man or woman spend time over the drawing board or the paint box except for the most casual sort of amusement? Academic subjects of the traditional kind provide exercise for the memory or for the faculties of reflection and analysis, but what training can be got out of drawing or painting?

The answer is simple and important; that the question needs to be asked at all is disturbing. Drawing and painting train the eye. Does our eye need training? Unfortunately it does. We depend upon it for the material upon which the mind works. Before we can philosophize about life, life must be observed. Some of our experience reaches us through other senses, through sound, for example, and one benefit of music study is an increase in the sensitiveness of the ear, but even a dull ear gathers at least what is said in ordinary conversation. The eye, however, upon which we depend for most of our primary information about life is in most cases not keen at all unless we teach it to be. We shudder at the thought of blindness, yet few of us use our eyesight.

Could you sketch offhand a portrait of your parents, or of your friends? I assume that you can't, and I dare say you would excuse your inability by the fact that you are not an artist. The truth, however, is that you haven't really looked at your father or mother. If you had, you would have seen the shape of the face, the eyes, mouth, nose, and ears, and you would know what lines or masses give the characteristic expression. If you had this knowledge you could draw a recognizable portrait, perhaps so crude as to seem a caricature, yet still a portrait. Why should this be surprising? If I ask you how to reach your home in the country, you'll have no difficulty in sketching a map of the roads or in indicating the approximate distances. Driving your car, you've been compelled to notice the road. Nothing has yet compelled you to look at your relative's face.

I stress here the educational value of drawing or painting, not because I underestimate the other values of the arts, but because there is no greater tragedy in life than to have eyesight and yet be blind. The quickest way to open our eyes is to make an attempt at a portrait. We can begin by looking out our front window and drawing the house across the street. There it has stood opposite us for perhaps ten years, but in our comings and goings our mind has been on other matters and we haven't noticed it. Now with pencil and pad we estimate the proportion of width to height, if there are a row of windows we count the number and notice their shape, we see whether they are equally spaced, we gauge the height of the floors, we study decorative details and the color of the material, whether the house is of painted wood or of brick and stone.

Our first sketches are important as eye-opening exercises, but if we continue to draw we soon encounter a central problem, the question whether we shall portray an object as it looks or as it is. Since the human animal is reluctant to use his eyesight, most of us can more easily draw what we know than what we see. Children and many grownups will draw a table with a rectangular top and four legs of equal length. Their information would be useful if they were carpenters about to build a table, but their drawing will look like thunder, since there is no possible angle from which the top of the table will seem rectangular and at the same time the legs will seem of equal length. You can record exact knowledge by a diagram, a blueprint; you can make a convincing portrait only if you are willing and able to obey your eye.

Primitive art, though perhaps exquisite in detail, is often indifferent to the truth of the picture as a whole. St. George on his horse may be killing a good-sized dragon in the foreground while peasants mow a field in the background some distance away. The indifference of the mowers to the dragon fight is not more remarkable than the fact that even far-off they are shown quite as tall as St. George near-to. Presumably the artist argued that he should paint them the same height since he knew their height really was equal. That is one kind of truth, a purely mental kind which forgets the eye. But there is another kind, which respects appearances, and which insists that appearances are a kind of reality. It is true that all the men in the picture are the same height, but it is a contradiction of human experience to represent them so. By distance they are modified to the eye, a very helpful change we must admit, since the modification gives us an idea of the distance.

It's a pretty cheap kind of criticism to say that modern painters give us still-life canvases in which plates, cups, and saucers are bent out of shape. The best modern art, the best art of any time, respects the eye. If we look honestly at the soup plate on the dinner table, it won't be round, not unless we lean over it and look down, and when we study it from a side angle it won't present an oval shape, though logically it should; soup plates and cups, plates of any kind, are not flat, and their sloping sides give them an eccentric appearance. But even if they were flat, they would still seem imperfectly oval when looked at from the side. The edge which is further from us will not correspond entirely to the edge which is nearer, any more than the six-foot man further away will look just as tall as the six-foot man nearer.

There are many ways of approaching the study and the practice of an art, but my personal conviction is that we should begin with the training of the eye, as in music we should begin with the training of the ear. A good teacher would save us time, but intelligent men and women, in drawing as in music, can, I think, do much by their own effort to develop their hearing and their eyesight. Carry with you a pencil and a notebook, and through the day, whenever or wherever you find a spare moment, sketch some simple object—the basket which someone is holding opposite you in the subway, the glass of water on the restaurant table. Don't worry about how the drawing will look; be concerned over the accuracy of your sight. As nearly as you can, draw exactly what you see. Don't bother about rules of perspective or any other rules. The laws of perspective are a record of the way the human eye sees, but there is no evidence that nature studied the laws of perspective before she got to work on the eye.

By the time we have learned to observe honestly, we have probably become interested in those matters which painters and sculptors refer to as design, mass, rhythm, or form.

Most artists have their own way of defining these terms. Perhaps the pleasure they take in philosophizing about their craft is a form of self-flattery; it is hard to explain otherwise a tendency to become over-subtle and long-winded about what is quite simple.

When the layman hears that such-and-such a painter is strong in design, or that a given picture is not well designed, he is probably bewildered, much more abashed than he need be by a sense of his ignorance. In the picture which is said to be weak in design, he sees, let us say, an easily recognizable landscape, very much as God made it, and in every detail apparently well drawn. Where is he to look for the design? When he finds it, how can he tell whether or not it is weak?

The four terms which I have named, refer in each case to the artist's point of view. We can put no design into something which is already made, but we can and do see a landscape from an angle of our own choosing. With experience we learn which angle gives us pleasure, or includes what we enjoy remembering. If the result pleases others as well as ourselves, the picture is said to be well designed.

When we use a camera, we sweep the lens around until what we want is in the picture. Since we aren't painters, we may not know it is a design we are after. The story teller does the same thing when he decides upon a plot. A plot is not a story; it is a point of view from which the story can be told. In other words, it is what the painter calls design. The story of *Hamlet* can be put into several plots. Shakespeare chose Hamlet's point of view. A different plot would tell the same story from the point of view of Hamlet's mother, or his uncle, or Ophelia.

You will hear a picture praised for the arrangement of its masses. About this term, as about all the others which are used in art criticism, much has been written, entirely too much. The word means what it says. When you arrange the furniture in your room, you don't put all the pieces in one corner or against the wall; since each chair, table, or chest of drawers has bulk or mass, you distribute these masses until they give you the impression of balance. If they all were on one side of the room, you'd have an unconscious fear that the house might capsize, and you'd brace yourself against such a catastrophe. But with an approximately equal distribution you can relax and feel secure. It would be possible to arrange the objects in a picture so that the canvas would always look tilted to one side, but we like a painting to seem as well as to be parallel with the floor.

One painter may see life in masses, as another may see it in lines. When you look at a table, you may have the kind of eye which delights in the outside edges, which sees the table defined by lines. If your mind works this way, you ought to draw well. You won't think it absurd to outline the shape of the table with a lead pencil trail a fraction of an inch wide; given this outline, you can imagine the table itself. But people of a different temperament would challenge that lead pencil line. They'd tell you the table is just so wide and just so long, and when it reaches its limits it comes to an end, without any pencil mark to frame it in. Those who think this way are painters. They see the table rather than the table's edge. They like to portray the whole surface.

Even though your talent is for line-drawing, you soon learn how important the masses are. If I were teaching a child to draw, I'd give it a very soft lead pencil and advise it to block a picture in masses rather than define it in lines. The edge-lines aren't there; why train yourself or anyone else to imagine them before you have learned to see the solid object, which *is* there? After you have noticed the solids, you can outline them to your heart's content. Let me remind you again, however, that when you portray an object by edge-lines you are in danger of obeying your mind rather than your eye. Masses, to be reproduced faithfully, must be honestly seen.

If I continue to speak as though my reader intended to draw or to paint, let me admit I hope the assumption will be justified. In my time I have read many volumes about all the arts, with the result that I know the theories of those who wrote the books, but I'm not at all sure the theories were sound. Any real knowledge I have of music I gathered from playing and from composing, and what little I know of drawing, painting, or modeling I learned from my own attempts. What I say here will, I hope, be found clear and simple, but I am sure it will have more meaning if you test me out by trying it yourself. You'll need only a pencil and a very small box of watercolors. Draw the objects nearest you and then paint them. I don't mean draw them in outline and then fill the outline with color; I mean, first outline them and then on a separate sheet paint the mass with no edge-line.

After this experiment, make a picture of at least half your room, blocking in the solid objects in their proper colors. Don't neglect the color of the carpet. The experiment will disclose, as no mere words could, the extent to which masses gain importance from color. A yellow lampshade in one spot will link itself with a bit of yellow upholstery five or six feet away; a touch of blue on wall or floor will re-enforce the tone of a vase or the mantel. Anyone with a natural taste for interior decoration will arrange balances between masses and echoes between colors. If you are not yet entirely aware of these effects, your painting of the room will drive them home.

The word rhythm, like the word form, is used in the discussion of all the arts. We speak of rhythm in poetry, in music, in dancing, in painting, in sculpture, and in architecture. But dealing with each art we may fall into the bad habit of using the word in a special sense. I call this a bad habit because none of the special meanings is so important as the central one, and the special meanings are not related to each other. Dance rhythms, or waltz rhythms, have reference to the number of beats in a measure or to the number of steps, but obviously this use of the word takes us far from what we have in mind when we speak of rhythm in a painting. The central meaning of the word is movement or motion, not outward motion but movement inside our minds, a sense of progress, an expectancy. Where rhythm does not exist, the music, so far as the audience is concerned, might as well stop. Or if it is a picture which has no rhythm, we are content to look at part of it and leave the rest alone. In each of the arts what we call rhythm is the special means by which the inward rhythm, the sense of expectancy is produced.

A correct understanding of rhythm in any art is of the utmost importance. For some reason hard to explain most of us think the essence of rhythm is mechanical repetition. We think a band plays in rhythm if it pounds out monotonously the beat by which soldiers march. We believe the leader of the band is employed to see that the beat doesn't vary. The truth is the band could keep time without a leader, but unless he is there, they can't alter the pace in their retards and accelerations.

A ticking clock doesn't illustrate rhythm, but ocean waves do, or the branches of a tree swaying in the wind. They move, not in

an absolutely dependable pattern but so regularly that we expect
their next movement, and when the variation does arrive it excites and holds our interest. If we drop a brick, the single thud
is not rhythmic. If we drop two bricks in close succession, a hint
of rhythm is created. Three bricks probably form a pattern—two
quick sounds, perhaps, and the third somewhat delayed. If this
whole pattern is repeated, we listen for it a third time, and we
recognize it with pleasure if the intervals between the repetitions,
though irregular, are sufficiently uniform.

We sometimes say that blank verse in English poetry is con-
structed of ten syllables with five beats. Very little verse answers
precisely this description, but ten syllables with five beats is the
mental pattern against which the variations are sounded. In dancing, where the music keeps strict time, great artists give us the
rhythm of a wave or a tree, not the unvarying up-and-down of a
steam pump. In a painting a touch of red in one corner and
another touch on some other part of the canvas will cause the eye
to look for more red elsewhere. Or the rhythm may be created
by the echo of a design. If the repetition has no variation in it, if
it is absolutely mechanical, the design will be static, as in wallpaper. The purpose of wallpaper, of course, is not to excite
interest or in any way to arouse emotions or stir thoughts. The
wallpaper pattern seeks to create an atmosphere of peace.

When painters speak of form they are using a very uncertain
word, and more often than not they are introducing an idea which
they aren't sure of. There is a difference between form and design,
between form and mass, but there is also a resemblance. Masses
are areas of design or of color which make on us somewhat the impression of solids, a two-dimensional impression. Forms in a painting are representations of three-dimensional objects. When we
use the word in the singular, however, we refer to the total meaning which the artist has put into his work. If you drop a piece of
string it may by chance fall in a pattern, but it won't have form.
We aren't likely to see meaning in it. The same could be said of
a knife and fork on the table, either laid beside the plate or
dropped carelessly, yet a painter observing the possibilities of
form in those casual objects could articulate it clearly for us
without rearranging the articles in the slightest; he could call

attention to the reflections of light on the table or on the metallic surface of knife and fork; he might make us feel the pleasant contrast between metal and wood; going deeper, he might emphasize in knife or fork the use or function of the utensil in handle, edge and point. We are told that the earth before the Creator took hold of it was without form. That doesn't mean that chaos was shapeless; it may have been symmetrical and round, like a globe of clay waiting for the potter. It remained a globe after it acquired meaning or form.

Design is near to form, but careful artists attach to the words different meanings. There may be design in color, but form is a spiritual thing, an inner structure not dependent on flesh or tint. Edna St. Vincent Millay described it in her magnificent sonnet, "Euclid alone hath looked on beauty bare." The bareness is peculiar to form. There couldn't be a bare design. There is design in the rosebud, or in the mature leaf of the flower, but form, the personality of the flower, lurks in the seed.

I mention these words and offer my understanding of them, merely because they are employed by artists and critics. I confess I have less and less use for them. I'd rather stick to the essential difference between nature and art. Say if you will that nature "is made better by no mean but nature makes that mean," yet it would be idle to paint a landscape if the painting were not different from the landscape—that is, if the painting didn't have in it something of the painter. In this opinion there is room to quarrel with me, but I can't help it, it's my opinion. If the painter has an original way of seeing the landscape, we'll discover design in his work, and form, and characteristic rhythms and masses. Of course the question will still remain whether we like his picture.

2.

The drawing and painting lessons which I had in my childhood did me, I'm sure, a certain amount of harm. For one thing, that color-mixing to imitate a spectrum disgusted me, as I told you, and when I became really interested in the plastic arts at the age of twenty-two or thereabouts, I avoided color and went in for etchings or engravings. Even earlier, in high school days, I tried my hand at pen-and-ink drawings, no doubt under the influence of du Maurier and Charles Dana Gibson, though I have been assured that my work was easily distinguished from theirs. A friend of mine in college was infatuated with the work of Charles Méryon, and through him I became acquainted with the genius of Honoré Daumier, who has done in his drawings what I wish I could do in novels. Are you familiar with Daumier's unforgettable *Endymion*—the love-sick moon gazing down on the sleeping shepherd, asleep with his mouth open, obviously snoring?

When I was teaching at Amherst College I had a few engravings and etchings on my study wall, and a colleague one evening remarked, as a friend will, "Do you know what's the matter with this room?"

The news that there *was* something the matter came as a shock.

"It's all black and white," he said. "There's no color except in the bindings of your books."

His words made an impression, but I learned nothing about painting until I came back to Columbia in 1909 and began to attend art exhibitions in New York. No doubt my eye got some training from the mere habit of looking at pictures, but my progress was nothing to boast of until one day I stumbled into 291 Fifth Avenue, the famous gallery then maintained in romantic altruism by Alfred Stieglitz. The small rooms were opened every morning and closed at dark by Mr. Stieglitz himself. During the day anyone could walk in there, and a small sign told you the exhibit was entrusted to the public. Not a single item, I believe, was ever stolen, though for one fortnight a group of Rodin drawings were exhibited, and every season some new works of Marin, who began his career, I fancy, in that place. Stieglitz held the sound doctrine that an artist learns from his public, and the still sounder doctrine that a young artist of talent learns more by exhibiting while he is finding himself than after he arrives.

I formed the habit of visiting "291" each week. Since the exhibitions ran for a fortnight, I had at least two looks at each, and if I showed up on the first day, Stieglitz would probably be there and I could have a little talk with him, always to my immense profit.

On one warmish winter afternoon, as I recall, "291" was filled with a perspiring crowd, all like myself a bit puzzled by a mess of pictures representing still-life of various domestic kinds—crockery on the table, lamps, rocking chairs, bric-a-brac. Each canvas was painted in high tones and each familiar object was bent into an eccentric shape. I pushed my way over to Stieglitz who was standing with his overcoat dropped down off his shoulders. "Usually," I said, "I can guess what the exhibition is about, but this one is too much for me. Why are you exhibiting it?" I spoke quietly, but he answered with all of his penetrating voice, "Because the artist is alive. If he were dead, I'd have no interest whatever in these pictures, but he isn't dead. He's the young man right behind you, who heard what you said."

I made what peace I could with the painter, and as he was a good sort he forgave me, or pretended to. He had been living in a remote New England spot, stretching out his few dollars as far as they would go, and reading in art magazines about modern tendencies. No one could be more modern than Stieglitz, but he wanted the boy to learn that the audience must always be reckoned with. He wanted him to learn sincerity, to be contemporary with himself, not to be an imitator of modernity.

Stieglitz taught me as well as the boy. From visits to "291" I acquired or recovered a love of color. It must have been in me always, and I marvel that I could have got on without it so long. Remembering my delight in Daumier, Goya, Hogarth, Holbein, Max Klinger, and other enthusiasms of my youth, I can still be loyal to them and yet crave something warmer than black and white.

Because I was late in discovering the world of color, my appreciation of obvious masters came slowly. Now I would put high on the list of my admirations certain well-known portraits—Titian's "Man with the Glove," Raphael's "Castiglione," the "Aesop" of Velasquez, the best work of Raeburn, Sargent's "Lord Ribbesdale," several portraits by George Bellows and Eugene Speicher. If you think my taste is uneven, you may be right. I am not entirely sure that some of the more famous painters are so good as some of the later.

Two of the greatest experiences in my life were my first sight of the Sistine Chapel and my first acquaintance with Michelangelo's drawings in his Florentine house. With the ceiling of the Sistine

Chapel I was already acquainted piecemeal through reproductions, and though I was willing to appreciate the whole wonderful achievement, I wasn't absolutely sure it would match its reputation. As I came to the modest side door through which the tourist enters the Chapel, I was almost sorry; perhaps it would be better not to go in; why risk disillusion with what had earned so large a name? I shall never forget the upsurge of spirit when a few seconds later I strained my neck to take in the miracle of art and science, the grandeur of the conception, the magnificence of the individual figures, the divine technique which solved the problem of painting on surfaces both curved and flat, managing proportions and perspectives so that the effect would be unified and simple.

Michelangelo's drawings I was prepared to revere, at least for their age, but they seemed the most modern things in that old city where you wouldn't be astonished if Dante or Boccaccio or a Medici came around the corner. The drawings gave me no impression of antiquity immortally prolonged; rather, they seemed fresh, as though the crayon had traced them yesterday, with a sort of immediate vitality which is just what we'd expect from Michelangelo, an immense urge to set down the emotion or idea, a have-at-you attitude toward the moment's inspiration. Genius so clearly reflected ought perhaps to discourage us but it doesn't. It prompts us to take inventory of ourselves, asking why every one of us in our measure should not strike out and have our say.

Among landscape painters I like especially Cézanne and van Gogh. English and American painters do fine landscapes, and in my own country I admire enormously the best of Grant Wood, Edward Bruce, Georgina Klitgaard, Benton, Kane, and many others. But in France the landscape, even before it is painted, is a work of art, with design, masses, and form, all contributed by the spirit of the people. For that reason landscape counts for more in French poetry than in English or American, and in Cézanne the French soul is revealed to the eye as in Debussy to the ear. Painting can function best when the subject it works on has been prepared by some previous instinct toward art. I mention French landscape painting with such emphasis and deliberately put American landscape painting in a lower place, because I hope we shall some day use our superb countryside not simply to wring crops out of it or to dig holes in it. We treat with whatever artistic foresight we have and preserve with care the rooms of our home. On the small scale we appreciate the importance of the atmosphere in which we pass our days. In time we'll learn that the landscape about us is only a larger room.

Twice in my life I've done some painting for an immediate purpose. Both times I used watercolors, a medium which I've never mastered; if any of my sketches survive they show clearly enough that I was thinking in terms of oils. When I came home after nearly two years in France during the first World War, that countryside even in its mutilated state haunted me, and finding it hard to describe, I made pictures of it for my small son's benefit. In recent years, having damaged my right hand in an accident, I took to painting again to exercise fingers and wrist, once more using watercolors because they were easily carried around.

From both these personal ventures I take courage to say again how much we can learn by practicing the art ourselves, what training we can give the eye, what insight we acquire into the artist's intention.

3.

If you draw or paint, no matter how amateurishly, you're practically certain to become interested in sculpture. Of course if you have a sculptor's talent, the interest was born in you; you naturally see objects in three dimensions, as an etcher sees the edge of the object or a painter sees the surface. But even without a special gift for sculpture, anyone who tries to represent on a flat surface objects which have three dimensions will consider the advantage of dealing directly with thickness or depth as well as with breadth and height.

Sculpture is a difficult art only because it compels sincerity. It offers little for the artist to hide behind. It presents the object as it is, relying to a small extent on illusion, but it also reveals the sculptor without disguise. To add an interpretation to life without distorting it is difficult.

Yet sculpture is an attractive art just because of this challenge. Those who work on flat surfaces usually pride themselves on their ability to make objects stand out as though they were sculptured. Great photographers have no higher praise for each other than that they can show life in the round. What is even more significant, many children find it easier to model in clay than to indicate depth and perspective with pad and crayon.

Yet we grownups are often blind to some obvious facts about sculpture. Some accidents of history break down our instinctive appreciation. The Greek sculpture, often fragmentary, which came to the attention of Western Europe after the Renaissance, was of heroic or life size because it originally was made for a public building or for some out-of-door space. Most of us think sculpture must always be large. Since marble and bronze examples are exhibited in museums, we conclude that sculpture must always be very heavy and very costly and therefore we are reconciled to leaving it strictly alone. Perhaps we don't see the relation between Benvenuto Cellini's small works, jewel-like in their perfection, and his larger things, but when we look at the beautiful silver and gold cups and other utensils in museums, archeological treasures from Mycenae, or headdresses and other ornaments from ancient Egypt, we are reminded that man's sculptural faculty has always been busy with things used daily. This is as true of us now as of the Pharaohs before Moses. We are not satisfied with doorknobs or lampstands or ash trays which serve only a useful purpose; we want pleasure from them as objects, as objects of three dimensions.

Any contact with sculpture brings us up sharply before a question which painting too should raise but usually doesn't. If there's a chance for us to own any sculpture large or small, we must ask where we can put it. If we haven't much taste and don't worry about the appearance of our rooms, we can hang a painting in any space that's large enough, but sculpture must rest on something at least as solid as itself. It forces three dimensions upon us relentlessly. We probably won't care to set it in the middle of the floor and walk around it. To put it against the wall, we must first move out the sofa. No matter where we locate it, the light will probably be wrong.

No great sculpture was ever intended to be shoved around experimentally. It was made for a special place and for special

surroundings. It's equally true, though far less obvious, that painting, to be at its best, should be designed for a definite surface
and looked at from one angle and from one distance. Our ignoring of these truths can be explained by some historical bad luck,
but even so, we should know better.

The Greek sculptors used marble, but they colored the stone.
They made statues for temples and public buildings, not for private homes. The coloring or other adornment of the marble, the
size and design of the statue, were calculated to reinforce a total
effect. In the eclipse of Greece during the Dark Ages temples were
destroyed and their sculptural elements scattered. What the
modern world dug up, either by chance or by search, was what
might fairly be called débris. Often the statue had lost a head or
an arm or a hand. Even so, the beauty of these fragments was
overwhelming, but we suspect they would be even more impressive if we could see them as integral parts of the original organic
whole. Unfortunately, the fact that they were recovered as débris,
isolated survivals, inspired sculptors to imitate them, and since
the paint was washed off, all marble statues thenceforth were
white.

Now one of the greatest modern problems in art is to drive
into the head of a sculptor or painter the idea that his work, if
conceived in his studio as an isolated masterpiece, will simply
clutter up the world. Is it reasonable or kind of the artist to create
his work exclusively for his own self-expression? Has he the right
to make a painting or statue in his studio without reference to
the needs of its future owner, and then expect you or me to
encourage him? Wouldn't it be rather intelligent as well as human
for the painter, before he perpetrates a canvas which measures
four feet by five or six, to inquire whether any such space is available? The question becomes acute, painfully so, when the sculptor
offers us a life-size figure, or even quarter-size or half-size. A few
rich collectors, if they don't live in museums, have attached to
their homes museum-like corridors, but there are not enough of
them to absorb all that busy sculptors produce.

For another reason it is a question, after twenty-five hundred
or three thousand years, whether the ancients were not wise to
use sculpture and even painting primarily for the embellishment

of public buildings. The artist who today finds private patrons is less fortunate than he at first thinks; his work has a market but paradoxically he remains obscure. Art in private homes is hidden. That's why a sculptor or painter, if he has sold you one of his things, will borrow it back for an exhibition. Success is all very well but he'd like some public credit.

It's a good omen for art that sculptor and painter begin again to collaborate in the ancient way with the architect. Once more we create not débris but integrated parts of a whole. The sculptor works not only with the designers of buildings but with landscape architects; the painter furnishes murals, indoors and out. From now on, we hope, art will be influenced more by public and social demands than by museum traditions.

Both painter and sculptor will of course continue to serve us in smaller and more personal ways, chiefly perhaps in portraiture, but also in the refinement of articles the home makes use of, doorknobs, dishes, chairs, tables. The association of art with daily life would have progressed faster if artists had not been snobbishly devoted to the creation of non-utilitarian débris. Once more they think of themselves as craftsmen. We feel new admiration for the early American carpenters who designed the houses they built and made even the doors things of beauty, spending affectionate care on the molding and the hand-wrought hinges.

Sculpture forces us to realize the essential purpose of art, and to consider the difference between good art and bad. A bad picture sometimes gets by, a bad statue less often. We may put up with the painting because we like its color or—heaven pardon us! —because we admire its frame, but a statue which is less than good becomes a nuisance.

The sculptor, like the painter, must record what he sees. The painter who sincerely reproduces the cup and saucer as he sees them will, as we said before, show us that to the eye their shape from various angles is not round nor even symmetrically oval. But if he trusts not to his eye but to his previous knowledge, and from memory bends the cup and saucer out of shape, his picture will look insincere; he has painted the object not as he saw it at that particular moment, but as, from previous experience, he thinks it should be. When he and the sculptor do your portrait, they are under the same obligation to set down precisely what is under their eyes. Since no two individuals see you the same way, no sincere portraits of you will be exactly alike.

It is quite possible, however, to reproduce your features with fatal precision. The sculptor can take a plaster cast, and from the cast get a bronze which is an exact copy, or he can make a copy in plaster and color the surface in exact imitation of your skin and your eyes and your hair. This kind of realism is found in exhibitions of wax works, where the figures are dressed in such clothes as living men wear, and we ask the doorman a question only to find that he's part of the show. The discovery always shocks us, not on esthetic grounds but because having taken him for a living man we find he's a dead one. If there is no other difference between a living person and his portrait, we'd prefer of course the living person. A literal copy is bad art. In any case, whether in paint, plaster, or bronze, the copy is dead; it can be brought to life only by the sincere and unconscious interpretation it has received from the personality of the artist.

The technique of every art is dictated by its medium. Even in literature the language of the orator differs from that of the philosopher or the essayist, yet this difference is for most of us hard to see, since in both cases identical words are used. It's easier to distinguish between watercolors, oils, crayons, and ink. We can understand how materials so unlike must impose upon the artist different techniques. The influence of the medium, however, is clearest in sculpture. If the work is to be cast in bronze, it is built up first in clay, and the human hand leaves its impress in the modeling. Before the clay model is cast in bronze or silver or some other metal, the artist will probably rub out all vestiges of the hand in order to take advantage of the surface which those metals provide. If the statue is to be in stone, it may of course be modeled first in clay and afterwards cut by mechanical means, but the sculptor usually prefers to cut the figure himself directly from the block. He is glad to leave convincing testimony, discernible at least by other sculptors, that he knows how to work in that particular material, marble needing one technique, granite another, soft stone a third. Greek statues are less monumental, far more subtle than Egyptian; the carvings in French cathedrals are less monumental and more subtle than Greek sculpture. The cathedral sculptors had a soft stone to work in, the Greeks had marble, the Egyptians had granite.

An energetic sculptor nowadays is likely to experiment with several mediums. Jo Davidson usually models his portraits and casts them in bronze, but some of his finest work is cut from the marble, and one exquisite head is in terra cotta colored. John Rood has in recent years carved his decorative and highly entertaining figures out of native American woods. Medieval wood carvers were often sculptors of great talent, but in our day it has been the fashion to use only the most durable material. John Rood revives an old craft to express extremely up-to-date ideas, and incidentally his work illustrates the influence of the medium on the style, oak calling for one treatment, pine or applewood for another. Boris Lovet-Lorski specializes in mediums for their own sake. He collects stones from far parts of the earth, or casts his figures in metals. His exhibitions are exciting not only for what he says but for the surprising materials through which he conveys his message—Sicilian lava, pewter, Swedish marble, silver, brass, stone of Xenozane, Belgium black marble, bronze, linden wood, Egyptian granite, Carrara marble, yellow brass, rose marble, ivory Carrara marble, slate, Madagascar marble, Cretan marble, terra cotta, Egyptian serpentine, Mexican onyx, jade.

4.

I offer from personal experience little illustration of what I've said. Never could I claim, not even in the most amateurish sense, to be a sculptor. In my late thirties I did become curious about this art and tried to practice it, probably because my son, then in kindergarten, was modeling in clay and I wanted to see if I could do as well as he. I couldn't.

Yet before I abandoned this chastening exercise I learned one thing about myself; I had more success with bas-relief than with a completely rounded figure. Was this a peculiarity of mine, or is it true of most beginners? I don't know, but I took it to mean that my disposition was toward painting rather than sculpture, and less toward painting than toward novel writing. Anything loses meaning for me when it stands alone. The prophets and patriarchs from the ceiling of the Sistine Chapel have been reproduced separately, but they seem far more wonderful in their place together. Michelangelo's David is no doubt a *tour de force,* but I prefer the figures of Dawn and Night on the Medici tomb. Sculpture which carries its background with it is a kind of bas-relief.

When my feeble attempts at modeling disclosed a tendency to put the face or figure always against some other aspect of life, I argued with myself; if a musical composition can be enjoyed for its own sake, why can't a statue stand alone? I don't know why not; I simply observe that it never does. Whether it is designed for a special place or created in the studio for any place that will house it, surroundings and background it will have; even the Christ of the Andes is seen against the mountains and the sky. Whatever spot a statue occupies, harmony of some sort between place and statue is good for the statue.

My education in sculpture advanced when a considerable number of Meunier's work were exhibited at Columbia University, some twenty-five years ago. Constantin Meunier (1831-1905) was a Belgian sculptor who portrayed the workers of his country, the miners and foundrymen, much as Walt Whitman might have drawn their portrait, or as Emile Verhaeren, another Belgian, drew it in poems reminiscent of Whitman. The purpose or meaning of Meunier's work I did not know when the exhibition was installed, but as I went to and from my classes I stopped at the Avery Library several times a day and let the statues make their effect on me. At the end of a fortnight the effect was threefold. I was sorry the statues were shown in a library; if ever works of art were weakened by the background, it was these poignant records of sweating humanity against placid shelves of well-bound architectural volumes. The emotional appeal of the statues, however, seemed increasingly strong, the more I looked at them; the background ceased to bother me. At last I concluded that the appeal was primarily humanitarian or sociological, that it could have been expressed just as well in painting and even better in words, and that the setting of the exhibition was not important since Meunier, excellent sculptor though he was, called attention to other than sculptural values.

Some years later I saw in France a number of Rodin's works and within a few days those unfinished blocks of Michelangelo's in the Accadémia di Belle Arti in Florence. The resemblances and the contrasts taught me much. Michelangelo has movement in his sculpture, as in his painting; his figures may stand or they may recline but they are at all times dynamic. Rodin's *John the Baptist* scandalized stupid critics, those who thought that because sculpture is associated with architecture a statue should be as restfully planted as a building. When Rodin gave us, as he liked to do, the male and female in some moment of rapture, it seemed to the ossified estheticians that he confused sculpture with dancing. They forgot those wind-blown figures, those divine athletes, in Michelangelo's great ceiling, or his Moses in the Roman Church, ready to spring to his feet; they forgot also the horses and riders of the Parthenon, or the Victory of Samothrace.

Those Rodin pieces which are cut from part of the marble and seem to rise out of it are I suppose inspired by the blocks of stone which Michelangelo left unfinished, tossed aside as though they were paper, as though the noble bodies half-emerging were a Titan's sketches. Here the incompleteness is no trick, no affectation. I admire Rodin, but it is well to cultivate an appreciation of his work before you have seen Michelangelo's.

From my own experience I believe we come to sculpture most easily through the famous single works or groups with which art books or school courses in appreciation make us familiar. As we progress, however, we see more clearly the point I have stressed, that sculpture in its sanest condition is a craft, and flourishes most sturdily while collaborating with other crafts to express a public idea or emotion. The best European sculpture is found, I think, not in museums but in medieval churches, in the figures of saints at the portals, in scenes of the Last Judgment, in the carvings of pulpits and choir stalls, in gargoyles and other embellishments. The medieval cathedral was the work of the community, or rather, it was a joint offering of all the artists, each contributing his specialty. If he had not previously specialized in theological subjects he was sometimes permitted to contribute human and even humorous scenes, or he would manage even in stone carvings to hint at the landscape he knew. The Middle Ages have left us few records more precious than glimpses of man at his work, of his way of living in each of the four seasons, of his manner of clothing himself.

This is as much as to say that folk art is very important. During my lifetime the intelligent appreciation of sculpture has gone far beyond the tradition of Greek art, modified and revived in the Renaissance. Even that tradition now includes contributions which preceded the Periclean age, and which came from other countries than Greece proper. The Egyptian crafts, for example, are now ranked high indeed, but it's a still healthier sign of intelligence that we study African sculpture, the sculpture of all peoples whom we call primitive, finding in their works a strange power, a revelation of other social habits, thoughts and feelings.

We begin to study our own folk art right here in the United States. We might have done it much earlier if like other human beings we hadn't recoiled from the idea that examples of primitiveness could be found among us. In my boyhood every cigar store had a wooden Indian in front of it. These figures are now collectors' items. As sculpture they really aren't worse than some Egyptian carvings I've seen, and they record quite as much of legend and custom. In my boyhood also there were more sailing ships than there are now, and many a vessel carried at its prow a wooden figure, a Viking, perhaps, or a mermaid. We were Victorian in those days, but it seemed quite proper that the wooden lady who took the brunt of the spray should be unclothed —that is, from the waist up, the only part of her which existed— and that her bosom should be as one might say robust. Her hair was long and waving and she wore a perpetual smile. These figureheads, like the cigar store Indians, are now sought after by connoisseurs. The history of their use on boats, their relation to old religions and ancient sea cults, deserves study.

5.

Architecture is at once the most public and the most private of the arts. Paintings are seen by a small proportion of us; if we don't like them, we usually don't have to look at them. Sculpture is forced upon our attention to a greater extent, yet we can escape it if we insist. A building, however, is hard to ignore. For that

reason the word architecture means for most of us the outside
of a building, the part we all have to look at. The study of architecture pays attention first of all to external styles. When we know
whether a column is Doric, Ionic, or Corinthian, we are supposed
to have a good start.

But the fact which distinguishes architecture from other arts
is that we not only must look at its masterpieces but we at least
visit their insides, and most buildings, the enormous majority of
them, are or should be made to live in. The inside purpose of
the building, the use for which it is intended, ought to show on
the outside. Ought, that is, in terms of economy and of common
sense. But for various reasons there is a clash between the external
and the internal approach to architecture, between the historical
approach and the functional.

The main reason is psychological, and it goes deep. The house
we live in will mean much to us; we prize it not only for utility
but for emotional associations, and we therefore continue prejudiced in its favor, even though we know it's a little ugly and very
inconvenient. Old styles of architecture which should have been
discarded long ago keep a firm grip on us even though with
modern materials another style would serve us better. In Colonial
times our churches, whether in the north or the south, imitated
Greek temples. Temples in ancient Greece were of course not
intended for congregations which sat in pews and were preached
at from pulpits, but the white church with portico and columns
and with the tall un-Greek spire is now so familiar in our landscape, suggesting so many historical occasions, that we're not likely
to do away with it. More recently it has become the fashion to
build Gothic churches. This style is modern compared with the
Greek temple, and it was developed in Europe to suit the needs
of the Catholic Church, but in the United States it is now cultivated by Protestant churches, to whose ritual it does not entirely
adapt itself.

But whether the church is Colonial or Gothic, it is usually the
pride of the architect and the congregation to keep it, as we say,
true to tradition; that is, to cherish the limitations under which
our forefathers worked before modern building materials were

invented. The Gothic church, for example, wanted as much light as possible, and in the development of this style the buttressed walls were gradually reduced to a minimum for the sake of window space, yet for safety the proportion of solid wall had to remain large, and old Gothic churches are characteristically dark. Most of us rather like the gloom; it suggests to us the mystery of religion. Today with steel construction the church might be all windows. We might invent a new kind of loveliness through new employment of colored glass. But there is little probability that such a church would be approved, not even though it were of jewel-like beauty. It wouldn't be what we are accustomed to. The Greeks associated God with sunlight. We don't.

Our conservatism is almost equally strong in domestic architecture. Our childhood home impressed us so deeply that when we build our own house we repeat the pattern, going in for more room and comfort, if we can afford it, but sticking to the same general plan. A house of any size will have a dining room, a living room, and something called either a sitting room or a library. It would be far more convenient to throw these three compartments into one. We don't need a separate room to eat in, nor a separate room to read a book in. Originally, perhaps, the separate dining room satisfied the primitive animal instinct to hide when eating, or perhaps a later wish to keep from the neighbors precise information as to how we live when we aren't giving a party. The parlor was once reserved for the formal stage of family courtings and funerals. If the dining room was then separate, perhaps we may deduce a commendable reluctance to cloud the pleasures of the palate with memories either mortuary or nuptial. But these speculations would take us far afield.

You know as well as I that the threefold division nowadays is designed not for privacy but in imitation of mansions or palaces where the number of rooms indicated wealth. We spend little of the day in the dining room; when we are not eating it stands idle. If we can afford it we have also a breakfast room, and if we are plain folk with a convenient porch on the house, we probably do our eating there in good weather.

Common sense would suggest one sizable room, with our

books lining the wall and with a table at the end nearest the kitchen, but as yet we find this provision in few houses and in few apartments. We cherish what we are accustomed to.

The architects themselves are not of one mind, and their guidance therefore is confused. Most of them are responsible for the fact that architecture in the United States is more traditional than in South America or Scandinavia. Yet we have vigorous pioneers who try to pull us along. Frank Lloyd Wright has been our apostle of the functional theory, what the layman likes to call modernistic architecture. Wright now has many disciples, and his ideas slowly find acceptance. We'd get on faster if the public did not live on the outside of most buildings while only one family lives inside. Modern architecture is more easily admired inside than out. There's no reason why a building which clearly indicates its function should not be good to look at, but quite a number of them, however practical within doors, seem outwardly unorganized and ugly. In New York City the Museum of Modern Art stands alongside St. Thomas' Church, a bare and unalluring façade in a losing competition with one of the loveliest of Gothic exteriors.

Not only does the functional architect neglect the outside of his building; at times he makes himself obnoxious to his client by presuming to know better than his client how the client wants to live. Not unreasonably those who put up the home, even though they accept the functional idea, want a house in which they can continue to enjoy their own habits. But the functional architect too often is fascinated by the possibility of telescoping several rooms into one. The feeling of spaciousness is lost, whereas the sense of spaciousness is all the more prized when the house by necessity must be rather small. If by combining living, dining, and sitting room, one spacious apartment is secured, the advantage is great, but if the combination merely saves space, nothing is gained.

The conflict between the modernistic architect, who perhaps pushes his theories a little far, and the memory-loving home maker, who clings too firmly to the past, can be easily understood from both points of view. But the architect who in more public buildings lags behind his age is a puzzle. Before the development of steel the walls of buildings were necessarily heavy; they had to stand up and they had to support the roof. If they were of wood, strength was supplied by a timber frame. If they were of stone or brick or mud, a wooden frame was still useful, but for complete safety they were built thick.

With the modern steel frame, however, architecture has arrived at an absurdity which we can see whenever an apartment house is put up in our neighborhood. The outside is faced with brick or stone, yet these false walls hold up nothing; they are suspended from the steel frame. Why should they be used to suggest a function they don't fulfil? Why shouldn't the rooms of the apartments have a maximum of light? The tradition of small windows is now senseless. Some wall space of course is needed as a background for furniture or for pictures, but for these purposes the inner wall is best. Some wall must be thick enough to enclose the plumbing, but here again the inner wall would serve.

Few apartment houses now display columns, whether Doric, Corinthian, or Ionic. The Greek porch has been banished. Since we have the steel frame there is nothing for the column to hold up. The modern architect, therefore, has some trouble with the entrance to his building. You may have noticed that the main door often looks best before the architect has finished it, while it is still nothing but a hole in the structure. Isn't that what a door essentially should be? The Greek porch was an elaborate approach or build-up, but a door in all honesty can be nothing but a door. It needs no emphasis unless the architect fears we shan't be able to find it. It's a fair guess that the new apartment house in our neighborhood has its doorway set off with metal trimmings for the greater convenience of the careless or the blind.

Our architecture in the United States is developing fast for several quite different reasons, of which even the layman is aware. New materials and new methods of construction make possible great advances in external appearance and in interior convenience. The new science of air conditioning improves the ventilation of small houses and small apartments. In the states near the Mexican border the influence of Mexican and Spanish architecture makes itself felt. In the northern cities new housing developments undertaken to relieve economic pressure on small incomes have uncovered helpful ideas about home planning, ideas which influence the design of costlier houses. We begin to question the traditional arrangement of the small American home on the village street, and fortunately we begin to realize that what we have accepted in American domestic architecture is indeed traditional without much reference to present needs. The long-accustomed appearance of our homes, the usual interior arrangement, the stereotyped placing of the building, will no doubt give way before the onslaughts of modernistic architects and in deference to a more intelligent popular demand.

The beautful porches and charming doorways of the Colonial home were adaptations of old-world magnificence. If you had such a porch and such a doorway, you had a fine house, and the house indicated your position in society. Your good fortune was further advertised by the extent of "grounds" around the house. In the old world the fortune of a gentleman was in land. In the northern Colonies or in the southern the gentleman's house was set back from the road, to be approached through lawns, if possible through a grove of trees. Two trees were enough. The age of the trees would suggest the date of the house and the stability of the family. This general rule, that the house should be set back as far as possible from the road, was modified in northern latitudes where in winter the path to the house had to be cleared of snow. The further north, the shorter the path. For convenience in other respects also a farmhouse in isolated districts was likely to be near the road.

But in all cases the house presented boldly its best foot forward; the parlor window was in front. If the home boasted some sculpture, a bit of marble, a portrait bust, the treasure was not infrequently placed on a pedestal in the window, and the curtains drawn back so it could show. The real business of the home would be attended to at the back door. The kitchen would be as far as possible out of sight. Until very recent times, the finer the home, whether in the city or the country, the more out of sight would the kitchen be, in many instances well beneath the ground level, in a damp and dim basement. This arrangement of course contradicted new-world ideals of efficiency, and the attitude which the new world theoretically held toward the dignity of labor.

When the house was moved nearer the street in northern climates there was no general compensation for the loss of the front lawn. What had formerly been a back yard remained a back yard, larger but not improved. If there was a fence around the property, it originally served to keep out the cows and other stray animals, and with time it answered a merely decorative ambition or was abandoned altogether. Fences had this quality, that they did not obstruct the view. In my childhood I was told that the absence of walls indicated a democratic feeling; we all had the right to enjoy the beauty of our neighbor's lawn. I regret to confess that the true explanation was quite different; if there had been walls, the grounds and the long path couldn't have performed their snobbish function, to advertise the family's social eminence.

Two influences, and perhaps several others, are now ending this tradition. From Spanish architecture the usefulness of garden walls has been learned. With the help of brick or concrete walls and partitions a small plot of ground can be varied and made interesting. Fruit and flowers can be grown against the wall, and even the noisiest street can be made endurable with a six-foot wall to keep out sounds. If the walled garden is behind the house, we can secure a greater degree of quiet, even of silence, and if the family wish to enjoy the garden without going through the kitchen, the old plan of the home can be reversed; the kitchen can be on the street, which is obviously the convenient place for it, easily approached by the grocer, the butcher, and all others who serve the house daily. In the rear the more intimate part of the home can open on a court or a terrace, and the walled garden can furnish an illusion of space and distance. Also, in the walled garden small children can play in safety.

Consideration for the children now affects city or town planning. In an age of crowded traffic it is no longer safe for children to play on the street. Modern housing projects assume that the streets will be only the approaches to a home, and that inside space will be used as a playground. We are still a bit unimaginative about the roofs of our homes, whether in the city apartment or the country house. Except in the northern districts where there are heavy snows, the roof might be a recreation area.

Whether we live in apartments or in separate houses, the home, as the modern architects tell us, should express our habits and our social ideals. If we are not satisfied to let the architect tell us what are our habits and ideals, we must tell him. To do this it is necessary to be ourselves, to some extent, an architect. Even though we never have occasion to build a house, we should at least inform ourselves about the problem of house-building so that we can choose our home with intelligence. What progress we have made toward this condition it would be difficult to say. Many of us still select a city apartment primarily on the basis of the condition it is in and the rent which is asked for it. A new apartment is usually more attractive than an older one, and a low rent of course has its appeal, but the renter may be wooed also by an ornate fireplace, burning gas or electricity. We have not yet learned what better use the household could make of a plain wall.

Of all the ideas which the new architecture brings us, the most valuable perhaps are those relating to light. Our apartments are still provided with bulbs hanging from the center of the ceiling, though few of us now use them. We prefer baseboard plugs in generous quantity so that low lamps can be placed where needed. We are not yet equally wise about daytime light; we still accept windows which are too small and which stop a foot or two from the ceiling. If they ran up the full height of the wall, we should have more sun, and as we said before, the largest part of the outside wall might be of glass. Curtains could be used to cut down the glare.

Our manner of planning and building the home is a test of our faith in ourselves. An age which develops new building materials and new methods of construction should use them boldly. If we cling to old architectural styles which prevent the use of our own inventions and improvements, we are living divided lives. If we study ourselves frankly today, we'll probably admit in most cases that the American bathroom is the only sincere part of the house. It serves superbly the uses for which it is designed; in its way it is as perfect as a Stradivarius violin. Perhaps the modern kitchen comes next, though few of our homes as yet have it in complete development. The rest of the house serves as a museum of out-worn fashions to which we cling through habit or sentiment, and for which we pay the large price of intellectual and spiritual insincerity.

I have listed in the bibliography of this book some works which I have found thought-provoking. A competent architect would supply a fuller bibliography, but I record what to me has been useful. An American today should, I think, know the ideas of Frank Lloyd Wright in his own statement of them, and the variation of his theories which other brave architects suggest. For a fair picture of the world we live in we should know also the doctrine of more conventional architects and the reasons for their conservativeness. Even a modest study of this important debate helps us to define our own ideals. Whether we are adventurous or timid, we might as well know our condition and be honest about it.

CHAPTER V

The Intimate Crafts

1.

THE CRAFTS WHICH I am taking the liberty of calling intimate are those which none of us can entirely avoid unless we have no home. I refer to three crafts especially, to the ordinary domestic carpentering, nail-driving, shelf-installing, to vegetable or flower-raising, and to cooking. You may be one of those persons who declare, as though in pride, that they never held saw or screwdriver in their hands, never raised an onion or a sweet pea, never boiled an egg. If you told the truth, I'd be sorry for you. These three homely crafts are so close to the conditions of our existence that to keep entirely out of reach of them indicates a tragic ineptitude for this world. The house is our shelter, and from time to time it needs patching to keep out the weather. Food is even more essential than a roof. The vegetable part of food we should know how to raise, and what cannot be eaten raw we should know how to cook. Most of us, men as well as women, have at moments dabbled in one or all of these crafts. Few of us practice them with skill. Our lives would be more complete if we acquired at least a modest technique.

Domestic carpentering, like domestic plumbing, is usually left to the man of the house, but the women too have a go at it, and so far as I've observed they often do no worse than brother or husband. The home plumber seldom attempts more than replacing a worn-out faucet washer with a fresh one. This operation is fool-proof once we have learned to cut off the water supply down below while making the change. Electric repairs consist usually of taking out a dead bulb and putting in a new one. This operation too succeeds without mishap if we first turn off the current. But the discussion of plumbing and electricity would take most of us beyond our depth. Let us keep to primitive matters. Man has managed to live very well indeed without electricity and without hot and cold water in the kitchen. He has never lived tolerably without a house, and he has never lived at all without food.

For domestic carpentering we need a hammer, a saw, a screw driver, a chisel, and a plane. These tools at least. If there's only one saw, it had better be a cross-cut, which as the name indicates cuts across the grain, but sooner or later we'll need a rip-saw, the saw that cuts with the grain. Sooner or later we'll use hammers of different weights, screw drivers, chisels and planes of various sizes, but we can start with smaller equipment.

We need the hammer, of course, to drive nails. The nails should be driven straight. What ghastly excavations can be made in a freshly painted wall, all by way of inserting a tack or a thin hook to hold a picture! No one knows better than I that the janitor of the apartment house would rather be called upstairs for a little nail-driving than be forced to rebuild the wall and repaint it, yet I was persuaded long ago that it's bad for us to accept our ignorance of elementary mechanics. If the hammer when you bring it in contact with the nail is going in exactly the same direction as the nail, and if the nail is hit squarely on the head, the result will be a nail in the plaster rather than plaster on the floor. In swinging the hammer the elbow and the arm are used but the chief hinge or pivot should be the wrist. A distinction might be made here between nail-driving and golf.

If the nail goes into wood instead of plaster and if its purpose is to anchor the wood rather than to stick out, for something to hang on, the problem will be to drive the nailhead flush with the surface without leaving a dent. If you sink the nail deep and putty up the cavity there'll be no problem at all, putty being the natural friend of poor artisans. But to drive a nail flush without leaving a dent is work for a master. If your muscles are under control, if your eyesight is excellent, if your nerves are sound, if your coordination is perfect, you can do it. That is, with practice. On the other hand, if you can't do it, not even approximately, it might be well to have a doctor look you over. If the doctor can't drive a nail flush either, try another doctor.

I pause to say that whether my reader is or is not a proficient carpenter disturbs me little so far as the carpentering itself is concerned—to say also that my own performances in this craft have been of no importance to the world, and a first-rate cabinet maker would smile at the simple things I here expound. But though my use of hammer and saw and plane resulted in nothing memorable, I did learn in the process much that has enriched my life, and since anybody could by the same practice acquire the same insights, I pass on my humble wisdom. No doubt I could have learned the same or deeper things from the use of the turning lathe or other machines, but I never went so far.

Working in wood increased the accuracy of my eye, drove home the value of precise measurements, made geometry come alive, and gradually persuaded me through a sequence of mishaps to respect the material I worked in. Wood is wood, but the hard woods differ from each other and from the soft. A little carpentering does as much for the mind as a modest experiment with water colors or with a pencil. After you have drawn a table or a chair you have eyesight for all tables and chairs; after you have built a shelf or two you become permanently a grand appreciator of shelves. Though as I have confessed I am not a virtuoso carpenter, I have learned to recognize the virtuoso quality.

I once thought, for example, that a screw was much like a nail and could be driven in by the same process, a gentle tap to set it in the wood, followed by more vigorous propulsion—the only difference being that for the screw propulsion is supplied by the twist of the screw driver instead of the blow of the hammer. If the screw is thin and the wood soft, this method will do. If, however, the screw is thick and the wood hard, this method won't do at all. Either the wood splits or you find it impossible to get the screwhead flush with the surface. To insert a screw in hard wood you must first bore a hole with an augur. The hole must be wide enough so that the wood won't split when the screw goes in, and narrow enough for the thread of the screw to take a firm grip at the sides. The mouth of the hole must be scooped out so that the head of the screw can sink flush with the surface. The entire operation calls for precision and delicacy of touch. A first-rate carpenter may impress you by the muscles of his arm, and if you're entirely ignorant of his craft you may think his chief equipment is vigor. Try a little carpentering yourself and you soon learn that this craft, like all others, is an art, to a certain extent a manual art, but depending more on sensitive mental qualities than on physical strength.

To plane a board smooth is less easy than it seems. If you don't go about it the right way, you simply create one kind of rough surface instead of another. It takes steadiness of eye and hand to rest the plane evenly on the surface so that there will be no mark from the edge of the plane iron. If you push against the grain none of the surface will be smooth. After you've once used a plane, however, you'll notice, whenever you pick up a piece of wood, which way the grain runs.

The use of a saw might seem a still simpler matter, but you'll know better when you try to cut two boards of exactly the same length. You'll probably lay the boards side by side and mark a line of right angles across them. You'll then cut along the line, one board after the other, but when you stand up the two boards on end, you'll discover that they don't match. If you are cutting these boards for shelves in a bookcase, you'll probably find that one fits precisely but the other won't go in at all unless you plane off the ends. You have forgotten that the saw has width, and the cut which you make across both boards must keep the same relation to that pencil line. The pencil line also has width, which may seem negligible before the board is cut but which will make a difference in the fit. In other words, when you measure the length and mark it by a pencil line, you must decide precisely whether the board is to end in the middle of that line, on the left side of it, or on the right, and you must aim the saw to end the board just there and nowhere else.

As I write these lines I think of an incident in my childhood which caused me anguish of spirit, but which also, as I later realized, provided a sizeable instalment of my education. I was trying to make a four-legged table for a Christmas gift to a defenseless and unsuspecting relative. The material was soft wood, but I hoped it would eventually polish as well as though it were hard. The top must of course be made smooth. I planed it this way and that till the surface looked like a skating rink at the end of a crowded day. Annoyed and humbled, I discarded the plane for sandpaper, and by muscle instead of science gradually wore down the board. I then cut the four legs, intending them to be of equal length. They weren't. It seemed impossible to make them so. The teetering could be cured, but then the top was no longer level. I sawed off a section here and a section there until the table was too low, and I had to begin again with four more legs. Since the Christmas gift was to be a surprise, I didn't feel like calling in mature help, and therefore not until the table had been bestowed and politely applauded did I learn how to saw to a line. My table in its final state, as I remember, was firm enough, but there was a difference in height between one corner and the corner opposite.

My next experiences with carpenter's tools were all connected with some form of boat. When I was twelve I received for a birthday or Christmas present *The American Boy's Handy Book* by Dan Beard. On its own terms this was the most stimulating piece of literature I ever encountered. It told how to make kites, especially war kites, how to make fishing tackle, how to make water telescopes, rafts and boats, how to make blow guns and squirt guns, sleds, chair sleighs, snowshoes, and iceboats. It told also how to make puppets and a puppet show, even how to make a magic lantern. It told how to do other things, but these are what I attempted during the next four or five years. I remember especially building a scow. You were to cut out the sides in an easy curve so that the prow and stern would both rise a little. The slope, Dan Beard led you to believe, would assist locomotion, but the results which I obtained were much the same as if the scow had remained an uncompromising oblong box. Having curved the sides, however, you nailed two pieces on the end and more pieces of exactly the same length across the bottom from curving side to curving side. This finished, you righted the tub, cut out thole pins for the oars—you hadn't yet made the oars—and midway down the sides you attached six-inch lengths of wood for a cross-board to rest on. This was to be the rower's seat. The real problem, however, was to get those boards along the bottom to match each other perfectly, and also to match the two end boards, which couldn't meet the bottom boards at right angles. I wonder now what pleasure a good man like Dan Beard could take in luring the inexperienced to try this. The hope was offered that when the scow was put in water the boards would swell and leaks would stop. My boards did swell, but not nearly enough to make up for errors in measurement. I hadn't curved the sides exactly alike, and I didn't know how to match those boards which had to be nailed on a curve. This first naval experiment of mine, after gathering dust and cobwebs in our cellar, went into firewood at last when my mother insisted on having the place tidied up.

When I was nineteen or twenty I built three or four model yachts. There wouldn't have been so many if the first had been successful, but failures drove me to try again. My people lived at the moment near my father's factory where there was a machine shop and good-natured mechanics who gave me valuable aid, as I shall describe. I had read descriptions of racing yachts which at the moment challenged or defended the international cup, and I had a clear idea of what the finished boat should look like, what its beam should be in proportion to its length, how high out of the water it should sit, what should be its relative draught, and how the bow and the stern should enter and leave the water. My procedure was something like this:

First I chose a block of wood an inch or so wider, longer, and deeper than I needed. On what was to be the top surface I drew a straight line down the middle. On each side of this line I drew the curve of the deck. For symmetry I first cut out a paper pattern, and having drawn the starboard side from this pattern, I turned it over and drew the port side. The cutting and shaping of the hull was done with chisel, draw-knife, and sandpaper. I got the machinist at the factory to bore a hole where the stem of the rudder would come up, and then to excavate the rest of the hull by boring large holes in it. I then finished the excavation myself with a chisel until the sides of the boat were no more than half an inch thick. There was one hole left, a deep cavity, into which the mast would be stepped. A cross-piece would be inserted later, just under the deck, to steady the mast.

Having reduced the hull to its approximate dimensions inside and out, I curved the sides so that the bow would be a little higher than the stern, and both higher than the middle. I then got a very thin board, no thicker than a quarter of an inch at most, the kind of board boys in those days used in their scroll saws. Having cut out roughly the deck pattern, I fixed this board to the sides, first with glue, then with pins—literally with pins, which I first cut in half. I then cut strips of the same board half an inch wide and bent them around the edge of the deck to form the gunwale. Then with a chisel I trimmed deck and gunwale flush with the hull.

For keel I relied again on my father's machinist, who very obligingly cast some lead in any shape I suggested. My most successful keel was a steel sheet of fin-like narrowness with a roll of lead at the bottom. That boat was guaranteed not to capsize. Until I lightened the keel considerably it was guaranteed also not to float. The varnishing of hull and deck, the construction of the rigging, the method by which the boat steered itself, I leave unsung. It was the making of the hull which showed me what I didn't know about the carpenter's craft. When I heard Stradivarius praised for his incomparable violin, the tone of which depends, among other things, on the exquisite molding and adjustment of flat and curved surfaces, I reflect with humility, not to say melancholy, on the reaches of wisdom which from some of us are withheld.

In mature life most of my carpentering has gone into book shelves. Except for the measurements nothing is easier, but few things are harder than getting the measurements right. Recently a true carpenter, a first-rate craftsman, built a set of shelves for me. They were to go into a space between two walls. He came one morning, measured and remeasured, wrote the figures on the rough design he had made, measured again, and went away in a peace of mind which, were he the sort of carpenter I am, would not have been justified. Some days later he brought the bookcase, and at his first attempt to push it into place, it stuck, to my evil delight. At the top it apparently was about a sixteenth of an inch too wide. I suggested as much. "No," he said, "the width is correct." He took the shelves out, started over again, and this time they slipped into place so snugly that they might have stood up without fastening.

Since I've had always a modest interest in the manual crafts, I wonder why I didn't go further with the carpentering. I suspect it's because I've spent so much of my life playing the piano. Carpentering and cabinet work of the finest kinds are not infrequently the hobbies of professional scholars, or of others whose work is chiefly mental. I remember one professor whose skill was great in delicate inlay work. He kept himself busy repairing valuable furniture, his own or his neighbors'. The pleasure derived from a beautiful craft, practiced with quite professional skill, complemented the satisfaction he drew from the rigorous processes of his professional research.

But however we learn to handle tools in childhood or youth, and in whatever hobbies we exercise ourselves, the intimate crafts serve a genuine purpose when they satisfy common needs. The carpenter's craft is properly employed in the building or the upkeep of a home. I once owned a house in the country, originally small and low-roofed, and with my own hands I repaired shingles and replaced rotting boards in the porch. On two occasions I painted the outside, and frequently I touched up the inside and revarnished the floors. The house was used all summer, but in winter only for Thanksgiving and Christmas visits. Cold and dampness played havoc with the doors. Every time the place was re-entered, hinges needed tightening, and even after the wood was dried out there were closets which wouldn't open or cupboards which wouldn't shut. To this day I hold that structure in affection, every panel with its peculiar crankiness, each door with its own character, like a human companion, steady and reliable, or temperamental and a little exasperating.

2.

My home had a garden which for six years I cared for entirely myself. There were a few rosebushes and other flowers around the place, but my gardening supplied the family with vegetables. By temperament I am a city person and it was a late surprise to me that work in the soil could fascinate. I made the discovery before

I bought the home of which I am speaking; perhaps I shouldn't have bought it if I hadn't made the discovery. Several years earlier I rented a summer place, extremely modest, from a man who was a fanatical gardener. In the goodness of his heart he plowed up about half the small lawn so that I could plant vegetables. When I saw the scar of bare earth I vowed he'd never hitch me to a spade or a hoe, but he would call on me almost daily and cast a sad eye at his plowed dirt and at the weeds which were making themselves at home in it. To end his reproaches I bought a few handfuls of radishes and beans and what-not and stamped them into disgracefully irregular rows. If I remember correctly the beans came up first. To give them a chance I did a little weeding. From then on I was lost. The soil had me.

When at last a house was my own, I'd visit it in early spring before the summer vacation began, planting a few rows each week to start the continuous supply. By this time I was something of a veteran; I planted with care, kept all the rows quite straight, estimated accurately the length of row needed for each vegetable, and I had wholesome respect for good fertilizer in generous quantities.

Those who do not work in a garden miss an essential experience. Without it we are deprived of an intimate sense of the elements, of earth, of air, of light, of water. Though fire does not count in gardening, heat does. Until my first planting I overlooked the importance of the sun. Several years later, when as I supposed I knew something about gardens, the spring promised to be mild and I planted a fortnight earlier than usual, telling myself that if the first row of peas rotted, the loss would be small, and if they didn't rot, I'd be ahead of my neighbors. One of those neighbors, venerable Samuel Lockwood, of good memory, whose farm was across the road, smiled at the experiment.

"Brother," he said, "those peas will come up when the sun says so, not a minute before."

He was quite right. I planted one row very early, a second row the following week, then a third row. Rows one and two came up simultaneously with row three, not a single pea sprouting before the sun gave permission.

In the autumn as in the spring a garden teaches patience. By the end of the season you've thought of a number of things which you'd like to try out at once—a vegetable which you've never raised, or a trick to make lettuce head up, or a new kind of corn or bean. But when the sun is finished with the year's gardening, you are finished too. Nothing can be done about it till the year comes around again. The garden never waits for you, and it never hurries. While you dig in it, you are far from the world in which men run after a train or a bus.

Generations of mankind have discovered that gardening is work for philosophers, and that the daily planting and weeding will make a philosopher out of him who never was before. I mean philosopher in the true sense, not simply a placid soul who can accept life without protest, but a mind awakened, fertile, discriminating. Gardening provokes thought on whatever subject may engage you. Why the intimate communion with half-grown carrots and onions should stimulate ideas, I don't know. I've heard it said that the crouching position of the weeder affects the spine, therefore the nervous system, therefore the brain. This hypothesis I reject. Crouching alone does nothing for the intellectual life; for good results the spine must bend in a garden. Those who weed on their knees are even less entitled, I think, to draw conclusions from their posture. So far as I know floor scrubbing does not kindle the imagination. What spurs the gardener's mind is probably the nearness of the elements. Carrots and onions in the garden row would be no more august than in the vegetable bin if it were not for earth, air, water and sun, building them up under your eyes. Your fingers touch earth reverently as you weed. You give thanks for light, for the air close to the ground, air both cool and warm, cool because the night dampness has not yet been baked out of it, warm because the sun starts up toward noon.

I have never had so many good ideas day after day as when I worked in the garden. The task is light if you keep at it steadily and know all the tricks. You can reduce the necessary weeding, for example, if you plant the rows of vegetables fairly close so that when the leaves are grown the soil will be shaded. The shade holds the dampness and prevents the sun from bringing on the weeds. You should get up early for the day's vegetable-picking. As you pick along the rows you remove all weeds, and after you have gathered enough, you keep on weeding through the rest of the garden, row by row. I used to finish the job in an hour and a half. Then I washed up, dressed for the day, and got at my writing, got at it with great eagerness, full of new ideas which clamored to be set down.

Gardening is not simply a summer aid to thought. If you know how to put up beans and other vegetables for the winter, your vacation efforts will keep on feeding you till the sun is high again, and when a dish of something you yourself raised comes on the table, it's likely to start your mind working. I used to wonder why food costs so much. I've had it explained to me many times and from many angles, but I still don't understand. The seeds for my garden didn't cost five dollars, yet they provided vegetables for a whole year, enough for a family of four and one servant and a pleasant sprinkling of guests. Since it's foolish to plant a niggardly garden if you plant at all, I always set out larger rows than I expected to eat. The surplus could be given to friends who had no garden, or if a bushel or two of spinach ripened all at once, I could exchange it at the village store for groceries. Gradually, however, during those six marvelous years, my gardening provided me with so many rich thoughts, and the thoughts so greatly improved my writing, and the writing brought in so much more money, that I hired other folks to do my gardening for me. It was a mistake, of course. In the extra hour and a half I could write more, but I had cut myself from the supply of ideas. What was less important but still interesting, the vegetables soon cost more than the amount I now paid the gardener. Here was a paradox, familiar to many households. My gardener was the most loyal and honest of friends, he was expert, he could raise vegetables for his own family much more cheaply, I'm sure, than I for mine, but when he took my garden in hand it soon cost more than his salary.

There is an explanation, of course, but I believe it is mystical rather than economic. Earth and sun discipline us when we work with them; we must be patient, we must plant and gather in the right order, we must be constant in our toil. So doing, we have our reward. But when we try to reap vicariously, from a distance, we pay. Nature rebukes us for deserting her.

3.

I suppose the most important craft is cooking. There's a sound reason for using skill in the kitchen as a standard by which to measure any civilization. To a large extent we can let others do our cooking for us, or so at least we Americans think, but unless we too know how to cook, those who prepare our food will prepare it any way they like and we must take what we get. That's about what we do. This country of ours doesn't know how to cook. When we go to the table we find there the means of subsistence rather than of nourishment; only in rare instances can we even pretend to find there an illustration of the complete life. The simon-pure American patriot can boil or fry an egg, can broil, fry or roast a chicken, can at a pinch bake pie or freeze ice cream, can even make a try at biscuit and bread—or we can do with a drugstore meal or a hot dog at the lunch wagon. In a manner of speaking we are fed. But if there's anyone around who knows how to cook, he's probably a foreigner.

Cooking is an art, and so is eating. If we don't know how to cook, we're not likely to know how to eat. The evening paper tells us of some football players who are taking a short course in cooking so they'll be useful to the army when they're inducted. War, any way you look at it, is hell. I recall a battalion of grand youngsters in the last war, taking over a sector to relieve the French. As soldiers they had had only a few months' training but they gave a handsome account of themselves. That is, as soldiers. When it came to cooking and eating, they supplied the poilus with something to talk about, the French army being full of chefs, professional or amateur. Our army had learned the art of the cuisine as it had learned the science of arms, overnight. We ate as we fought, with courage. The tin plates could and did hold all at the same time a slab of meat buried in gravy, a miscellany of vegetables, a biscuit and a wedge of pie. On top of the pie the soldier, unless he was clumsy, balanced his tin cup, filled with soup or coffee or both. He ate where he stood, beginning on whichever end of the meal was handiest.

You can see that kind of trough-feeding without going to war.

You can see it in any high school cafeteria, in any college com-
mons. I suggest that an acquaintance with the art of cooking
should be a prerequisite to a diploma or a degree. Some colleges
won't graduate a boy or girl who can't swim; why graduate any
who can't cook? Let's tackle our ignorance where it's most firmly
intrenched. What campus boarding house is remembered by
gourmets as the birthplace of their ideals? If you know of a
faculty club in which the table isn't damned by the professors, tell
me where it is; I'd like to see at least one before I die. Stewed
chicken for dinner with heavy gray dumplings and string beans
boiled black, scrambled eggs on cold toast for supper or thickened
codfish—if these are not the victuals of American scholarship and
culture, what is?

Of course instruction in cooking is already given in schools.
The school catalog says so. In the universities cooking is listed as
a subject of the domestic science department. But so long as the
results remain what they are we don't make the case better by
recalling how much effort goes into teaching of the wrong kind.
Domestic science in our schools is taught not by professional
cooks but by people, usually women, who are graduates of a
domestic science course. I don't say they can't assemble certain
forms of nutritious food; I do say that when restaurants or hotels
want a fine chef they look elsewhere than among the product of a
domestic science course. They apply at professional schools, where
the teachers have made their reputation and earned their living
cooking, or more probably they promote the assistant of a noted
chef, someone who has mastered the art by thorough apprentice-
ship. They would apply at a domestic science school only if they
wanted someone who had the disposition and the skill to run a tea-
room and print the number of calories on the menu alongside the
items of fried chicken, hot biscuit, salad and stewed fruit.

When we propose that cooking should be taught in our schools
by competent professional cooks, quite as competent as the football coach, we may expect opposition from those who talk of
culture, by which they mean degrees and barnacles. They wouldn't
let Escoffier himself teach cooking in their school unless the poor
fellow first took their courses, lecture courses where the pupil
merely listens; the best cook in the world couldn't communicate

his art in an American school unless he first proved he knew also some things which his colleagues would be capable of understanding. This in institutions which pretend to concern themselves with all the arts and sciences! If the holders of the educational citadel remain stubborn, those professors who believe that the arts can be taught by talking and learned by listening, I'd gladly put cooking in the athletic department, where the demands of so-called culture are not allowed to interfere with an honest piece of work. In football, basketball, baseball, swimming or track a successful result is wanted, and if the coach can't produce he gets fired. Did a domestic science teacher ever lose her job when it was discovered that a pupil could pass her course and still not be able to cook?

But I mustn't put on the schools the entire blame for this nation-wide ignorance of ours. The schools, I believe, could correct it gradually, working on successive younger generations and leaving the elders to wallow in their miserable condition. Something can be learned from horrible examples. The plight of the elders is demonstrated, in my opinion, not only by the domestic science cooking they support and pay for, not only by their contentment with their own inadequate cooking, but by the newspaper and magazine departments which dispense advice as to how to cook in the home. These departments or columns wouldn't be maintained if they hadn't a pathetically large number of readers, not one of whom apparently asks who conducts the department or column, or whether any of the advice handed out is based on experience. In rare instances a really qualified cook, a well-known chef, gives his recipes to the public through a newspaper, but in most cases the cooking column is conducted by anyone around the office who is willing to try it. Friends are besieged over the telephone for a recipe to fill out a paragraph. Knowledge of cooking is a prerequisite neither in the amiable friends nor in the columnist, nor even an interest in the food mentioned. I know one column which is run by a vegetarian. I know a woman who became a cook after she had handed out considerable advice on the subject, and then only by an accident which might have been a tragedy. She began with the usual method, asking chance acquaintances for their favorite recipes and printing whatever they said. One of her readers, as trusting as herself, tried out a recipe and all but died. The newspaper was threatened with a law suit. From then on the columnist sampled the recipes herself before she published them. It cost time and it put a strain on her health, but she learned to cook.

Most of us Americans, if we ever have encountered cooking of the finest sort, have met it only in the homes of the wealthy or in expensive eating places where a foreign chef presides. It is therefore a deep-rooted conviction among us, a mistaken idea but firmly held, that good cooking is more expensive than bad. The truth is that all great national cuisines have been developed not among the rich but among the poor—that is, in the households which, because they could afford no great quantity of food and little variety, learned to delight the palate by the seasoning of each dish and by contrast of flavor between one dish and another. The best seasoning is still the herbs which can be found in the fields or raised in the garden. French or Spanish peasants, Chinese or Mexican farmers, perhaps developed their distinctive cuisines without realizing the soundness of the instincts they followed. Food, to be satisfactory, must be not only nourishing but pleasant to eat. Correct flavoring is essential to the pleasure, and the pleasure is essential to the nourishment. What we don't enjoy eating does us little good. We could all eat less and get far more out of it if even our simplest meal were, as it easily might be, well cooked and well flavored, and if the succession of dishes, where there are more than one, were a symphony of taste.

Our land compared with France or China or some of the other countries which have developed characteristic and masterly cuisines is naturally rich in food material. I have heard that fact offered as an explanation of our poorly cooked and poorly served meals. Where the raw material is so good, we haven't been compelled to improve it by art. American corn on the cob, for example, is difficult to ruin by incorrect boiling, and we can make a meal, if we choose, out of a few ears. If butter is added it isn't a meal, it's a feast.

But still it isn't cooking. No art has been needed to boil the ear or to add a flavor. Nature has done it all for us. Let me tell you a personal memory by way of contrast. When those American boys of whom I spoke, the indiscriminate and heroic eaters, were standing about their field kitchen at the French front, the poilus who looked on were, as I said, extremely competent chefs, whether they had cooked to earn a living or merely to excel in the most human and necessary of arts. One of those who looked on was in peacetime a journalist. He had grown up in poverty, the eldest of five children, all supported in their childhood by their mother, a widow. When she went to work each morning she left my friend, the future journalist, to get lunch for his brothers and sisters and to have dinner ready when she came home. At the age of twelve he was a first-rate cook within a limited range, and by the time I met him in the war he was recognized, though an amateur, as one of the supreme chefs of France.

I have reason to know his merit. Our regiment was quartered at Haudainville, a small village which once had roofs on its houses, but now had none. Since we ate our meals in the mud wherever we pleased, my journalist friend set up a private mess for three or four of us, he doing the cooking with one hand, as it were, as we sat at the plank which served for table. He had picked up a small wood stove somewhere, appropriating it, soldier fashion, from one of the wrecked houses. The rations we drew from the commissary were uninspiring—meat which had already been boiled for the benefit of wounded in hospitals, black beans, on rare occasions a potato, no sugar, milk, or butter, pepper or salt, but Bar-le-duc jam and Gruyère cheese. From the canteen we could get coffee or chocolate, both sweetened in advance, by what method I don't know.

With these materials the journalist gave us night after night a meal full of new flavors and unexpected combinations. He got his ideas, as it seemed to me, through his pores as he went about his military tasks during the day. One evening we had a delicious salad. I had seen him gather it. It was late winter, and our errands had taken us across some fields which were beginning to soften. Every yard or so he'd stoop down and with his knife dig up a dandelion root. When we came back his pockets were full of this plunder, which after patient washing and drying emerged, if you'll believe me, as something altogether appetizing.

For another meal he got a pound of rice from the commissary

and a cup of sweetened chocolate from the canteen. To cook rice properly is difficult, as you may know; every kernel should be cooked to a melting softness, yet each kernel should stand out distinct. On his rickety wood stove he did the trick. Then he warmed the sweetened chocolate and mixed it with the rice so deftly that every kernel was covered yet not a drop was left in the bottom of the dish.

Nothing could be cheaper, please notice, than the materials which made these two meals memorable experiences in my life. But my friend's skill was not cheap. His mother had taught him the art of cooking, and obviously she must have known what she was talking about. I dare say the clamor of his hungry juniors spurred him on to make the little he had go a long way. He is in my mind when I wish that our schools taught the real art of cooking. The boy or girl who learned that art could transform the meals at home without buying a cent more than the family had been in the habit of spending.

Though our country in all sections is rich in food materials, some states enjoy a special prestige for their fruits, or for their wheat, for their vegetables, or for their meat. Few states, however, are equally famous for skill in cooking what they produce. There are exceptions, of course, some of which it would be unjust not to mention. Excellent cuisines can be found in San Antonio, Texas, and in some other places in that state, particularly along the Gulf of Mexico, where marvelous fish is cooked to perfection. In New Orleans there is the incomparable Antoine's, one of the great restaurants of the world. Other cities, the length and breadth of the land, will rise up against me to mention good eating places which I've omitted here. My own town, New York, I leave out; the neglect may be a form of boasting. If I don't make myself a guide to fine cooking in San Francisco and Los Angeles it isn't because I haven't been there or haven't been appreciative. In spite of the exceptions I believe my main point is overwhelmingly true, that the quality of our food exceeds our skill in preparing it. Without a knowledge of cooking and a sensitiveness to the kind of meal which is a work of art, no man or woman makes the impression of complete culture, and it's with cities as it is with persons. If I have two friends, both of them widely traveled, both of them college graduates, but one of them able to tell whether his food is or is not properly cooked, and why it is or isn't, competent also to choose the right sequence of flavors, and the other content to feed at a lunch wagon or out of tin cans at home—I know which man is completely cultured.

I can learn their cultural condition by probing a little, to see if the principles of good cooking are in them. These principles are few but very important. All cooking is a matter of time. In general, the more time the better. Cooking also is a matter of heat; just how hot the fire should be is as important as just how long the food should be on it. If you order your boiled eggs by time alone, you're not much of a cook. "Three minutes?" asked the boy at the lunch counter, and you probably nod consent. Why don't you ask him how hot the fire is? An egg boiled very slowly at not much more than a simmer becomes a different egg from one blasted in a fierce bubble, as though cooking could be done on a blow-pipe. And good cooking is a matter of flavoring.

Some dishes of course must be cooked fast, some meats especially. If your Texas filet is served to you entirely unburned on the outside but dry and hard throughout, you know it has been on the fire too long and the fire hasn't been hot enough. You can draw conclusions also from the absence or presence of grease on your plate. It seems that few of us know the difference between grease and gravy. There should never be any grease. If you are frying bacon, drain the grease off each piece after it's cooked by letting it rest for a minute on soft paper. Bacon without grease is a tid-bit.

Whether or not you go in for sauces or gravies is a matter of taste, but an inflexible rule of good cooking prescribes that the gravy should not be used as an incompetent carpenter sometimes uses putty and paint, to hide a bad job. If the meat doesn't satisfy without the gravy, your cooking is a failure. The sauce or gravy should supply an additional flavor worthwhile in its own right.

Do you know how to broil chops? Most housewives think they do, but the result as I've encountered it in American restaurants and American homes is usually this, that the meat of the chop is cooked dry and perhaps tough, while the fat on the edge has been cooked into a grease, conveyed to your plate for the chop to float in. The right way is to stand the chop up on the bone side with the rim of fat near the flame, so that the fat can melt off and run down over the meat into the broiler below. Then brown the chop quickly on both sides and serve. The meat will be tender and there won't be any grease.

Do you know how to make an omelette? There are many kinds of omelette, and we may say that all are excellent, except the kind you get in most American restaurants. We Americans usually turn out an omelette which is a fair substitute for a piece of meat, being quite solid and of substantial weight. If that's the effect you want from eggs, why not boil the eggs hard or fry them stiff? The labor and skill which go into a good omelette have for their purpose to produce an extremely delicate dish, delicate in flavor and delicate in weight, something which, as we say, will melt in the mouth. You can't make that kind of omelette by the slow process. It must be an improvisation, a *tour de force*.

'All first-rate omelettes are made with speed and dash. The eggs must be entirely fresh and they must be thoroughly beaten. Whether you should beat the whites and yolks separately or together is a disputed point. I beat them separately and then mix them pretty thoroughly before pouring into the frying pan, or whatever you cook the omelette in. The frying pan should be a heavy iron affair. You need enough metal to hold the heat, because the cooking is done on the pan rather than on the stove. When the pan is very hot, put in sufficient shortening to swish around and grease the whole surface, the sides as well as the bottom. I use butter, but it's tricky because you must pour in the beaten eggs before the butter starts to burn. Rotate the pan, holding it in your left hand. If you don't do this, the omelette will stick to the sides. If you rotate the pan steadily, the omelette will float on the butter and slide off when you want it to. You learn by practice when the omelette is done, but a good sign to go by is the black smoke rising from the edges. I take it as a signal to slide the omelette on a platter, folding it over when the sliding is halfway finished. If you don't wish to fold it over, you can have a hot oven ready and stick the pan in for thirty seconds, just long enough to brown the top of the omelette.

If the school your children go to doesn't yet provide sound

teaching in the art of the kitchen, start the youngsters off yourself. The knowledge of correct egg-boiling, they will probably feel, is too elementary; chop-broiling, on the other hand, is rather high up in the art, and omelette-making is higher still. Begin with a simple exercise in flavoring. Tell the children that lunch will consist of a baked potato, to be cooked and flavored by themselves. Mention the flavoring to encourage them, and promise that if they don't like the taste they may change it to suit their individual palates. By bringing the seasoning into the foreground you emphasize what makes cooking an art and eating an intelligent delight.

Let the children put the potatoes into the oven and watch the clock for an hour or slightly more, the oven being at a good heat. If the potatoes are not thoroughly baked, the children will at least have learned something about the importance of time and temperature. Slice off one side of the potato. I'm now talking to the children. Dig out the potato and mash it, softening with butter and a little milk. Then fry three slices of bacon for each potato, fry almost to burning, and drain the strips on a sheet of paper till there is no grease. Break up the bacon into small particles—use a fork. For each potato put a small onion through the meatchopper, taking care not to lose any of the juice. Mash into the potato the onion, the onion juice and the particles of almost-burnt bacon, mixing thoroughly. Then put the mixture back into the potato skin, butter it, and brown slightly in the oven.

If you like the onion flavor, try less burnt bacon. If you prefer burnt bacon, try less onion. Diminish the flavor you don't like instead of increasing the flavor you do.

4.

These recipes, though I use them myself, are offered merely to illustrate elementary principles. Chop-broiling involves the correct application of heat, omelette-making is a question of time, much or little, and the baked potato is, as I said, an exercise in flavoring. So far I presume as an amateur to discuss the general subject, but since I'm not a professional chef nor even an all-around cook in the amateur class, I refer you to those who really know. Not only in cooking but in gardening and carpentering.

I suggest in the appendix a few books which contain professional advice about the use of tools and about the care of a garden; also about cooking. But here a word of caution may be inserted about all cooking advice, beginning with my own. There are two kinds of cook books, those written by experts who, like other artists, have a personality, a consistent philosophy, a point of view; and those put together by connoisseurs of food who do not themselves cook and who therefore gather recipes from various sources on no unifying principle. From these anthologists we can learn of excellent dishes but not the art which invented them.

Everyone has to some extent and for some purposes used a hammer and otherwise handled tools, most of us have at least once or twice planted flowers and vegetables, practically all of us have on occasion cooked. We are ready to profit by seeing how an expert does well what we perhaps do awkwardly. Cook books of the kind I mentioned first, the kind written by practical authorities, may be divided into those intended for you and me and those intended for experienced chefs. You and I, amateurs though we are, can learn from the advanced texts as well as from the elementary, but we'd better begin with the elementary.

There are many good books of the elementary sort. The mark of them all is that they teach you the essential processes, what no cook, domestic or professional, can afford not to know. I use *The Boston Cooking School Cook Book*. We go to such a work to correct our methods, to simplify them, to get new ideas. In the early stages of our self-education we learn most by consulting recipes for dishes we think we already know how to prepare.

Since flavoring and the mixture of flavors is the essence of cooking, we can't get far by preparing only separate and unrelated dishes. *The Complete Menu Book,* by Gladys T. Lang, has given me many ideas about meals planned as a whole. It is in all respects an excellent cook book, but it is a grade higher than the sort of text which imparts fundamentals; its service is to stimulate the imagination toward the combination of flavors which, though they are familiar, are rarely brought together.

Among the most advanced works is, of course, Escoffier's book, a classic. Others, of great value, have not yet been translated and are difficult to secure. I prize the *Guide du Maitre-d'Hotel et du*

Restaurateur, by J. Rey, a supreme chef whose sons have carried the family skill to various parts of the world. As the title shows, the book is designed for head-waiters and all who know thoroughly the art of the restaurant, yet it contains suggestions of an amazing simplicity, illustrating that economy of means which distinguishes all art and fine cooking in particular, and reminding us that an educated palate likes an understatement in the seasoning.

Notice, for instance, what Rey says about poaching eggs. You and I know that egg-poaching is a fool-proof operation; a child can do it. You drop an egg into boiling water, move the water off the fire, let the egg cook as the water cools, and what you get is called a poached egg, a rather tasteless morsel, if the truth is faced. Particularly on dining cars, for some reason.

It is well to use a poacher, to shape up the white of the egg and to get the whole thing out of the water when it's done. Rey suggests also that we put into the water salt and vinegar, to hold the egg together and season it. But there should be more seasoning than that. He further suggests herbs in the water as it comes to a boil, tarragon or mint or whatever you prefer. I like basil myself, and chervil is excellent. An egg poached in slightly salted water, with a sifting of your favorite herb and a dash of vinegar, is a tantalizing mystery, a smooth astonishment.

Whether we become good cooks, remember, depends on our ability to correct ourselves by the examples of the masters. We learn from them the elementary processes. We learn from them how to season. We learn from them the sequence of dishes and flavors which are necessary for a distinguished meal.

And chiefly we learn from them to have ideas of our own.

CHAPTER VI

Conversation

1.

WE ARE STILL considering the arts, those which all of us should know something about if our lives are to be complete. Conversation is more than mere talk. It is a diplomatic exchange of opinion and idea, carried on like a game, according to rules which all the players understand. Those rules, a few centuries ago, were handed down as part of the education of gentlefolk. Today we trust, and with passable results, to our general feeling for the sport, but we might get more out of it if we glanced at the rules once more, to be clear about what we're doing.

Conversation, in the ancient meaning of the word, is a social condition, the state in which man moves among his fellows. The King James translation of the Bible, you recall, says that our conversation is in heaven. Later shifts of meaning in the word leave undisturbed the social implication, the idea that mankind is surrounded by mankind and therefore tact is needed, and even more, a technique. The art of conversation is the technique for getting on in company when everybody wants to talk at once.

Conversation is possible, of course, between two people, but it can't be much of an art unless there are at least three. The larger the number, the greater becomes the difficulty of assuring each person a just share in the talk, and of preventing the group from breaking up into fragments. The mark of good conversation is that every member of the company takes part in it, and that all discuss the same theme.

It isn't difficult to find subjects which excite a number of people simultaneously, and it isn't hard to stir a group to speak, but an angry mob does not produce conversation. If emotions are roused, the result will be action; the assembly which can do nothing else, at least proposes and seconds a motion, votes, and goes home. The purpose of conversation as an art is not to send the company home, nor to arrive at any decision, not even to discuss or consult, as in a committee or legislature. Conversation aims at entertainment which subtly enlightens. If the enlightenment doesn't remain subtle, the conversation will be no more entertaining than a lecture. The subject upon which the illumination is bestowed is life in general. The topic may seem narrower, the exchange of talk may be inspired by any event of interest to the speaker, but it cannot be handled in polite conversation until it is translated into universal values.

The chief hindrances to conversation are certain natural impulses. The rules of the art, therefore, tend to be negative. Only if we can restrain ourselves is conversation possible. Good talk rises upon much self-discipline.

The first rule of the game is that all voices must be kept subdued. In a numerous company, well-disposed toward self-expression, the tendency will of course be toward clamor. The proper art for democratic gatherings, it has been said, is oratory; a single voice guides the multitude by kindling emotion, and the multitude responds by shouting. In contrast the art of conversation is ill-adapted to democratic assemblies but suitable for groups which are sophisticated, thoughtful and refined. In conversation the speaker gets and holds attention not by raising his voice, but by what he says and the way he says it. Our almost universal neglect of the art in the United States is betrayed by the deafening chatter in restaurants. The food patrons lift their voices, as they would say, to make themselves heard, but if voices were lowered hearing would be easy. The loudness has not much to do with the problem of being heard; it is rather a release of cordial emotions, an attempt to express good will by whooping it up. Haven't you heard some of your neighbors praise another neighbor for his or her hearty laugh? And when you are in the hearty laugher's company, haven't you questioned at times the felicity of greeting a witticism with a war whoop?

If we speak louder than others we risk stopping the talk. Since we make such a point of being heard, the company may decide to do nothing but listen. What should be an exchange of ideas may degenerate into a monologue or harangue, and once the talk falls so low, it's hard to recover it. But there are other ways of shipwrecking a conversation, and the rules to guard against that catastrophe are many. It is a mistake, for example, in a general conversation to offer an illustration out of your personal experience. If the others have no private confessions to match yours, it's hard for the next speaker to go on from where you leave off. If they can indeed furnish parallels, the talk may break up into miscellaneous anecdotes. Such stories are told because they are unusual. For that reason, therefore, anecdotes and jokes, personal experiences, and whatever the company cannot be expected to discuss with the same intimate knowledge as yourself, should be avoided. The point is that we must leave the conversation in as flourishing a condition as when we entered it. To settle the topic under discussion so that there's nothing more to be said, is as fatal an error as to call for a vote and adjourn the meeting. The topic should be developed; when we've had our turn at it we should pass it on to someone else, preferably to the person in the group who so far has said least. This transfer may be accomplished by a question, or by the shift of our attention, imitating the actor's technique, who, when he has said his piece, hands over the audience to the next speaker by the manner in which he listens.

Listening is an art by itself. We needn't lean forward, bulge our eyes, or hang out an eager tongue; relaxation in the listener has the same value as a quiet voice in the speaker, but it is the body which is relaxed, not the brain. To listen well we hold the speaker with our eyes. If from moment to moment the expression of our face shows the effect of what is said, well and good, but this response should be unconscious. If our features are by nature masklike, once more well and good. Only the eyes are important, and if they indicate attention, the speaker will soon be addressing us. Fix your eyes on him, if you wish to cut in as soon as he's through.

The speaker hands over the conversation to someone else by looking at him and by putting on the listener's attitude. On the other hand, if you want to speak next, you take the floor by listening to the person who is doing the talking. Some simple souls just wave a hand and call out, "It's my turn, let me talk next," but this isn't art. Of course there may be some in the group who don't understand the technique of conversation as well as you do; even though you have your eye on the speaker and he has his eye on you, someone may try to cut in before you get under way. It's surprising how easily this catastrophe may be avoided, not by cutting in over-quickly yourself, but continuing in the same rhythm as the previous speaker and at the same pace.

The method of cutting in calls for alertness, intelligence, all the qualities which go with quickness of mind, but the technique of dropping the conversation is more difficult; it calls not only for mental agility but for moral character as well. The art of conversation is possible only so long as we remain unselfish. Once we have the floor we must yield it quickly to another or the interest of the group will flag. Three fairly short sentences at the outside are all that we're entitled to, on each sally. One sentence gets us into the talk, the second makes our point, the third gets us out gracefully.

I've heard it said that a reliable formula for stepping out of the conversation and handing it on to the next speaker is a question; we can pick our successor by asking whether he does or does not agree with us. But I've never seen this rule work well, and quite frequently it works very badly. Nothing irritates the average human being more than a pseudo-question which really asks nothing, the kind of sentence in which the speaker first dogmatizes a bit, then turns to you and says, "Don't you think so?" My impulse is to say I don't, even when I do. The method is little better if the inquiry is put at the beginning: "Don't you think Wagner's music is wonderful?" We suspect, if we do not see clearly, the speaker's point of view, and we feel as though we were invited, not to discuss the subject, but to stand up and be counted for or against. A speaker who wants to keep conversation alive will match his ideas against what has been said, inviting comparison but avoiding a compulsory vote.

These rules for conversation may seem in one sense artificial; it is no longer our custom, as in the eighteenth century, to hold salons, evening parties in which the chief amusement was good talk. The art of conversation has lapsed somewhat, we admit, but if the changes in our habits have left no further occasion for it, some of us ask why shouldn't it lapse? No doubt you have heard the remark, as I have, that conversation has art enough in it if it says what we mean and if it says it kindly, clearly, and with satisfaction to all concerned. Yet though the formal salon has disappeared, we still give dinner parties, groups of friends still meet in the evening in each other's home, and though the talk is good, it might be far better. We might as well note the respects in which it could be improved.

At most dinner tables the hostess would be worried if there were no conversation at all. Imagine a meal at which the guests fed in silence. Talk, even if it's no more than amiable chatter, at least indicates that the company and the hosts have no grudge against each other. Yet in the party there may be one or two persons who listen without contributing a remark. They may be enjoying themselves, but they certainly keep their condition a secret; even their presence may be forgotten. This means, of course, that someone else is doing the talking for them. Haven't you dined out on occasions when one of the guests, perhaps a neighbor famed for her brightness, has put on a monologue? If you dined out again and encountered the same neighbor, wasn't there another monologue, or the same one over again? The art of conversation isn't a fad or a frill; society invented it in self-defense, and we in the United States may revive it for the same purpose.

Since it's our custom to seat men and women alternately at a dinner table, the simplest method for distributing conversation is to talk as much to your partner on your right as to your partner on your left. Though we have progressed no further in the art of conversation, we usually observe this rule. Not always, however. Through thoughtlessness or selfishness we sometimes cling to a partner we know is interesting rather than turn to the one as yet untried. In that case the dinner breaks up into twosomes, or a guest may have bad luck indeed and be deserted by the group on the left before being noticed by the group on the right. To avoid this embarrassment some hostesses suggest, if necessary in very plain terms, that the moment has arrived to aim conversation in the other direction. A still more elementary method is to move the male guests around after each course. Just when you and your neighbor have established heart-to-heart or mind-to-mind communication, you are invited to collect your knife and fork, napkin and glass of water, and move on. Both these methods are to say the least crude, and the second is a desperate confession that host and hostess are afraid the party will get out of hand. True artists would keep the conversation out in the open, pursuing topics in which all are interested. If the talk threatens to disintegrate into small units, the guests can be recalled by a question, which is a little obvious, or more subtly by the mention of a name. If Mary is lost in a tête-à-tête with George, put Mary's name into whatever you're saying at your end of the table. Pronounce it ever so softly, and note the promptness with which Mary will ask who's talking about her.

Even in our informal world there are still men and women who at least at dinner tables keep the talk flowing on a high plane of social art. Those who had the privilege of knowing Corinne Roosevelt Robinson remember evenings at her unique table where she conveyed her interest in her guests and stimulated their interest in each other, so that ideas, serious or amusing, criss-crossed the board. Hers was the studied art of the old-fashioned salon. She did not depend upon her guests to furnish the entertainment; before the evening was over they had reason to know that she had prepared for their coming by hours of thought. I recall one dinner party at the end of which she read out a brief poem addressed to each guest. Knowing her friends, she could foretell what thoughts they would have when brought together, and her clever verses turned out to be lucky guesses, comments on what, by that hour of the evening, each guest had actually said.

Though I speak of dinner parties and salons, I don't mean to limit the art of conversation to formal or elaborate gatherings. I'd be sorry to call up for the reader the picture of any life not familiar to all of us in the United States. We ask our friends to eat with us though the men are wearing neither black nor white tie. They may be wearing no tie at all; we may be enjoying the meal in summer on the porch, or perhaps we're picnicking with our coats off and our sleeves rolled up. Yet whatever the setting, there will still be talk, and it will be worth remembering if there's some art in it. In the French Army during the World War I was deeply impressed by the persistence of fine social habits. A dog will carry his bone to a private nook and do his gnawing undisturbed, but civilized man wants companions who can talk, to nourish his mind as well as his body. The French soldiers liked to eat in groups of at least four. In any dry place in the mud, they'd make themselves comfortable and strike at once into a grand exchange of ideas and opinions, parrying the thrusts of argument, sharpening wit on wit.

2.

If we know how to talk, what do we talk about? This question leads straight to the best reason for knowing how to talk. Those who have the art of conversation can discuss any subject whatever in any company. Those who haven't this art can only say certain things to certain people.

The principle of the art is this: If you are talking to another about an intimate matter, involving deep emotion, and if a third person joins you, the topic can be continued without embarrassment if you treat it in more general terms, a little less specifically, and if you reduce it, as it were, to a lower temperature. The more numerous the group, the less personal and the less emotional should be the conversation.

Suppose you are talking to a dear friend about a death in his family or yours, and suppose that another friend joins you, someone who perhaps knew but slightly the relative of whom you have just spoken. Many of us would drop the subject abruptly and start a new one. This course, though instinctive, is awkward, and for the newcomer it may be painful, since he knows by the expression on our face and by the tone of our voice that we have been discussing something more than the weather, something that we are keeping from him. Among my own friends I can think of several who though rich in natural kindness, always change the subject when a newcomer joins in. They give the impression, disturbing to others and unfair to themselves, that they are occupied always with a secret.

Artists in conversation consider themselves defeated if a new arrival, merely by happening along, can force them off their topic.

They would rather transpose to a lower emotional temperature and go on. If a fourth person joins them, they continue with another emotional transposition. Their manner becomes lighter, their ideas have a more public application, but they stick to their purpose, and the friend who is with them from the beginning hears only one theme, though through several keys.

The themes which most often call for tactful transposition as the group enlarges itself, are love, death, and politics. We can discuss with venom or ecstasy the representative we ourselves elected, or our taxes, or foreign affairs, so long as all in the group hold the same opinions, but when a friend joins us who belongs to the other side, unless we change our tone we'll soon have on our hands not a conversation but a row. To drop the subject altogether or to be untrue to our convictions, just because a critic has come within hearing, would be somewhat ignoble and not a little stupid. Decency requires us to continue what we were saying, but with such moderation of tone as courtesy to the newcomer demands, and with at least a pretense at weighing the views we don't agree with.

In general conversation the theme of death is avoided, and when a small group is suddenly enlarged, talk of personal sorrow usually stops, yet the seventeenth and eighteenth centuries, when the art of conversation reached an exquisite perfection, had the courage and the skill to transpose grief into graceful tributes, almost into personal compliment. Many epitaphs carry understatement so far that they have the effect of wit, yet as expressions of grief they are none the less convincing. To write of death in a courtly tone was a skill which had first been acquired in conversation. The best examples suggest not the grave but the drawing room. Thomas Carew wrote of Lady Mary Wentworth, dead at the age of eighteen:

> "Good to the Poor, to kindred dear,
>   To servants kind, to friendship clear:
>   To nothing but herself severe."

Sir Henry Wotton said, on the death of Sir Albert Morton's wife,

> "She first deceased; he for a little tried
>   To live without her, liked it not, and died."

The essence of tragic matters, however transposed, is interpreted by the tone of the voice, and such understatements as these
poems illustrate make their full effect only if they ring true. To
talk well we must not only be sincere but we must sound so. An
affected manner, an artificial diction, an obviously acquired pronunciation, will put our hearers on guard against us.

If ever the impression of sincerity is an aid to the speaker, it is
at those rare moments when the topic of conversation is love,
personal affection. It's the last thing we'll touch on in general
conversation, yet exceptional cases do occur, and they demand the
technique of an artist. There was a man, for example, some eighty
years ago, who called on a girl just before taking a long journey.
He intended to propose as soon as he returned, but his emotions
were too much for him, and with the formality no longer in
fashion he started in to offer then and there his heart and hand.
Before he had got well into his second sentence two neighbors
rang the doorbell and made themselves comfortable for a visit
which evidently would stretch beyond his train time. Rather than
accept defeat or postponement he wove his proposal into apparently
casual talk, and she with the same skill accepted him, without
giving the intruders an inkling of what was going on. If we had
a record of that conversation, speech by speech, we could study
the art at its best.

Conversation as badly practiced by improperly educated people
has been immortalized by many satirists, notably by Jonathan
Swift in his *Compleat Collection of Genteel and Ingenious Conversation,* published in 1738. In his preface to this bitter attack
on the so-called good society of his day, Swift says he took pains
to write down on three separate occasions the small talk with
which good society kills time. Whether the dialogues were real
or imaginary, we needn't inquire too closely. None but students
of eighteenth century manners will recognize how lifelike the
talk is. Instead of looking up the old book, I'd advise the reader
to imitate Swift and make a word-for-word record of the talk in
any chatty gathering of friends. Beneath the satire of his preface
we detect the rules of conversation. He invites us, for example, to
applaud the numerous quotations, all of them from the best
known authors; or quotations lacking, the well-known jokes; or

at least the phrases which all the best people use. Stating the principles directly, we'd say that in good conversation there are no
quotations, no quoted jokes, no anecdotes, and no trite phrases.

Swift reminds us that uncultured people are sometimes at a
loss for "questions, answers, replies, and rejoinders." His satire
shows the ladies and gentlemen talking glibly but never giving
an answer which connects with the question, and never observing
the difference between answer, reply, and rejoinder. Or if they
know the difference, they cannot handle them all with equal facility. The passage which makes this point gives by inference an
excellent idea of how the art should really be practiced.

"I have passed perhaps more time than any other man of my
age and country in visits and assemblies, where the polite persons of both sexes distinguish themselves; and could not without much grief observe how frequently both gentlemen and
ladies are at a loss for questions, answers, replies and rejoinders:
However, my concern was much abated, when I found that
these defects were not occasioned by any want of materials, but
because those materials were not in every hand: For instance,
one lady can give an answer better than ask a question: One
gentleman is happy at a reply; another excels in a rejoinder;
One can revive a languishing conversation by a sudden surprising sentence; another is more dexterous in seconding; a
third can fill the gap with laughing, or commending what hath
been said: Thus fresh hints may be started, and the ball of
discourse kept up.

"But, alas! this is too seldom the case, even in the most select
companies: How often do we see at court, at public visiting
days, at great men's levees, and other places of general meeting,
that the conversation falls and drops to nothing, like a fire without supply of fuel; this is what we ought to lament; and against
this dangerous evil I take upon me to affirm, that I have in the
following papers provided an infallible remedy."

We might examine the phrase "questions, answers, replies, and
rejoinders." An answer completely satisfies a question. A reply
or a rejoinder counters the question without answering it. The
word "reply" means a folding back. I reply to your question by

throwing it back to you in one form or another, or by asking a question in return, or even by changing the subject. If you then reply to my reply, you are said to make a rejoinder. The word carries the meaning of a joint or a splicing. In a reply there is usually an evasion of the original question, for the simple reason that if you could give the answer, or wished to, you would. At its best a reply is gracefully diplomatic; at its crudest a reply is a retort, a retaliation. As employed by the unskilled a rejoinder, too, may be only a retort, and since the reply has preceded it, the rejoinder, seeking to out-do the reply, may verge on insult. Where courtesy prevails, or where conversation is practiced as an art, the evasive element in a reply is understood to have a social purpose, to keep the talk in motion, to avoid closing the subject by a complete answer. Where the motives and the art are good-natured and accomplished, the rejoinder tries to excel the reply in wit.

We are aware of these distinctions even though we haven't names for all of them. Those friends who are clever talkers we describe as having a good come-back. Replies and rejoinders are come-backs. The rejoinder, the second come-back, ought to be better than the first, but it usually isn't.

Swift begins his satire with a question, a reply, and a rejoinder, of the weak sort which with little change we can identify still in our conversational efforts. The impulse to make a reply or a rejoinder is always strong, but unless our mind is working the result is flat and silly. It would be painfully silly if we were not accustomed to the silliness, and therefore fortified by callousness. Swift makes one character say, "How do you do, Tom?" Tom replies, "Never the better for you." The first speaker comes back with, "I hope you're never the worse." The content of this intellectual exchange is meagre, but unfortunately it's not below our average today.

3.

I said we must not only be sincere but we must sound as though we were. The art of conversation is impossible unless we know how to use our voice. To speak well, to manage lips and throat and lungs so that musical and significant sounds come out of them, is an art rare but simple. Correct pronunciation follows from correct vocal technique. If in our speech we have some local peculiarity which marks us as a westerner, a middle westerner, a New Englander, or a southerner, there is less reason to be proud of this provincialism than perhaps we think; if we spoke correctly, all of us, from whatever district, would utter approximately the same sounds. A soprano from New England and a soprano from Texas, if well trained, produce the same tones and pronounce the words the same way. Local oddities which for local vanity we cherish are nothing more nor less than defects of speech. The New Englander talks through his nose because he doesn't breathe deep, doesn't relax his throat, doesn't open his mouth. The ladies from certain parts of the South who specialize in flat A's, who drawl indolently, and omit final G's, do indeed astonish, at times fascinate, but when they speak in public their voice doesn't carry, and even in private conversation they are not always clearly understood. Their ideal apparently is to deprive their voice of all resonance; they are proud of sounding like a violin with the sides and the back removed.

If you are familiar with the structure of a pipe organ, you can easily understand, in a rough parallel, the mechanism of human speech. There must be a bellows to pump air into a wind chamber, and the pressure in the wind chamber must be kept steady. From the wind chamber the air is carried through a flue to the pipes, where vibrations are set up which produce the tone. With the diaphragm we draw or pump air into the lungs, which constitute the wind chamber. To speak or sing properly we must keep the pressure fairly even in the lungs. The throat is the flue which carries the breath to the vocal cords, and the nasal chambers like the organ pipe receive the vibrations and magnify them by a sounding-board effect. The only muscular effort is permissible in the manipulation of the bellows. The throat or flue should never be contracted or pinched. The vocal cords should not be forced. The resonance should be established not in the throat, but in the front of the head, and the mouth should of course be open, for the same reason that a trumpet flares out in a bell. Of course you can stick something in the mouth of a trumpet to stop the tone or change its quality. Many of us unfortunately mute our voices by closing our jaws on the sound.

Deep and steady breathing is essential to good speech. It is almost equally important that the voice should be correctly placed, that the resonance should be set up in the front of the face rather than further back. We don't speak through the nose, but when the mouth is open we can feel the sound vibrating in the nasal chambers, in the bones of the forehead, through all the front of the head. Singers have an elementary exercise which most of us have heard; they sound the vowels with an m in front of them— me, my, mo, mah. Since it's impossible to sound m anywhere but on the lips, this exercise tends to bring the vowel forward, where it belongs. After a few minutes with me, my, mo, you feel the vibrations in your nose, but the breath and the sound issue of course through the lips, not through the nostrils.

Anyone who speaks with relaxed throat, with plenty of breath, and with the mouth open, will produce a pleasant sound, even though the words are imperfectly pronounced. A relaxed voice helps the listener to relax, but tenseness in the speaker tightens up the listener. People who live out of doors, in what we call primitive conditions, on the soil or in the mountains or on the sea, usually are distinguished by splendid speech, brought about by no education or training but by the health of nerves and the relaxation of muscles. Moreover, since such people are as far as possible removed from artificiality, they don't change their way of speaking when they meet a stranger. In more sophisticated society it is hard to find such health or such naturalness, or such freedom from self-consciousness. For this reason the art of conversation, courtesy in speech, correct voice production, is for most of us difficult, yet if once mastered, extremely rewarding.

When I mention out-of-doors people who by instinct and habit speak well, I think of a guide in Maine whose quiet deep tones, even though you didn't know what he was saying, imparted a kind of healing. I think of an Irish child on a moor in County Kerry, whose exquisite inflections haunt my remembrance after thirty-five years. I think of a gigantic rancher in Texas whose casual syllables in a bus, though he spoke softly, seemed to make the windows vibrate. Either we have such gifts by inheritance and have preserved them by natural habits, or we must give our voice a thorough education. There is no middle course. If our voice is but half-trained, our speech may sound affected or distorted. Relaxation, resonance and clear diction are either entirely instinctive or they result from complete training.

But fortunately much of this training we can give ourselves. Once we become interested in speech and know the general principles of breathing, of relaxing the throat, bringing the resonance well forward, opening the mouth, we gather more wisdom, bit by bit, listening to good speakers or discussing with them their technique.

One bit of technique, however, which can be observed even among those whose ideas are worth listening to, we had better not imitate. Most lecture platforms and some pulpits are supplied with a glass of water for the rescue of the speaker when his throat gives out. If it is known that his throat has a trick of giving out on a large scale, a pitcher of water will be furnished. These preparations should warn the audience that the speaker doesn't know how to use his voice. Singers get through their concert without drinking; on the opera stage the artists are not followed by a water-boy. Dryness of the throat or huskiness comes from nervous tension, and no permanent remedy can be supplied by water or any other liquid. For a moment they would feel better, probably because the act of drinking relaxes their throat, but at once their state would be more tense than before. They can get out of trouble only by relaxing the throat and breathing deep.

We progress in the mechanics of speaking when we give careful attention to the words we use. Most of us get along with fewer words than we should. The easiest way to enlarge our vocabulary is to note every new word we hear, look it up in the dictionary to be certain of its meaning, and employ it ourselves as soon as possible, to fix it in our memory. Most professional speakers and writers make a habit of reading the dictionary. If you have ten minutes to spare, open the book anywhere. Whether the words are old acquaintances or new to you, in either case examine the definitions with care. We are liable to use words in the wrong sense. We are in still greater danger of using words because their sound is familiar rather than because we know precisely what they mean. Uncertainty as to the meaning may have a disastrous effect on the voice. Subconsciously our ignorance makes us nervous. We are bluffing, or at least are taking a chance, and conscience will trip up a speaker as it does a piano player who hasn't thoroughly practiced the piece, numbing the fingers in the hard places, tightening the throat on an uncertain word. But if we study the dictionary a few moments each day, perhaps we shan't need that glass of water.

Even though we know the precise meaning of a word, we sometimes get the accent wrong. Though the fault is probably not ours, we should correct it promptly. The people among whom we live may at any time develop new pronunciations. If everyone adopts it, the dictionaries in up-to-date editions will tell us so, and we'll be justified in going with the new fashions, but while the novelty is only a fad, we needn't encourage it without reason. In most cases, at least in the United States, the excuses for new pronunciations are weak. Since our population is recruited from other lands, the newcomers more often than not learn English late. That they should distort some pronunciations is inevitable, and no harm comes of it if we don't imitate them.

In the neighborhood of New York, for example, it is the almost universal custom to pronounce "inquiry" with the accent on the first syllable. The result is an unlovely sound which might be spelled "*ink*ery." The reason for this innovation is, I suppose, that many of our foreign-born citizens have observed the tendency in English to push the accent forward. If "subsidy" has the accent on the first syllable, why shouldn't "inquiry" have it there? But the parallel is not genuine. "Subsidy," the noun, is related to "subsidize," the verb. "In*quiry*," the noun, is related to "inquire," the verb. The correct accent, therefore, is on the second syllable, not the first. Even if the dictionary didn't set us straight, we might be guided by our ear for the music of words. As mere sound there is no comparison between "inquiry" and "*ink*ery."

4.

I've postponed as long as I could the most delicate problem in the art of conversation. However adept we are in keeping the talk going, we must have something to say. We must? No, it's not obligatory. Dean Swift satirized the well-born men and women of his day who maintained a steady chatter without a single interesting or creditable idea. He bore down heavily on the clumsiness with which the outside technique of the art was managed, but the essence of his criticism was that the talkers had nothing inside their heads. Most of us, no matter what our opportunities or our education, are open to the same charge. Few of us, very few, feel the obligation to have ideas, but we all talk. Our motives are of the best; we feel a kindly urge to be sociable, to remain in communication with those near us, even for no other purpose than to let them know we are well disposed. I could never see a virtue in taciturnity. When a man boasts that he's silent in my company because he has nothing to say, I blame him on two accounts—first, because he doesn't feel the urge to be friendly, and second, because by his own confession, his brain, when he meets me, stops working. We shouldn't talk less; we should exercise our brains and talk better.

If one person has ideas and the other has none, the difference may be in natural talents, but I'm disposed to look for it rather in energy or in indolence. To think at all is hard, not to say painful, and the further we push our thoughts, the easier it is to stop and rest. Some of the worst conversation comes from intelligent people encountering each other, no doubt with good will, but beyond question after they've done their thinking for the day. When both sides are reluctant to start the machinery again, they satisfy social obligation by chattering.

On a train recently I heard two men talking, two pleasant-looking and no doubt intelligent men, energetic, keen, no doubt successful in business, and either neighbors at home or accustomed to meet elsewhere. When I saw them they were going to the races. One had a fairly high voice, the other a deep baritone, but both talked without opening the lips. The baritone, having developed an exaggerated nasal resonance, could make himself heard through the barrier of locked teeth. They were courteous, never for a moment was the chatter allowed to die, but they proceeded almost exclusively by alternate question and answer. Replies and rejoinders would have put a load on the brain. When each fatuous inquiry had its fatuous response, good will hurried them on to a sillier question and a sillier answer. Their performance, as I remember it, came to this:

"Your wife didn't come."

"No, she didn't come."

"Doesn't she enjoy the races?"

"Sometimes. But she'd rather stay home."

"She came last year."

"Remember that horse I liked?"

"The large bay?"

"That's the one. That's the prettiest horse I ever saw."

"Didn't that horse lose?"

"The jockey didn't know his business. He should have let him out earlier."

"He couldn't, he was pocketed."

"He should have let him out before he was pocketed."

"He was pocketed right at the start."

"Well, anyway, he should have let him out."

"I liked the other bay better."

"But you bet on the large one, same as I did."

"I liked the other one. I should have followed my hunch."

"I always follow my hunch."

"But the horse lost."

The train crossed a bridge over a stream.

"Oh, did you see the fish?"

"What fish?"

"In the river."

"How could you see it in the river?"

"It jumped out."

"Why?"

"It was a shad."

"Oh, shad don't jump."

"This one did."

"How do you know?"

"I saw it."

"I mean, how do you know it was a shad?"

"Well, this is the season for them, isn't it?"

"Might of been a catfish."

"No, this one was large."

"Of course, a large catfish."

"How do you know?"

"It must of been."

"But you didn't see it."

"It must of been a cat."

"It *looked* like a shad."

"Have you ever seen a cat?"

"Small ones."

"Well, this was a large one. That is, you said it was large."

"Well, you should of seen it yourself."

"Wished I had."

I can't write down the good comradeship in the voices, the willingness to keep gnawing at an unpromising bone, for friendship's sake. It was pretty bad, but no worse, I dare say, than can be heard in any crowd if we care to listen—no worse, perhaps, than the exchange of drivel which you and I carry on when we are too tired or too lazy to think.

Conversation is the one art, unfortunately, which we cannot practice alone. There must always be at least one person in the group as skilful as ourselves and as ready to keep his end up, otherwise we may fall into the habit, not of good talk, but of monologue. Even worse, we may enjoy our own monologue. Have you any friends who think they are doing you a good turn by entertaining your other friends for you? Most of us have been guilty at one time or another. I do not at this moment feel disposed to discuss further what is a serious fault of my own. Yet I can say in self-defense that my docile friends should behave as my family do; for the sake of a complete life, a life equally shared, they should interrupt and talk back.

CHAPTER VII

Manners

1.

IN OUR CHILDHOOD, when my mother got me ready for a party at the neighbors, she usually sent me off with a final caution, "Remember to behave naturally."

She didn't mean it, of course. She was altogether too familiar with my behavior whenever I relapsed to the state of nature. Her hope was that I might behave as though my good manners were natural.

Most of us trail all through life some memory of this kind, and draw from it a wrong deduction; we feel that manners are artificial, something imposed upon us by an elder generation, and however great our affection for our elders, we like to believe we should have been better off if they hadn't tried to improve us. In a restaurant the other day I overheard a woman declare that she wanted her friends to accept her for what she was. Of course I don't know what she was, and I don't see how even her friends could tell, but perhaps she was revolting against the supposed tyranny of manners or etiquette.

Etiquette is the better word. "Manners" covers too much ground, suggesting the total behavior of individuals or of society, but etiquette means precisely what my mother had in mind, the correct way of greeting or of saying good-by, of conducting a conversation, of expressing thanks, of handling knife and fork. Etiquette is the French word which gives us our "ticket," and the French more than other people have developed the philosophy of manners, and have raised it to a fine art. Since it is difficult to make one's self at home in a system of etiquette which has been acquired, we excuse our own shortcomings by saying that elaborately-mannered folk are artificial. Nations less polite than the French like to say that the French are in their daily manners stilted and entirely unnatural. But all etiquette is unnatural. So is all art. Between art and nature there is an inevitable contrast. Nature, as the philosophers have told us, is the condition into which we are born, and art is the improvement we make in that condition. When we have practiced good manners long enough, they become natural to us. Of course our amusement or even our contempt has a good target when stupid people deliberately cultivate formality and rigidity in their behavior. If their purpose is the snobbish one, to make themselves seem different from their fellows, at least they may have the satisfaction of knowing that their fellows gladly testify to the difference. But though manners, since they are an art, are to that extent artificial, their purpose springs from something very deep in human nature, and for that reason the importance of etiquette will remain so long as mankind would rise from merely animal existence to something higher.

The French "etiquette" or the English "ticket" both suggest travel. Your ticket entitles you to reach a certain place. The particular etiquette which you use takes you forward and upward in the spiritual progress that you desire. Manners, therefore, are not a silly veneer, but an essential means to an important end. Since different people, in different times, wish to progress in slightly different directions, the rules of etiquette may change, but the basic principle is constant.

The easiest illustration, I think, is table etiquette. If we were entirely natural, the dinner table would be a place where animals feed. Since hunger is the most primitive and permanent of human wants, men always eat, but since their wish not to be a mere animal is also profound, they have always attended with special care to the manners which conceal the fact that at the table we are animals feeding. It is therefore impolite to reach for things, or to grab the food, or to eat fast, or to smack the lips, or in any way to seem ravenous. It is good manners to enjoy our food as it were incidentally and to balance the animal character of the performance by an exercise of intelligence, of wit, of good humor, preferably on subjects of permanent and general interest. Dinner parties have therefore become occasions for exhibiting the least animal, the most graceful and spiritual aspects of character.

This purpose and this result can be noticed in the table manners of all peoples, ancient or modern. In ancient Greece a dinner party was called a symposium, a "drinking together," perhaps because Greek food was poor and the wine better, or because the wine-drinking had a religious significance. But after Plato wrote his marvelous story of the dinner party the poet Agathon gave, where Socrates was a guest, a symposium has meant an interchange of noble thoughts and emotions.

Most of us are curiously prejudiced against etiquette. If we live in a quiet corner where we need only a small supply of manners, we are tempted to make fun of the more elaborate etiquette which others employ in a more complicated world. If I were raising cattle on the prairie, I'd have no occasion to use the etiquette of diplomatic society in Washington, and I might hastily conclude, therefore, that the government would get on faster if everyone dressed and behaved and kept house the way I did, but the opinion would reveal a certain confusion of mind. I'd be overlooking the fact that in my own sphere I knew and employed the proper etiquette for that sphere; no doubt I would treat other cattle raisers with the manners to which they were accustomed, and they would show the same good manners toward me. We wouldn't wear top hats or tail coats, but we'd conform to the etiquette of the region; we'd all wear broad-brimmed sombreros, chaps and high-heeled boots, though high heels are no more natural than high hats. The principle underlying our etiquette would be the same as underlies the etiquette of diplomats.

My prejudice against tail coat and top hat shows that I don't understand the importance of conventions, nor the difference between conventions and etiquette. Any regimented costume is a convention, arrived at by experience, and conventions justify themselves in those conditions of life which generated them. The cowboy costume would be as ridiculous in Washington as the top hat on the prairie.

Etiquette, as we said, is the formula which shows where we are going. In France you see the word at the end of a freight car, where the label shows the car's destination. For a different destination different etiquettes are needed. A convention, on the other hand, is both an agreement and a convenience. Representatives of political bodies meet in a convention, or they sign a convention, the underlying idea in either case being that they have come to an agreement or hope to do so. The word convenience, like the word convention, means a coming together, an agreement, but the purpose of the agreement here is not the settling of grave international issues but economy of effort in ordinary social life.

In the eighteenth century, for example, there was little agreement in masculine dress. A man wore as good a costume as he could think up and afford. He dressed in all the colors of the rainbow, and when he walked on the street or entered the drawing room, he outshone those who couldn't afford to keep up with him. Now that fashions in men's clothes are more nearly conventional for day wear and altogether conventional at night, the convenience is great. Men are free of the obligation, which is still upon women, to design original evening clothes for themselves. They don't feel compelled to buy a new dinner coat until the old one wears out. Best of all, though some coats cost more than others, they look alike so long as they are equally well cut— or at least they look so nearly alike that this most conventional dress, like any other uniform, is democratic.

It is a convention, or convenience, for people in a given community to observe approximately the same dinner hour. In South America that hour is nine or ten. In most of the large cities in the United States it is half past seven or eight. In smaller towns and in the country it is earlier. For each of these differences there is a good reason, yet any fixed hour is conventional. It is well not to shy off at the word. The western cattle men in the roughest days of the frontier, like the miners in the gold camps, were strictly conventional, and their special conveniences were invented to make life possible. In the mining camps no unnecessary questions were permitted about a new arrival's past, not so long as he behaved. This convention was enforced far beyond any diplomatic protocol. The slightest infraction might start gun-play.

In Mrs. Gaskell's *Cranford,* that famous story of a small village which is the portrait essentially of all simple communities, it was proper to serve your friends only the simplest refreshment, tea and buttered bread, with perhaps a little jam. Cranford citizens had narrow pocketbooks, and to practice a more elaborate hospitality was for most of them impossible. In delicacy and perhaps for self-protection they established a convention of good taste which was within the means of all. Those who could afford more and demonstrated their ability, were condemned as vulgar.

The oldest conventions are those which try to make men a little more comfortable in the face of poverty and shortage of food. If I drop in at your house some afternoon and you are reading a book, you feel under no compulsion to present me with the volume, or with another volume from the same set. But if you are eating anything, you will offer me some of it. Here is a convention still in force, though older than history. As early as 1000 B.C. it had been elaborated and refined to suit the needs of various societies, but the main outlines of it were everywhere recognized. You and I are familiar with illustrations in the stories of the Old Testament, or in the pre-Homeric legends as they are developed in the *Iliad* and the *Odyssey*. The soil of Greece is rocky and parched. Food on the mainland or in the islands was always scarce. Hospitality therefore meant a literal sharing of life. In an age which had no hotel systems for traveling salesmen, only two classes did any traveling, business men and those who were out of luck. The business men of the day were the pirates. Their manners were not influenced by ideals of hospitality, but their too-frequent arrival on unprotected shores contributed to hospitality a constant risk. Odysseus, trying to make his way home from Troy, represents the honest travelers, those who journeyed against their will. Normally a man stayed as near home as possible, within easy access to the barn where he had stored the winter's food. After a good harvest the family could eat heartily until next year's crops were gathered, but there was slight chance of surplus. If the harvest was bad, or if a guest dropped in, the household went on short rations.

The guest was rarely invited. More often than not he was a total stranger, a shipwrecked mariner or a footsore wayfarer who arrived at nightfall. To refuse him food would be to kill him. For him to stay too long or eat too much, would be to kill you.

The convention, therefore, was to take him in for three days and to feed him no matter who he might be, friend or enemy. Against the awkward chance that he might indeed be someone you hated, you were forbidden to ask his name. If he felt at ease with you, he might tell it, as Odysseus did in the house of Alcinous, but he would be within the proprieties if he went away as anonymous as he came. In the marvelous scene where old Priam, in the *Iliad,* comes to the Grecian camp by night, to the tent of Achilles, and claims the privileges of a guest, neither man can pretend he doesn't know the other. Priam is the father of Hector, whom Achilles has just slain. Hector killed Patroclos, the dearest friend of Achilles. Priam is in the camp of his enemies, but since he comes as a guest, Achilles cannot take him prisoner nor harm him. When Priam begs for the corpse of his son to give it decent burial, Achilles can't refuse, though he had intended to offer Hector's body as sacrifice to his friend's ghost. He and the old king lift dead Hector on a cart, and Priam drives back to Troy unmolested, but first the two deadly enemies, the old man and the young, must sit down and eat together; the convention of hospitality demanded this sacrament. It wasn't easy for Achilles to go through with it. "Stir my heart no more amid my troubles," he said, "lest I leave not even thee in peace, old sire, within my hut, albeit thou art my suppliant."

If the guest stayed beyond three days, it was all right for the host to kill him. Few over-stayed their time, but in the *Odyssey,* as you remember, Penelope's suitors cluttered up the house while Odysseus was trying to reach home. Their devouring of the food store was unpardonable. A guest at a wedding was expected to stay not three days but seven, but even a wedding guest at the end of the week moved on. The crowd of suitors stayed for months, and there was little to eat in Ithaca when Odysseus got back. Just before that exciting moment the goddess Athena, appearing to his son Telemachus, exclaimed, "What feast is this? Is it a wedding feast? Here is no banquet where each man brings his share." Telemachus answers, in effect, that what the goddess saw was no wedding, but a murder. Modern readers perhaps think Odysseus slew the suitors out of jealousy, because they all had tried to make his wife untrue to him, but the ancient Greeks understood that he was dealing justly with guests who had out-stayed their welcome.

I called attention to the purpose of table manners, to conceal or disguise mere animal feeding. Ancient hospitality had to do with food. You fed the wanderer who came to your door, and when you traveled, some other man fed you. You surrendered often at serious risk a share of your bread and wine, knowing that the same charity might some day save your life. But to disguise your concern with food or to raise your thoughts to more than self-preservation, you gave the parting guest a present, and he left a gift with you. This exchange is described at length in Homer; it persists among us to this day. The traveler encumbered himself with no large stock; he needed to start out with only one article since at the house where he left it he would receive another, which in turn would come to rest for a while under the next roof. When the guest was friendly with his host, he would tell who gave him what he was now passing on. In time the guest gift gathered value from the famous hands through which it had passed. In the *Odyssey,* as Telemachus was ending his visit to Menelaos, his father's friend, the elder man said to him, "Of the gifts, such as are treasures stored in my house, I will give thee the goodliest and greatest of price. I will give thee a mixing bowl beautifully wrought; it is all of silver, and the lips thereof are finished with gold, the work of Hephaestus; and the hero Phaedimus, the king of the Sidonians, gave it me, when his house sheltered me on my coming thither, and to thee now would I give it."

This graceful convention after thousands of years begins to wear a little thin, at least in our country. In Europe there is usually an exchange of gifts, but most Americans feel that the host is excused, and only the guest brings a present. We also reverse the ancient sentiment about the age or newness of the gift. Instead of handing on a venerable relic which some other guest has bestowed upon us, we try to bring a gift suitable to one particular host or hostess and to no one else. If possible, we wish the gift to be characteristic also of ourselves, so that by proxy and by constant remembrance we may keep a place in the home where we have enjoyed happy hours. If there is here a slight difference of convention, we hope there is a deeper meaning.

The difference between manners and conventions is important. We should notice also the difference between conventions and fashion, though a discussion of fashion takes us somewhat away from our subject. In manners we have the fine impulse of the race to raise itself higher, in conventions we have common agreements which show on the whole good sense, but in fashions we are face to face with weakness of character. At its best the fashion of the moment is a compliment paid to a strong character by those who have no originality of their own. Dianne de Poitiers, widowed in youth, for the rest of her life dressed in black and white. Her marvelous beauty was enhanced by that severity, as homely features might be sorely tried. For a hundred years every fine lady in western Europe, rather than admit that she needed more merciful treatment, dressed in black and white. Washington, Napoleon, Andrew Jackson, all set the fashion in one respect or another. The imitation was a tribute to men who themselves were independent of fashion.

Willingness to follow one's betters is the sheep-like quality upon which fashion merchants build their trade. If they can persuade someone prominent and admired, a moving picture actress, an athlete or a singer, to wear a new design or to recommend a cigarette, they count on the mass of the population to fall in line. Their expectations are on the whole justified. It isn't an inspiring revelation of human nature. The hat which becomes one skull is ridiculous on another, but once the fashion is set, all empty heads wear the same covering. The purpose of those who pull the marionnette strings each season is not to improve the style but to change it. Since few of the customers have the backbone to wear a garment which is out of style, fresh purchases must be made twice a year. Occasionally we do meet a character who, having learned what suits her or him, continues to wear that style in season and out, but these are heroic exceptions. If women's skirts are shorter this year, in twelve months they'll be longer. The short skirt must be discarded, though as material or as garment it is still in excellent condition. I use the women as example because they are the principal target of the fashion merchants, and in the United States they allow themselves to be exploited on a fantastic scale, but men have their share of the sheep instinct; if a bow tie is the fashion with a double-breasted coat, most of us are uneasy wearing a single-breasted garment with vest and four-in-hand.

2.

Let us get back to higher ground. Where do manners begin? Are they the work of unguided instinct? Are they like the fashion invented by clever individuals who have an axe to grind? Do they date back to the beginnings of our race, or does their history when examined turn out to be rather short?

The instinct to invent manners seems planted in our very bones, but it manifests itself chiefly at certain fruitful crises, at moments of hope when large sections of mankind see, or believe they see, a prospect of perfection, or at least of improvement. Some of our manners today, the less formal, date from the Revolutionary end of the eighteenth century, when Rousseau's doctrine of naturalness had a wide appeal. In place of careful etiquette, spontaneity was accepted then as it is now so long as the spontaneous were sincere and, we may add, so long as they were young. Spontaneousness, however precious at any age, is a substitute for social technique only in children and infants. The best manners for mature characters in the midst of mature experience must be learned by experience, either the experience stored up by the race over centuries and articulated at last by the creative ability of an individual, or precipitated by new conditions which impose new forms of behavior.

The younger generation, just before the first World War and just after it, favored the impromptu manners of the eighteenth century revolutionaries. They knew little about the revolutionaries, but that's what they favored. You might say that the revolutionaries were more courtly than the flappers and their boyfriends, yet the modern informality was the long-postponed upshot of Rousseau's optimism. Those of us, old or young, who today still set value on the etiquette which is an art, admire the code of manners which was invented in the late Middle Ages and the early Renaissance. We might leave the Middle Ages out and content ourselves with tracing our ideals back to a few influential conduct books, the earliest of them written not much more than four hundred years ago. We might place the beginnings so late, I say, except for one or two of our habits which began earlier. We take off our hat to a woman, and when we are very polite, to a man. We'd rather not shake hands with our glove on if the other man has his off, or we apologize for not removing our own glove. Both these habits are said to derive from the dark ages, when knights were simply armed men on horseback, with no tradition of delicate manners, with frankly confessed distrust of each other, and when the word chivalry carried an image of the horse instead of describing the character of the rider. Mounted men casually meeting would either attack each other at sight, like dogs not yet properly introduced—or they would remove their helmets while still at a distance, each watching the other so that both helmets would come off at the same time. With the head uncovered they were practically out of commission; with the gauntlet drawn from the right hand, they were completely disarmed. The overlord or king permitted no subject to stand before him helmeted. Indeed, few monarchs had subjects they could entirely trust. Later these rituals or prudence, outlasting the occasions for them, assumed a creditable and finally a noble significance. The subject bared his head to express a spontaneous admiration or deference; the glove came off in order that warm hands might clasp; the hat was lifted to a woman in homage, not to her only but to her sex. These manners, in other words, no longer recorded the dangers against which the knight on the road guarded himself, but had come to express certain impulses of gentle nature, for which no other language served so well. Yet the long survival or evolution marched with a different pace in different lands. In France, polite country though it is, men are as careful to take off their hat to each other as to women; unconsciously they recall the origin of the custom, when knights on the highway removed their helmets and respect for women had nothing to do with it, there being no ladies present.

Our tradition of etiquette began, as I said, in the fifteenth and sixteenth centuries with a cluster of books, most of them written

in Italy. The new world had been stumbled on, the Greek masterpieces rediscovered, science was beginning its modern advance,
and men who were at once thoughtful and enthusiastic raised the
question how best to take advantage of their dazzling opportunities, opportunities for the mind and the spirit as well as for the
senses. The Middle Ages were beginning to recede—that is, to be
undervalued and misunderstood. For fourteen or fifteen centuries
men had striven to prepare for the next world; in the Renaissance
they trained themselves for life here. They made the contrast no
less sharply than I have stated it, ignoring the fact that Medieval
man, though preoccupied with the next life, had not been indifferent to this one, nor ignorant of it. They forgot that the Middle
Ages had manners which satisfied their needs and expressed their
ideals. They shut their eyes, it seems, though such blindness must
have been difficult, to the triumphs of Medieval art and science,
the architectural wonders, the miracles of engineering skill.

Our age begins to see that the Renaissance, which historians
used to speak of as a total advance beyond the Middle Ages, was
a progress only in certain areas of life. We are ready now to admit
that Dante's mind, for example, was concerned with the universe,
whereas Shakespeare avoided cosmic themes almost as though he
were afraid of them. When the youngsters of the flapper years said
that their elders were inadequately equipped for living, they
were right, or would have been if they intended a contrast between Renaissance and Medieval education. Whether they, the
youngsters at that time, had grasped a more complete philosophy,
remains to be seen. Most of them are now fifty years old, sobered
down and silent. So far as the courage of their thinking was concerned and so far as their thinking went, I admired them, but
though almost as young as they, I was troubled by this, that they
discarded the manners of their elders without creating a code of
their own. They all went in for spontaneity and impulsiveness,
but each exploded in a different way. I should think a sincere
philosophy would try to get expressed clearly and reasonably.
Dynamic social philosophies have hitherto found expression in
new codes of manners.

Those who in the Renaissance invented the code of manners
which, if we have manners at all, we still practice, were the

younger generation of their time. As youth will, they settled the problems of their universe in talk, and they criticized their parents for not having brought them up correctly. This sounds familiar. They soon advanced, however, beyond blaming their immediate elders; they ignored them. When there was need of antiquity, they drew upon the old Greeks, of whom they knew little except what could be read in newly discovered manuscripts and recently published texts. They could give no accurate account of daily life in Athens, but thanks to Homer they felt prepared to describe life in Troy. Their main interest, however, was in themselves and their own day. If their parents had fallen short of perfection, how should they, the younger generation, now bring up their children? How should a boy be educated? How should a girl?

Conversation and formal debates on these questions were frequent during the fifteenth century, and a body of ideas fell gradually into recognizable pattern. The purpose of educating a boy was to make a courtier of him, or as we should say, a gentleman, and by a parallel discipline the girl was to become a lady. We may misunderstand these terms if we read into them snobbish or class distinctions which the Renaissance cared little about. It is, or ought to be, an advantage to be born of wealthy and educated parents, who themselves enjoyed the best advantages, but this good fortune was in those centuries uncommon. The great dukes of Italy, the great commercial families such as the Medici, were self-made. They were ancestors rather than descendants. Had they come of parents who were already gentle folk, they wouldn't have occupied themselves deciding what was a gentleman, or what training would produce one.

The conversations found their way into popular books, which, after so much talk, took the natural form of dialogue. The most famous of these was *Il Cortegiano,* by Baldesar Castiglione, 1528, translated into English by Thomas Hoby in 1561, just before Shakespeare was born. Hoby's translation is one of the masterpieces of English literature, but its language begins to seem forbidding. Castiglione was an up-to-date person, and his book is now best read in the modern version by Leonard Eckstein Opdycke. *Il Cortegiano,* or as we call it, *The Book of the Courtier,* records certain discussions which took place at the little court of

Urbino during a quarantine. Castiglione, distinguished in diplomacy and letters, was among the gentlemen and ladies who during their enforced leisure practiced the art of conversation. No doubt Castiglione put his own ideas into his book, but he probably followed in general what the others had said. Since he was a practical statesman, a shrewd observer, we are not surprised that he presents the speakers dramatically, letting each character outline itself clearly by word and action. Two persons attract us especially, Lady Emilia and Lord Gaspar. Both were young and perhaps more than a little in love; at least Castiglione represents them so. Gaspar found it difficult to speak without teasing Emilia, and she seems aware of him in everything she says. They remind us óf Benedick and Beatrice in *Much Ado About Nothing,* and it is thought they supplied Shakespeare with the hero and heroine of his great comedy.

One of the little circle at Urbino proposed a subject for discussion, not a new subject, by any means. "I would that this evening's game might be, that we select some one of the company and give him the task of portraying a perfect courtier, explaining all the conditions and special qualities requisite in one who deserves this title; and as to those things that shall not appear sound let everyone be allowed to contradict, as in the schools of the philosophers it is allowed to contradict anyone who proposes a thesis." Here is the great theme of the age which invented our manners.

The man chosen to lead the debate began promptly, having formulated his ideals in advance. If there were a choice, he would have his gentleman wellborn. All very fine to be social pioneers, but heaven knows it's a task, and if some day we reach that condition in which others have done the spade work for us, we'll be in luck. Gaspar, who agreed with nobody if he could help it, here urged that good birth was not essential, indeed might be a handicap, since fortunate people are often lazy, whereas he who must exert himself will go far.

The pioneer type of character should imitate whatever gentleness, softness, and sensitiveness is found in the wellborn, in those moments when life is not a struggle; on the other hand, the well born should acquire the initiative, the daring, and the strength which belong to those who win their place by hard struggle. "Let the man we are seeking be very bold, stern, and always among the first where the enemy are to be seen; and in every other place, gentle, modest, reserved, above all things avoiding ostentation and that impudent self-praise by which men ever excite hatred and disgust in all who hear them."

Here begins that double ideal of the gentleman in peace and in war, at home and in business, which still embarrasses us. The Medieval doctrine in Christianity was simple and clear, though difficult to follow in this world; a saint was not expected to have two sets of manners. The Renaissance, however, wished to retain only so much of the Christian ideal as wouldn't interfere with earthly success. The gentleman was to be courteous among his friends and in all the conditions of peace, but in war he should be prepared to give his enemies hell. If in the grim process he could exhibit sportsmanship or be a little generous without risking defeat, so much the better, but he must act like a fiend whenever fiendishness was called for in the hell-giving process. War was to be his profession, and the sports and exercises he indulged in should be warlike. Hunting on horseback, the chase, was a gentleman's recreation. In England the young man of family still seeks a commission, even in peacetime, and rides to hounds.

One rule is laid down for the behavior of the courtier in all circumstances; though the use of arms and the management of a horse in battle and in the hunting field are a science or an art, they should be practiced with studied ease so that they may seem natural. "You see how ungraceful a rider is who sits bolt upright in the saddle, as compared with another who seems not to be thinking about it yet sits his horse as free and steady as if he were afoot." The difference between the gentleman and the parvenu is that the new arrival is still preoccupied trying to remember the rules.

The gentleman should practice all the arts, beginning with the art of conversation and the management of his voice. He should avoid an affected speech, peculiarities of diction, anything that could divert attention from the good sense and sincerity of his thought. His voice should not be thin or soft like a woman's, nor on the other hand should it be rough and combative, but sonorous, rather, "clear, sweet and well-sounding, with distinct enunciation, with proper bearing and gestures; which consist of certain movements of the whole body, not affected or violent, but tempered by a calm face and with a play of the eyes which shall give an effect of grace, accord with the words, and as far as possible express also, together with the gestures, the speaker's intent and feeling."

The courtier should know Latin and Greek and modern languages, not only to read but to speak them. Who can say when unforeseen emergency will send us abroad on an important errand for ourselves or for others, or bring us into the company of the learned? The purpose of all accomplishment is to make accessible to us the proper manners for any occasion, and if we come among those who speak another language than ours, either we have equipped ourselves in advance with their language, or we must remain silent like a bump on a log. Don't argue that the others should speak *our* language; so long as a complete education in manners prepares us for any society, we need not concern ourselves with the plight of the ill-equipped.

The courtier, or gentleman, should not only speak well but he should know how to write. Here the Renaissance ideal as Castiglione states it is remarkably fine, in the best tradition of literary art. He says the gentleman should write as he talks, so that the written word will be merely the spoken word lingering on after the voice is silent. If the gentleman writes as he talks, it is equally true that he should talk as he writes, in one interchangeable manner, so that on the page or in conversation we shall meet the same personality. To this rule, faithfully followed, we owe the great writings of the Elizabethans. Sailors, soldiers, and diplomats in those days wrote and spoke like themselves. Literary theories of style, especially the atrocious vogue called euphuism, had a bad effect, but only here and there, and only temporarily.

Every courtier, trained soldier though he was, should practice the art of versification so that when he falls in love he may compose acceptable tribute to his lady. This quaint advice, as we recall, was not rejected by Philip Sidney, nor Walter Raleigh, nor indeed by any of the Elizabethan well-bred.

The speaker in the dialogue was here asked a very significant question. Were these accomplishments, literary and otherwise, to be acquired in order to make the courtier more efficient in the business of his life, which might sometimes be diplomacy but most often would be war? Is so large an equipment needed as a mere aid to fighting, or might not the military education of the gentleman be considered secondary to accomplishments so admirable and so varied? The answer is, that so long as one profession is the center of a man's life, everything else he studies should spring from that central interest, and should in some way aid him to success in it. By implication, though the idea is not clearly brought out, if the gentleman's profession were riding to hounds, or writing verse, or speaking a language, then his other accomplishments should in some way bear on that activity. This ideal has not yet taken firm root in our systems of education, and therefore not yet in our manners, but it has appealed to shrewd men, both practical persons and theorists. A training which branches out of one central interest will not be narrow; the Renaissance conception of a warrior who could read and speak ancient and modern languages, was far from narrow, and those individuals, like Philip Sidney, whose marvellously rounded personalities touched life at many points, were noted for the consistency of their manners at all times. Perhaps in this passage of the dialogue Castiglione was setting up a balance to that passage in which the courtier was advised to be gentle in peace but stern, even primitively brutal, in war.

As though to exaggerate the paradox which the question had raised, the leader in the dialogue added quickly that the gentleman should have not only languages and literary arts, but he should be a musician, trained to play or sing and to read music. He should be not only a connoisseur of painting and sculpture, but he should paint and carve. He should be also, as we have noticed, a trained diplomat, not only because a wise commander sometimes wins his ends by negotiation rather than by combat, but also because the ruler of his country may send him on a mission in peace, ambassadors being no less convincing if they have already proved skilful fighters.

How should the gentleman dress? On the same principles that govern all his manners. He should strive for an under-statement in clothes as in speech. Preferably his costume should be black, or at least dark colored, and though the material might be rich, there should be no ostentation. His dress should express the man, the seriousness of his work, and the single-minded devotion which he gives to it.

His friends also should express his character, thus becoming as it were, part of his manners. In a wide acquaintance he will know many amusing or brilliant fellows, but unless their character is the complement or extension of his, they are not the friends for him.

This rough summary falls short of Castiglione's subtlety and thoroughness. In the dialogue each of these specifications is argued backward and forward until the reasons for the ideal are clear. By much the same process he sets forth the rules for the lady. She is to enjoy the same education as the gentleman, and to lead much the same life, with a few obvious exceptions. Her main business will be domestic rule rather than war, yet she may be called upon to play a diplomat's part, or to govern a state. Her education must prepare for the emergency. Like her husband, she will know how to ride a horse, she will have command of languages, ancient and modern, she will be skilled in the arts and in politics, and she will be well read in history. Some games or sports, however, she will refrain from, and some virtues she will cultivate more thoroughly than a man, just because she is a woman. Since it is woman's destiny to be loved by men, nothing in her manners should break the illusion she has created in their hearts. Let her practice music then, but let her not play the drum or the trombone. Let her be as athletic as she will, so long as she doesn't box or wrestle. If a man should be modest, she should be far more so, never seeking praise, always seeming astonished at it, never envious of compliments to other ladies—at least never showing on her face or in her speech what she really thinks of her rivals.

The Book of the Courtier is divided into four sections, the first two dealing with the education of a gentleman, the third with the education of a lady, and the fourth with the reasons why any such education should be undertaken at all. This last section is a noble passage. The speaker is Pietro Bembo, famous scholar and philosopher, who after a full Renaissance career entered the Church and was made a cardinal. In Castiglione's book he is portrayed as a mature man, steeped in the philosophy of Plato. He astonishes us a little by proclaiming that the end of education is to enable men and women to love adequately, but as we listen to his magnificent eloquence we soon recognize the doctrine of Plato's *Symposium,* that the soul loves the highest beauty it is aware of, but through love becomes aware of still higher beauty, so that beginning with love for a beautiful body it learns to love the idea of beauty, and step by step rises to the vision of the beauty of holiness.

"The soul,—freed from vice, purged by studies of true philosophy, versed in spiritual life, and practiced in matters of the intellect, devoted to the contemplation of her own substance,—as if awakened from deepest sleep, opens those eyes which all possess but few use, and sees in herself a ray of that light which is the true image of the angelic beauty communicated to her, and of which she then communicates a faint shadow to the body. Grown blind to things earthly, the soul thus becomes very keen-sighted to things heavenly; and sometimes, when the motive forces of the body are absorbed by earnest contemplation or fretted by sleep, being unhampered by them, she is conscious of a certain far-off perfume of true angelic beauty, and ravished by the splendour of that light, she begins to kindle and pursues it so eagerly that she almost becomes phrensied with desire to unite herself to that beauty, thinking that she has found God's footstep, in the contemplation of which she seeks to rest as in her beatific end. And thus, glowing in this most happy flame, she rises to her noblest part, which is the intellect; and here, no longer darkened by the gloomy night of things earthly, she sees the divine beauty; but still she does not yet quite enjoy it perfectly, because she contemplates it in her own particular intellect only, which cannot be capable of the vast universal beauty. . . .

" 'Deign, then, O Lord, to hear our prayers, pour thyself upon our hearts, and with the splendour of thy most holy fire illumine our darkness and, like a trusted guide, in this blind labyrinth show us the true path. Correct the falseness of our senses, and after our long pursuit of vanities give us true and solid good; make us to inhale those spiritual odours that quicken the powers of the intellect, and to hear the celestial harmony with such accord that there may no longer be room in us for any discord of passion; fill us at that inexhaustible fountain of content which ever delights and never satiates, and gives a taste of true beatitude to all who drink of its living and limpid waters; with the beams of thy light purge our eyes of misty ignorance, to the end that they may no longer prize mortal beauty, and may know that the things which first they seemed to see, are not, and that those which they saw not, really are.

" 'Accept our souls, which are offered thee in sacrifice; burn them in that living flame which consumes all mortal dross, to the end that, being wholly separated from the body, they may unite with divine beauty by a perpetual and very sweet bond, and that we, being severed from ourselves, may, like true lovers, be able to transform ourselves into the beloved, and rising above the earth may be admitted to the angels' feast, where, fed on ambrosia and immortal nectar, we may at last die a most happy and living death, as died of old those ancient fathers whose souls thou, by the most glowing power of contemplation, didst ravish from the body and united with God.'

"Having thus far spoken, with such vehemence that he almost seemed transported and beside himself, Bembo remained silent and motionless, keeping his eyes toward heaven, as if wrapped in ecstasy; when my lady Emilia, who with the others had been listening most attentively to his discourse, took him by the border of his robe, and shaking him a little, said:

" 'Have a care, messer Pietro, that with these thoughts your soul, also, does not forsake your body.'

" 'My Lady,' replied messer Pietro, 'that would not be the first miracle that love has wrought upon me.' "

The purpose of education then is not, as we were first told, to prepare a gentleman for the profession of war—or rather, it is still to prepare him for that profession, but warfare is to become a metaphor of earthly life, where our enemies are physical or material temptations and whatever else detains or imprisons the soul. At every stage of the progress our manners should continue to express our character, our purpose becoming nobler, our etiquette more refined, more spiritual. Instead of external rules, such as were laid down in the first dialogue, the gentleman will guide his employment and his behavior by his own nature—not the set of impulses which were his while he was still uneducated, but his character now after he has become his best self. He may safely obey his instincts, indeed he must obey them, now that the crude nature which was once his has itself been transformed into a work of art.

This old book in Hoby's translation became for the youth of England a kind of secular Bible. The literature of the sixteenth and seventeenth centuries is filled with portraits of young men and women such as they would be if they followed completely Castiglione's teaching. Some individuals, a very few, represented to their contemporaries those ideals incarnate—Philip Sidney, for example, in one century, John Milton in the next. But Sidney and Milton both excelled in manners the lords and ladies at Urbino, even Pietro Bembo himself. No wonder that the poet Edmund Spenser, creating the most spiritual pattern of behavior which western literature contains, took Philip Sidney for one of his examples.

3.

The first three Books of Spenser's *Faerie Queene* were published in 1590, and an additional three in 1596. The finished poem would have contained twelve Books, but Spenser died before he completed the work. The meaning of the six Books we have would not be clear if Spenser hadn't explained his purpose in a letter to Sir Walter Raleigh, published as a sort of preface. There is a legend about this letter which throws light on Spenser's temperament. He showed the manuscript of the first three Books to Sir Walter, explaining perhaps, as later he did in the introduction, that the plot of the story would become clear in the final Book, the Twelfth, where he would describe how the Red Cross Knight and the other champions started on their various quests. If our guess is correct, Raleigh then pointed out that Spenser's readers might not live till the Twelfth Book appeared; it would be well, therefore, to let them into the secret at once.

We are grateful to Sir Walter. Spenser had ideas of his own about telling a story. In his day he was as deliberately original and experimental as Gertrude Stein or James Joyce, though there is little other similarity between his work and theirs. He thought it would be a good idea to tell his long story backwards. The subject, as the prefatory letter tells us, was the fashioning of a gentleman or noble person in virtuous and gentle discipline, but he presents this ideal person to us, not at first as a complete character, but section by section, as it were, building him up by gradual addition of his virtues. In Aristotle's *Nicomachean Ethics* Spenser found, or thought he found, a list of twelve central virtues. One virtue was to be represented in each of the twelve Books. The puzzle here, which we needn't stop over, is that Spenser names some virtues which are not in Aristotle. Even if the work had been completed there would have been insufficient room for all of Aristotle's virtues. But the six virtues which Spenser's unfinished poem presents are important enough in themselves—holiness, temperance, chastity, friendship, justice, courtesy. Perhaps the Sixth Book deals a little more directly than the others with etiquette, but throughout the poem the finest kind of manners are illustrated—and also the lowest kind by the way of instructive contrast.

Spenser's treatment of manners goes on from where Castiglione's book left off. If manners are, or ought to be, the direct expression of a well-educated and noble character, we can hardly put thought on them without considering some challenging questions. There are defects in human nature, base impulses, which we must fight against, but there are also difficulties in life itself, the result of no fault of ours yet waylaying us at every turn in the road. What is the virtue of holiness? The Elizabethan reader, taking up the book for the first time, must have expected to read of a spiritual condition, and that is indeed what Spenser writes about, yet he defines holiness in a novel way. He makes it a corrective for the natural illusions which prevent human beings from seeing truth. To the saint as well as the scientist, a false hypothesis or a wrong decision may wear the guise of right. Holiness is that condition of the soul which gives us, at least in rare moments, clear vision, even in this world where for the most part we see through a glass darkly.

In the Book of Temperance Spenser presents life in another aspect, not as a condition of partial blindness, but as a state in which our moral eyesight is clear, and the choice between good and evil is obvious, our only problem being to make the right choice. The strength to choose is called temperance. Falsehood, in the Book of Holiness, looks like a beautiful woman, but when she is found out and stripped she is a horrible hag, almost a beast. The temptress in the Book of Temperance is equally beautiful, but her beauty is not false; she is evil only because the Knight, if he allowed himself to be detained by her, would be diverted from his proper destiny.

Book Three must have surprised the Elizabethan reader even more than Book One. Chastity when Spenser wrote meant only one thing, conquest of sexual impulses, refraining from love or marriage. The champion of chastity in the *Faerie Queene* is Britomart, a girl warrior, in search of Artegall, to marry him and bear his children. He doesn't know she is looking for him. The ideal she represents anticipates George Bernard Shaw by centuries. Britomart represents what might be called creative chastity, an absolute purity of mind which should be natural to well-educated and well-mannered people. Her woman's destiny is to marry and have children. The manners of another age taught that only the man should do the proposing, and the woman should pretend to have no desires of her own. Later on, when she was bearing her child, she should walk out for her exercise only after dark, and when the baby came she could say she found it in a cabbage. Obviously, one set of manners would be needed for this hypocritical philosophy, and quite another for Britomart's pure faith in the processes of life as God made them.

The Book of Friendship raises a question dear to the Greeks and to the people of the Renaissance, the question which Castiglione glanced at when he said the courtier should choose as friends men like himself. How many men are like us? We have few absolute friends, perhaps only one. Where complete friendship does occur it seems, as the Greeks said, like a sharing of a single soul, and each soul, however shared, will emerge in one consistent set of manners.

In the Fifth Book Spenser states the conflict between justice and equity. He here takes, naturally, the English point of view. The English have a name for administering justice, but to other nations, to us in the United States, for example, as to the French and the Italians, the genius of the English seems to be for law and order, which is not necessarily the same thing as justice. If a murder is committed in England, someone is hanged for it, and hanged promptly. When a murder is committed in the United States, someone is arrested for it, but he may or may not be hanged, and in any case he won't be hanged promptly. This uncertainty of punishment and this delay seem to the English scandalous. We are equally disturbed by their simple and speedy procedure, which has ended more than once in hanging the wrong man, or at least in condemning to death persons whose guilt is still in doubt. Justice to us demands that the innocent should be protected. Enforcement of law to an Englishman demands that the guilty be punished.

Which view is right philosophers have never decided, but they agree that mercy interferes with law enforcement. Shakespeare's head was full of this problem, as we know from many passages and from one entire play, *Measure for Measure*. In Spenser's allegory the champion of justice comes on a wretch who is about to murder a defenseless man. Because the rascal is half-witted and otherwise handicapped for distinguishing between right and wrong, the champion reprimands and punishes him, but spares his life. After the champion has gone his way, the rascal returns to his mischief, resumes from where he left off, and finishes his murder. Through reluctance to execute the guilty, the champion assumed responsibility for death of the innocent.

The reason Spenser gives in the Sixth Book for the practice of courtesy sounds strange, but his age understood it; the purpose of good manners, he says, is to make ourselves eligible for fame. Many a man at Elizabeth's court was no less thoughtful than Sir Walter Raleigh, no less self-sacrificing, but Raleigh is remembered because he threw down his cloak in the mud for Queen Elizabeth to walk on. The gesture is unforgettable. All good manners are dramatic gestures, and if the gestures are perfect, they are memorable; they make it easy for fame to fasten on us.

Why did the Renaissance desire fame, that last infirmity of noble mind? The noble mind admitted that the desire was a weakness, yet when Renaissance men turned away from the Medieval philosophy to throw themselves heart and soul into the enjoyment of this life, they began to fear that, even though their pleasures here were fine and spiritual, they might as well seek immortality here also, since perhaps they would find it nowhere else. The desire for immortality in this world balanced the loss of faith in another to be.

Whatever our philosophy today, we need a different argument for manners. Perhaps *The Book of the Courtier* in this one respect serves us better than the *Faerie Queene*.

4.

These famous books show us how in another age admirable conduct was dreamt of and planned. If we are fully trained in these codes or in any others, etiquette may be an art in which we need to progress no further. But it would be a pity to have our manners exclusively from tradition. The Renaissance invented its manners; if we find ourselves in new situations, why not adapt the old formulas or devise fresh ones? Taking a leaf out of Castiglione and Spenser, why shouldn't an educated person write his own conduct book?

Some education, I'm afraid, is necessary. We should at least be familiar with the code we intend to improve on. Accepting in essence the ideals of Pietro Bembo in *The Book of the Courtier,* we could try to base our manners directly and sincerely on our character. Don't tell me at this point that I retrace my steps and am now advising the natural spontaneity of the flapper generation! I'm doing nothing of the kind. The spontaneous impulses of an educated person, a person who has already been trained in a system of etiquette, are not the spontaneous impulses of a person still in a state of nature.

In a state of nature, for example, our impulses are usually selfish, but all good manners are dictated primarily by unselfishness. If it is easy for us to ignore those around us, politeness won't be our specialty. If we can remain seated, undisturbed, while someone else must stand, we are as yet not so rude as callous. Perhaps callow is the word. On the other hand, if we rise high enough in the Platonic scale of love, as Bembo described it, to wish for our fellows at every moment the same enjoyment, the same comfort, the same privileges, the same opportunities as may fall to us, then our good sense and our good taste will hit on the right technique for any occasion.

I've brought in the good taste casually and at the last moment, but it's important. Also, we can acquire it or develop it, if we try hard enough. It's only a more subtle form of unselfishness. Loud laughs, guffaws, are not good manners, nor is loud talking. If we are not making the noise, we don't enjoy it; we need no other reason for having mercy on the folks around us who may be engaged in conversation, or who may be reading, or who may wish quiet for thought.

Common sense and taste teach us the usefulness of restraint, or understatement. If I'm very fond of you but see you only once a year, you won't object to considerable warmth in my greeting, but if we run into each other every day, the temperature of my greeting had better come down to the point which can be sustained through many repetitions. Manners, to be good, must wear well.

The same moderation, the same judgment, should prompt and guide our conversation, especially when we come among those whose superiority in some respect we feel and before whom we stand perhaps slightly embarrassed. At such a moment our manners are severely tested. The inferiority complex is foolish, but if it takes possession of us, good behavior is impossible; through nervousness we become over-bold and assertive, in which case we are a nuisance, or timid and self-effacing, in which case we are a nonentity. Yet all the while we have a right to our own character, to our own thoughts, and so long as we are sincere and so long as we are unselfishly interested in those we talk to, they will like us better for being ourselves.

The incompletely educated avoid those who are further advanced in experience, who have had more advantages or were born with greater talents. This modesty is an error; only by consorting with our betters do we learn. Some men of genius, cursed with the inferiority complex, are at a loss among their equals but thoughtful, gracious and at ease among young people and children. For a mature person to get on best with the immature is a bad sign. Our manners are precisely as mature as the people with whom we get on well—unless indeed we have attained that versatile ripeness which remembers to be young even while growing old.

CHAPTER VIII

Foreigners

1.

To FEEL THAT others equally with ourselves are members of the human race is the most difficult of arts. The idea of equality, as an idea, is easy to accept, but it is hard to translate into an emotion.

The word foreigner originally meant out-of-doors, as against what was inside the home. He who took a step beyond the household entered at once a foreign world, even though he still moved among neighbors. If neighbors can be foreigners, people who live at a distance will be more so. When to distance is added strangeness of language, the foreigner becomes not only alien but potentially hostile. These definitions are found in the dictionary, but unfortunately they can be checked by your experience and mine.

We are by nature egocentric; we see ourselves as the hub of the wheel, with spokes of sympathy radiating out to those who belong to us and who therefore are not foreign, but who none the less are relegated to the rim of our private universe. Even in the family there may be one person who seems not to belong. We say he is a strange child, exactly as we say a visitor from abroad is an odd person. This strange child of ours may look like us and certainly our blood is in his veins; the visitor from another land may also look like us, and though our parents are not the same, we might find ourselves of the same stock if we traced our ancestry to the beginning. The strangeness or oddness lies in manners which are not ours, in an unaccustomed accent, or in a difference of taste. Ideas seldom keep us apart; the prejudiced are seldom influenced by ideas.

Of course if these judgments were pronounced from the other end, the family member or the visitor would say that *we* are the foreigner. The amount of queerness in the world is constant, and only one person at a time is free from it. That generous person, of course, is always ourselves, whether we contemplate the stranger in our family, the new arrival in our land, or those complete foreigners with whom we associate when we go abroad. It is one of the ultimate ideals of civilized people to rise above this primitive antagonism toward those who, in small matters or large, differ from us. I call it an ultimate ideal, not because I think it necessarily the highest, but because it is probably the most difficult to attain.

We might cure ourselves more easily of this particular narrow-mindedness if certain virtues, or halfway desirable qualities, were not tied up with our perception of foreigners. What is extremely beautiful seems to come from another world. The person we love is somewhat removed by our admiration from all other people. Perhaps you recall how Emerson, in his Journals, comments with his usual penetration on this tangled phenomenon. "It is singular," he says, "how slight and indescribable are the tokens by which we anticipate the qualities of sanity, of prudence, of probity in the countenance of a stranger.

"We see with a certain degree of terror the new physique of a foreign man; as a Japanese, a New Zealander, a Calabrian. In a new country how should we look at a large Indian moving in the landscape on his own errand? He would be to us as a lion or a wild elephant.

"In such proximity stand the virtues and defects of character that a disgust at some foible will blind man oftener to a grandeur in the same soul."

In another place he writes: "What is the meaning of that? The fork falling sticks upright in the floor, and the children say, a stranger is coming. A stranger is expected or announced, and an uneasiness betwixt pleasure and pain invades all the hearts of the household."

In still another place, he celebrates the precious rather than the distressing quality of strangeness. "The lover delights in surprise of face and form yet so dearly related to him. The more foreign

the better. The lady's eye seemed always looking at distant lands
and distant people; she could never be domesticated. It was like
a young deer or a young leopard, or a forest bird, newly caught
and brought into your yard. Still descend to him, prefer him, but
for Heaven's sake do not lose this exotic charm, which fills his
imagination."

More exalted even than the strangeness of beauty and the
strangeness of the loved one, and far more profound, has been
the mood of some men, the most sensitive spirits of our race, who
see our brief mortal days as but a far voyage, a visit to a land
which however interesting is not our home. "I am a stranger with
thee," sang the Psalmist, "and a sojourner, as all my fathers were."

Much of our defensive attitude toward foreigners is bound up
with admirable loyalties, chiefly with loyalty to the place where
we were born. We may be narrow-minded, of course, but the cure
would not lie in rooting out the instincts of faithfulness and affection. I have small admiration for that type of international idealist whose largeness of heart does not include his own people. No
man is true to himself who belittles or neglects what belongs to
him. Here is the precise problem, to love one's own home, one's
own land, with the special devotion which is natural, and at the
same time to make ourselves, in the noble eighteenth century
phrase, a citizen of the world, fitting ourselves by education of
mind and heart for membership in the human race, our larger
family.

The eighteenth century believed we might become citizens of
the world by educating chiefly the mind, sharing, believing, and
practicing certain universal ideas. We were to become brothers
through enlightenment. We were to recognize the distinction between those attitudes toward life which all men share, and those
attitudes which are found only in places and respond to local
needs. The universal attitudes bring us together, the local attitudes divide us. The eighteenth century invented fables about
Chinese or other remote folk who, visiting Europe, seemed at first
like men from another planet, so strange was their dress, their
language, their etiquette; yet after they had stayed long enough
to establish a technique of communication, they were discovered
to be only Europeans disguised. They themselves, of course, dis-

covered that the Europeans were only Chinese disguised. The story usually stressed the superiority, intellectual and moral, of the visitor who had first seemed foreign.

Our day puts its trust less in enlightenment than in propaganda, which might be the same thing but usually isn't. A widely popular school of thought holds that universal brotherhood will come through political leagues or through international adjustment of economic inequalities. In these hopes there is much good sense and considerable promise of success; decent men and women everywhere do what they can to hasten the abolition of tariffs, to let down barriers between nations, even—hardest of all—to abolish the cruel walls which men of one color usually set up between themselves and men of other colors, or even between themselves and men of the same color. Yet the best ideals are handicapped by our contempt of enlightenment, of intelligence—by our unwillingness to observe what happens under our eyes. The black man asks equality with the white. There is no valid reason why he shouldn't have it, yet his demand for justice is only part of the picture; there are whites who deny equality to other whites, there are blacks who claim superiority to other blacks. There are restrictions, indefensible I believe, against the immigration of Orientals to our land, but the Oriental in his own country restricts immigration and discourages the foreigner—us—from owning property. The brotherhood of man demonstrates itself most clearly on the lowest level, the level of prejudice.

2.

Agreed, then, that our international and inter-racial attitudes need reforming, and that the reform may be hastened by juster laws and by some kind of world federation. The individual must still meet the obligation to enlighten himself. Laws and federations are not self-made; they are the creation of man and man, working together. Let there be more opportunity for us all, yet the complete life can never be conferred or imposed from outside. Our human nature will remain for us to deal with. Among ourselves, even in more fortunate conditions, there will be strangers and foreigners.

The first step toward enlightenment is to assume that we are the foreigner, and that the other fellow is partly correct in thinking us so. Essentially he is wrong, since we all are human beings, but he is justified so far as we cannot or will not see life from his angle—so far, that is, as we fail to use our imagination. There is an art in being a foreigner, and small excuse at this late day for being ignorant of it, since the errors which we commit when we travel are the same errors which men from other lands commit when they visit us. If we have been irritated or offended by an unimaginative stranger, why should we not, when the positions are reversed, avoid inflicting on him those very irritations and offenses?

The art of being a foreigner contains warnings and rules, formulated thousands of years ago yet somewhat depressing in their utterly modern application. The warnings seem more up-to-date than the rules, for the sad reason that the art of being a foreigner is constantly annotated by the blunders of unsuccessful practitioners. Let me remind you of our commonest mistakes, by citing the rules for avoiding them.

Never measure the other man by yourself, or if you do, don't let him know it. This rule is a warning against an estranging kind of comment, not less estranging when the comment is favorable. When we visit another town we inevitably compare it with our own; in so doing we may give offense, unless we are careful, by implying that our town is the standard. It is obviously boorish to announce in a place where we are guests that the Town Hall or the main street doesn't come up to ours. A quick way to earn unpopularity is to advise our hosts how to mend their civic defects. But it's also an error to say that their Town Hall and their chief thoroughfare are quite as remarkable as anything we have at home, or even a little better. They'll want to ask how in thunder we acquired the right to travel abroad like school teachers, examining and handing out marks.

Practically all foreigners make this mistake, for the simple reason that the body travels more easily than the mind, and until we have limbered up our imagination we continue to think as though we had stayed home. We have not really budged a step until we take up residence in someone else's point of view. Our comparisons, even the favorable ones, give offense because man in his native habitat is loyal to his surroundings without comparing them with other places. If you see a fine Town Hall, say it's a fine Town Hall, and stop there.

Comparisons between different lands, each with its own needs and its own customs, are stupid as well as harmful unless we seek the reasons for the difference. The informed and imaginative traveler soon learns that the other man knows what he is doing, in some cases that he knows better than we. I've heard many an American, after a superficial tour, declare that our trains are more comfortable than European, and that our dining cars serve better meals. Personally I think the opposite is true, but I admit the point can be argued either way. Our Pullmans were intended to provide rooms and restaurants as nearly as possible like those to be found in stationary hotels. We certainly come nearer than the European does toward the realization of this ideal. But this ideal the European does not try for; he thinks it amazing—and somewhat ridiculous. His *wagon-lits* are what they are called, beds on wheels, and his train restaurants are restaurants on trains. He accepts the conditions of travel, he provides for a state of life in motion.

Hotel restaurants are open between certain hours, in some cases continuously. The room service of large hotels will answer a call for almost any food at almost any time. The American ideal of comfortable travel is an approximate duplication in miniature of this plentiful luxury. The dining car offers us a choice of dishes of astounding variety, almost incredible for train pantries and kitchens. Private meals are brought, for a slight extra charge, to the compartments. The Pullman lounge, except while passing through prohibition states, is an open bar. Isn't this efficiency? The American thinks it is, or he wouldn't maintain such a system.

Yet there are certain shortcomings which strike the European at once. Our train kitchens can't do justice to the number of choices they offer. Unless you go early to lunch or dinner the supply of this or that may be exhausted. The quality of the cooking, what with haste and congestion, is not always praiseworthy; the service, through no fault of the waiters, must be a sleight-of-hand performance under high pressure. Since the passengers may go to the dining room at any time, they are likely to go all at

once, so that while you eat you are goaded by the consciousness
that the hungry watch your progress, to slip into your place the
moment you remove yourself. To the European this experience
is not admirable, not even civilized. He would call it childish
rather than efficient.

Any meal worth paying for, he thinks, whether in a restaurant
or on a train, should be well prepared and well served, and it
should be eaten in leisure and peace. Shortly in advance of lunch
time or dinner, he expects the *maître-d'hôtel* to come through the
train with bundles of tickets in his hand, marked *premier service,
deuxième service, troisième service*. There are as many tickets in
each service as there are seats in the diner. You ask for one, two, or
three, as you prefer, but if all the ones are taken by the time the
maître-d'hôtel reaches you, he gives you a ticket for the second
service. When your number is called, you go to the diner and
find the tables in neat order, waiting for you. The same meal is
served to all passengers, with one alternative main dish and a
slight choice of dessert. The courses are brought to all tables at
the same moment. You are expected to eat slowly and enjoy your
meal. When your coffee is drunk you pay your bill, a small one,
and the diner is clear for the next service.

The train meals in South America are of this European type.
Our friends down there think we are in many directions efficient,
but they wouldn't mention our dining cars as an illustration.

The use of tickets to prevent crowding is common in Europe,
elsewhere than on trains. We Americans are known for our hustle
and push, and our subway rush-hours are a legend. Europe hasn't
found the answer to subway overcrowding, but it has a system
for establishing priority among street-car patrons. In France I've
often watched a crowd gather at a car stop. Each person arriving
would pull off the top ticket from a package fixed to the lamp
post. The tickets are numbered in series. When the car arrives the
conductor calls for the lowest number, the holder of that ticket
shows it and gets on, the others follow in order. There is no pushing and shoving. The system encourages good manners, and its
fairness is beyond challenge.

It is a primitive instinct in all men to consider the foreigner in
some sense inferior. We correct this stupidity in ourselves follow-

ing the advice already suggested here, to imagine ourselves the foreigner and to adopt the attitude of learning rather than criticizing. Immigrants to our country usually herd together as long as they can, continue their old customs, protect themselves against our ideas. Since we all of us were at one time immigrants, we wonder why more recent arrivals, if they come at all, don't come all the way and join us. More recently the war refugees, who come because they must, show a tendency to emphasize their foreignness, sometimes to our inconvenience and irritation. But before we condemn them we should remember how Americans and every other people behaved in the good days when the tourists roamed the earth. In France, Italy, Germany, we always flocked together, patronized hotels which catered to us and furnished their version of American cooking, spoke no language but our own. The English wherever they went stayed close to the English colony, avoided the caravans of touring Americans, and magnificently ignored what they called the "natives." The French, content with the lot to which God had called them, traveled almost not at all. We are all alike. On our summer tours we were temporary immigrants, and we behaved like immigrants.

On my first trip abroad, years ago, a wise Englishman gave me a few rules, to my life-long profit. "In a foreign restaurant," he said, "never ask for a dish which you could get anywhere at home. What's the use of travel if you avoid new experiences? Learn the cuisine of the country. Wherever you eat, ask for the *specialité de la maison,* the dish on which that restaurant prides itself. In fact, when you're in a new land never order the meal, least of all the wine; ask the waiter what he would recommend. Such a request is a great compliment, as from one connoisseur to another. The waiter will outdo himself for your sake. Had you been insensitive to good food, as he knows by long experience, you would have insisted on selecting it yourself."

He told me this also: "Go to the hotels which the people of the country patronize, but tourists do not. Eat in restaurants which cater to the local citizens, and be sure you try restaurants of all grades. Find the places where cab-drivers take their lunch, the cafés where workmen eat and drink, or where they celebrate a holiday with their wife and children. Eat and talk with them all, if you can. Also with the shopkeeper, the local doctor, the post-man. You will learn something of the country, of its ideas, preju-dices, ambitions; you will also be guided, incidentally, to the best and cheapest food on the various economic levels."

My friend did not tell me what is a cardinal rule: the foreigner should never show surprise. The omission was perhaps a compli-ment; since I was fresh from university Latin my English friend may have assumed that I knew the ancient and perennial advice to all who would be courteous to their fellowman—*nihil admirari,* be astonished at nothing. When we receive visitors from abroad or when we go on our own journeys we shall, we hope, see novel-ties, but we knew in advance that there are more things than we dreamt of in heaven and earth. If we advertise our amazement we overstress our previous ignorance; what is far more serious, those who are foreign to us or those to whom we are foreign are at once reminded that we are still removed from them. A true citizen of the world, coming on something new, feels that he has come home.

If what has astonished us is a fault, we should postpone con-sideration of it until we are thoroughly acquainted with the peo-ple in whom it is observed. To notice faults first is to overlook what makes an individual or a country worth knowing at all. This point needs no elaboration. There is no land in which admirable qualities cannot be found, but there are folks who would see cracks in Paradise. To such travelers passports should be denied.

When I was a boy our nearest neighbor went to Europe on his vacation, and the evening of his return my father talked with him in the twilight, over the hedge between the two gardens. I listened by my father's side, knowing his passion for Latin countries and disposed by temperament if not yet by experience to agree with him.

"Of course you saw Venice," said Father.

"Venice? Venice? Oh, yes! I stopped at Venice."

"A magic city, isn't it!"

"Maybe, but in my opinion there are too many canals."

"Too *many?*" You should have seen Father's face.

"It's damp," said our neighbor. "Inexcusably damp."

Poor Venice! Poor neighbor! The poet Wordsworth was a better foreigner:

> "Once did she hold the gorgeous east in fee,
> And was the safeguard of the west; the worth
> Of Venice did not fall below her birth,
> Venice, the eldest Child of Liberty.
> She was a maiden city, bright and free;
> No guile seduced, no force could violate;
> And, when she took unto herself a Mate,
> She must espouse the everlasting Sea."

3.

Since the problem of the foreigner springs from a natural prejudice, and since our prejudices are as old as our race, rules for dealing with the stranger date from the beginning of time. There is surprisingly little difference between primitive and recent versions of the art of being a foreigner. Our culture is drawn mainly from two great sources, the Hebraic and the Greek. From both we derive a sense of duty toward the stranger who is within our gates, and specific regulations as to his treatment, but these rules are for him in particular, as for a creature different from ourselves. The Hebrews thought of him as a Gentile; the Greeks called him a barbarian. The Old Testament is rich in beautiful stories about foreigners. Human nature rises at times above its prejudices, charity stretches beyond frontiers, angels are entertained unawares. In the New Testament Jesus attacks our prejudice toward those who are not of us, when he speaks of the Good Samaritan.

One of Plato's works, known to most readers by title only, but as I've said, a great favorite of mine, is *The Laws,* a voluminous collection of rules, or rather suggestions for rules, to govern an ideal city. He described a Utopia in his famous *Republic,* but in his old age he seems to have mulled over the same subject at greater length, and, as I think, with greater penetration and occasionally with delightful humor. In the *Republic* his eye was on a theoretical framework for society; in *The Laws* he seems occupied less with the abstract scheme than with actual experience.

Inevitably he talks about foreigners, about those who visit us, and about ourselves when we go visiting. Strangers, he says, are of four kinds—merchants or traders, tourists, ambassadors, and philosophers or scientists. In every respect but one they should receive, he thinks, different treatment. For all alike he would lay down this hard and fast rule, that the visitor should not be permitted to criticize or to suggest innovations. In Plato's day also, it appears, foreigners told you how to improve your town. To avoid anger, or in extreme cases murder, Plato prescribes that they should go home and work out their good ideas there.

For merchants and traders he had, of course, little esteem, since even in the later Greek world wandering peddlers often carried stolen goods, a clear distinction not yet having been established between the traffic of business and the traffic of piracy. He advised that the traveling salesmen be closely watched. They should be received by designated officials who should make them comfortable, not inside the town but just beyond the walls. The appointed officials or, as we should say, the local Chamber of Commerce, should regulate prices, and most important of all, should send the visitors on their way after a reasonable time.

The tourists would come, Plato says, to see plays and dances, to hear music, and to admire architecture. There was then as now no reason, of course, why tourists should not be interested in other matters, but Plato says they seldom were. We are not prepared to argue that our own travel before the war was for satisfactions much wider or more profound. Tourists, Plato advises, should be received hospitably in the places provided for them, and officers of the city, selected from the reputable and sedate, should attend to their wants. For the sake of its reputation the city should put its best foot forward, but they'd better not clutter up the place. After a stay of the same length permitted the merchants, they should move on.

Ambassadors were an easy problem, Plato thought. The diplomats of his time did not reside in foreign capitols; their function was chiefly that of heralds, to bring an important message or to take one back. They would have neither the intention nor the wish to stay. Their reception would of course be formal, with public honors; any city of consequence would know all about that without special instruction.

Scientists or philosophers, the pleasantest of all visitors, are also, says Plato, the rarest. They illustrate in perfection the art of being a foreigner—they come to learn. If the city has wise men of its own, let them receive the visiting sages. The group altogether won't be large. Let them go off to a quiet corner and talk as much as they like, or if the visitors prefer, let them knock at all doors, let them seek, without further introduction, whoever directs the education of youth, or whoever has received a prize for any virtue. Let them ask whatever question they choose, and let them in turn be questioned, for the enlightenment of all concerned. When they are ready to depart, escort them to the city gates, and wish them a safe journey.

Here the impression is unavoidable that if all Greeks were like Plato, they must have questioned the value of travel. As a matter of fact, they did, except in the case of scientists and philosophers. Plato himself, and historians like Herodotus, were praised for receiving honors in far lands, and for the renown of their own country. In an ideal state everyone should stay home except the prize citizens, who should be let out to wander freely as Exhibit A. But Plato knew too much about ordinary men to expect them to stay home. There would always be plenty of restless feet. For them he advised the following regulations: The would-be tourist should apply to the public Assembly for a travel permit, or as we should say, for a passport. The application should be public in order that the neighbors might check the tourist's pretensions. He should give the name of the places in his proposed itinerary, stating clearly in what respect he thought the trip would improve him. On his return he should report to the same public Assembly which had authorized him to go. If it seemed to them that he really was a better man than when he set out, he should receive on the spot an olive crown and other congratulations. If he seemed neither better nor worse than before, no olive crown should be his, but he should be complimented on the physical energy which had taken him so far and brought him back undamaged. If, however, he was clearly a worse man than when he set forth, the

Assembly should order his instant execution. Obviously the deteriorating tourist is a threat to his country, first by giving it an evil reputation abroad, and second, by bringing home with him certain additions to his country's stock of bad habits.

In his discussion of foreigners, whether other men or we do the visiting, Plato must have felt strongly the two difficulties which still bother us and which still fan prejudice. The stranger still arrives at our shores, and almost before landing advises us how to improve ourselves. He is not aware of his rudeness nor of the hostility he provokes. It makes no difference that his criticism may be just and his suggested remedy excellent; the harm lies in the fact that he has spoken out of turn. We ought to forgive him more easily, since we in our travels commit the same blunder, but of course we haven't noticed the failing in ourselves. When Plato made rules for tourists from his ideal city, he didn't warn them against passing judgment; perhaps even he, among the wisest of men, forgot for the moment that folks from his ideal city could be stupid in that particular regard.

His suggestion to execute the tourist who comes back in a worse state than he went, makes in the original text a quaint climax, as though he permitted himself a humorous exaggeration, but the idea is serious. In the Renaissance Englishmen who could afford the costly and dangerous journey began to make what afterwards was called "the grand tour" on the Continent, giving themselves a glimpse of the chief cities in France, Spain, Italy, Switzerland, Germany. Later on, young men and women from the United States made the same pilgrimage, so far as their dollars held out. To travel in the old Mediterranean world, and to see the best of that region toward the north which challenged the Roman world and brought about the fall of Rome, was thought to be a crowning education. Yet in England and in America there were plenty of Jeremiahs to say that foreign travel skirted the edge of hell, that the tourist acquired a respect for strange gods, that he forgot his country and discarded his morals. Those against whom this criticism was directed evidently liked the foreigner too much rather than too little. They should have taken the relatives along, to cure their prejudices also.

The dire results which the censorious perceived in them were

probably nothing but surface mannerisms. Some American
Rhodes scholars from the middle west, admirable fellows in every
way and a credit to the place which produced them, brought back
from Oxford a hastily and none too securely acquired accent
which paralyzed the old neighbors and made Mother and the
aunts weep; something in the boy who had been the pride of
the family was now changed beyond recognition. In time, of
course, the accent would wear off, or the home town would become used to it and would forgive, yet the genial intention of
Cecil Rhodes to weld us together sometimes results in prying us
apart. Apart, mind you, only as to non-essentials, but in this
matter of foreignness the non-essentials count heavily.

4.

So far I have called your attention to the effect of strangeness
in those whom we visit and in those who visit us, and I have
suggested that the art of being a foreigner is acquired by travel
abroad. I write these words while we are in the midst of a great
war which reduces, almost terminates, the possibility of travel,
either abroad or in our own large country. Lacking rubber and
gasoline we surrender our automobiles, and only on necessary
occasions do we use the bus or the train. The stranger and the
foreigner, however, are still with us, and the art of understanding
them needs more than ever to be learned. Wide divisions among
us are a luxury which we cannot at the moment afford.

I was about to say here that all wars interrupt our understanding of each other and cause loss of ground in the struggle for
enlightenment, but on second thought I'm not sure such a statement is entirely true. At this point I hesitate to set down my beliefs for fear you will read into them a praise of war, a diabolical
advocacy of large-scale killings as a means of promoting brotherly
love. I take the risk, however, trusting in your good sense. War
is a ghastly business, but in some wars and for some ideals decent
men must take part, the more whole-heartedly, the more civilized
they are. If out of the horror some good is salvaged, why not recognize that fact thankfully?

The truth is, I believe, that wars increase hostility and hatred
among those behind the lines, the on-lookers; but the men who

confront each other in the trenches or on the battlefields who
endure the same misery, who exercise the same ingenuity and
courage, who deal out to each other the same agonies—those men
learn, in that awful school, that an enemy can be respected, even
admired. If any war lasts long enough, the fighters become friends,
but the folks at home who have loyally backed up their men by
training their emotions on one target, wishing everything good
for their own and everything bad for the foe, end up in a condition of irreconcilability. An intelligent man who has been
active in one war will, I think, get into the next if he can, not
only for the defense of his people but because he knows that in
war chivalrous ideals and civilized manners flourish most sturdily,
not in safe places of government and supply and self-profit, but
among the fighters who stand or move in the presence of death.
If treaties of peace were made by the survivors of the mêlée and
by no one else, there would be fewer foreigners in the world and
more comrades.

I am optimistic enough to believe also that science, which
progresses by necessary strides in war, thereby brings us, in spite
of ourselves, nearer to the date, however far, when we shall be
citizens of the world. I take comfort and hope, sad though these
days are, from a passage in Raymond B. Fosdick's review of the
Rockefeller Foundation's work for 1941.

"Whether we wish it or not," he said, "an indelible pattern of
unity has been woven into the society of mankind. There is not
an area of activity in which this cannot be illustrated. An American soldier wounded on a battlefield in the Far East owes his life
to the Japanese scientist, Kitasato, who isolated the bacillus of
tetanus. A Russian soldier saved by a blood transfusion is indebted to Landsteiner, an Austrian. A German soldier is shielded
from typhoid fever with the help of a Russian, Metchnikoff. A
Dutch marine in the East Indies is protected from malaria because
of the experiments of an Italian, Grassi; while a British aviator
in North Africa escapes death from surgical infection because a
Frenchman, Pasteur, and a German, Koch, elaborated a new
technique.

"In peace as in war we are all of us the beneficiaries of contributions to knowledge made by every nation in the world. Our

children are guarded from diphtheria by what a Japanese and a German did; they are protected from smallpox by an Englishman's work; they are saved from rabies because of a Frenchman; they are cured of pellagra through the researches of an Austrian. From birth to death they are surrounded by an invisible host— the spirits of men who never served a lesser loyalty than the welfare of mankind. The best that every individual or group has produced anywhere in the world has always been available to serve the race of men, regardless of nation or color."

5.

If we cannot travel, we may find a substitute in reading. I wouldn't say that we are chiefly drawn to a good book, or should be, by the desire to become a citizen of the world, but among the other services which good books render, they may teach us to be at home with people not like ourselves. This service may be rendered by our own literature, studied chronologically from remote periods down, or by books of our day, read as it were horizontally in the literature of several countries. To read contemporary literature widely yields in this respect much the same profit as to read the books of one country consecutively. The books of other lands are almost as helpful in translation, at least for the purpose of world citizenship, as in the original.

We may seek in literature, as in all the arts, whatever is constant in human interest, whatever is peculiar to a time or a place. In general, I believe we should look for the constant and enduring elements, but for the kind of education which we now discuss, idiosyncrasies and peculiarities should have our first attention. Tolstoy, Victor Hugo, Dickens, can be read for their immense sympathy for the poor, the over-worked, the under-paid, and for their generous satirizing of injustice and stupidity. From this point of view the three giants are alike, brothers in arms against the powers of darkness, but Tolstoy is very Russian, Hugo very French, and Dickens very English. I am suggesting that we re-read them to notice the differences. The Russians, the French, and the English whom we meet in New York or San Francisco today, illustrate the same national traits as these geniuses, and therefore seem to some extent foreign. In the war books of the moment we have a solid unity of condemnation against Naziism and Fascism; to that extent the writers, whether British, French, Polish, Norwegian, Chinese, or American, seem like blood brothers. Yet if we met them, one by one, they would still seem foreigners. Why would they? Their books on the war contain the answer, if we choose to read for it. They all condemn Hitler, but the manner of condemning is in one case Scandinavian, in another case Polish, in the other case Chinese. German bombs fall on a Russian home or on an English; the tragedy is the same but the homes are not. Read the details of the wreckage, or look at the rotogravures; if you care to attend to such matters in the face of the larger tragedy, you may observe that the English make their homes different from ours, and cling, as we say, to different conveniences and comforts. We, of course, do just as much "clinging." All peoples are equally conservative, and all believe themselves equally progressive, but in the details of this conceit, varying from land to land, we produce on each other the effect of strangeness. There is no land which does not deserve the love of its own people; every people, if we know and understand them, have their own good qualities.

6.

At the beginning of this chapter I said that the stranger is often found in the family circle; some one of the household does not quite understand. Husbands and wives are often strangers, divided by personal faults, or more fatally by subtle disharmonies. There is no greater cause of division, for example, between two persons than for one to believe what both profess to believe. There is no misfortune more common or more natural than for one character to mature further and faster than the other. With the years both characters will change, and in mathematical probability there is small hope that the change will be in the same direction and at the same pace.

A similar fortune for better or worse overtakes nations, even those related by blood. England today is not the England of the Victorian period nor the England of the eighteenth century. Canada, Australia, and New Zealand today are not precisely what they were a hundred years ago, and it may be doubted whether they have grown more like England or more like each other. The United States, with a population which increases much faster than in any of these lands, a cosmopolitan population, less and less Anglo-Saxon, has changed perhaps more than any other country on earth. To be a world citizen is harder than it once was.

Yet I come back to where I started—the art of being a foreigner begins in the home, with the immediate neighbors, with our locality. Before we abolish the larger irritations, the impression of foreignness between country and country, brothers and sisters must learn to understand each other, some light from heaven must descend upon husbands and wives, so that wedlock may be a sacrament and not an endurance test. Of all the matters touched on in this book, the problem of ourselves as strangers to each other is, I think, the most challenging and the most impenetrable. It is at the root of color prejudice, race prejudice, religious prejudice. It varies in individuals. Like any other disease, it must be cured where it breaks out, case by case.

As I write I think of a cartoon in *Punch,* forty years ago. Two men walk along one side of the street with their hands in their pockets. On the other side passes a Frenchman, his mustache waxed, his costume from the Boulevards.

One of the two says to the other, " 'E's a foreigner, ayn't 'e? 'Eave arf a brick at 'im!"

CHAPTER IX

Religion

1.

IT WOULD BE grossly improper for me in this book, and it is far from my intention, to discuss your personal religion or my own. Yet I believe a life is incomplete indeed, abnormally so, if it does not include an intelligent interest in religion. Most men and women, I have observed, whether they do or do not adhere to a definite faith, whether they obey or neglect the discipline of the faith to which theoretically they belong, still have a deep concern with religion. In most cases this concern is emotional and it shows itself, unfortunately, in occasional outbursts against the religion of some other person, but on the whole men revere, more profoundly than perhaps they realize, the indubitable prophets and saints, the mysteries and revelations of this life, and of a life beyond this.

The emotional element in all faith is large, and it is this portion of our neighbor's religion which we are most bound to respect as something intimate and in a way sacred. I doubt, however, if any life is complete which does not use intelligence to clarify and define its emotions. There are certain directions in which by the use of our intelligence we might partake more completely in the religious life of our place and time. Since I write primarily for readers in the United States, I find my illustrations in this country.

Many religions are represented among us. With due respect for them all, I shall let three large bodies stand for certain general principles. If a man from Mars should visit us and report on what he found, he could reasonably say that in this country, as in Europe and other parts of the world, he found these three groups present in varying proportions, but always in the same approximate relation historically and philosophically. He would say that the ancient religion of the Hebrews, slowly unfolding and revealing itself through thousands of years, produced at last a supreme prophet, who to some Jews of his time and to innumerable non-Jews seemed more than a prophet, seemed indeed an incarnation of divinity. The worship of Jesus developed, the man from Mars might observe, into the Catholic Church, but the ancient Hebrew religion continued, those adhering to it who could not accept Jesus as more than a human prophet.

From the Catholic Church four or five centuries ago a number of protesting or critical groups split off, all having this in common, that they thought the tradition was in some respects developing amiss and they wished to reform it. These Protestant bodies as a group come to a formidable total, but they keep on subdividing and splitting up into fragments of varying size and influence. The Catholic Church meanwhile continues on its way, influenced perhaps by Protestantism but maintaining its essential character, and the ancient Hebrew religion likewise continues, influenced by Catholicism and Protestantism, yet still invincibly itself.

The man from Mars, if he observed all this, would be doing pretty well. His account would not be entirely satisfying to Jews, nor to Catholics, nor to Protestants, but it would do justice to a striking historical phenomenon, that the religion which Jesus himself practiced and the doctrine which he taught were the climax of ancient faith and the inspiration of a later religion.

The man from Mars might add something which he probably observed first of all, that the ancient and bitter antagonism between Jew and Christian survives among us in the form of mortal prejudice; that the less ancient hostility between Catholics and Protestants survives among us in a prejudice even more virulent; that well-bred Americans like to pretend that these two prejudices don't exist; that the leaders of the three religions treat each other with marked politeness; that different types of Protestants dislike each other almost as much as they disapprove of Catholics and Jews; that there are liberal-minded Catholics and other kinds; that there are variations within the Jewish faith, some congregations being extremely liberal and others firmly orthodox.

The other side of the picture the man from Mars might easily overlook. To balance off these antagonisms and prejudices there are subtle and unexpected ties. In philosophy and temperament the Jewish religion is very close to the Protestant. Protestantism generally goes to the Old Testament for a large part of its doctrine and inspiration. On the other hand, the Jewish religion has certain affinities with the Catholic in a common liturgical genius, which some Protestant bodies lack and seem determined not to acquire.

The man from Mars, if he observed all this, would do so because he came here with his eyes open. You and I, if we are equally curious, may observe the same phenomena. In a thousand ways they color our American life. Whether we are Jew, Catholic, or Protestant, a minimum degree of curiosity might be expected of us. Our lives would be more complete if we knew in a general way what are the doctrines of the Jewish Church, of the Catholic, of the different Protestant bodies. What we call our general culture, our conception of a man's total inheritance, would be broader if we knew something of the liturgies employed in the Jewish and Catholic worship and in those Protestant churches which are liturgical, and something of the plain bareness which non-liturgical Protestantism strives for and achieves. All three religions are important sources of the art of music as we know it today. Even the non-liturgical Protestant bodies have made permanent contributions to music and to literature, which is surprising, since in their worship the arts have little or no recognized place.

The best result of knowing something about the religions among which we live, and among the members of which prejudices survive, would be the decrease of prejudice through understanding. I have asked two friends of mine, Dr. George N. Schuster, President of Hunter College, a Catholic scholar, and Rabbi Solomon Freehof, of Pittsburgh, a Jewish scholar, to suggest some reading which would represent the point of view of their different faiths. The titles will be found at the end of this volume, in the section of the Bibliography devoted to this chapter. I asked a leading Protestant divine to give me the same aid on behalf of Protestantism. His answer, after due reflection—an answer in which other Protestants concur—is that the various Protestant bodies differ so widely in their point of view, and each within itself divides into so many parties, that they cannot be studied as a single group or movement. My advice to the reader therefore is that he look up in a good encyclopedia the article on Protestantism. He can then look up the article describing each branch of Protestantism, most or all of which the main article will probably name. The encyclopedia will furnish for each subject a helpful bibliography. Whether the encyclopedia is written from the Jewish point of view, the Catholic, or the Protestant, will make little difference. Consult the one you are most comfortable with.

If you and I were living in Asia, I'd choose other religions for my examples. I couldn't there neglect, for example, Buddhism, or Mohammedanism, or Confucianism. To some extent these faiths are represented among us. If your curiosity is great enough, you will at least inform yourself of their doctrines and practices. If you have studied Greek or Roman literature, you must have learned something about Greek and Roman religion, and if your interest has spread so far you may have some insight into Egyptian philosophy, or your reading in English literature may have taught you something of Norse and Germanic mythology. I could wish for any friend that he should be acquainted intelligently and sympathetically with many religions, ancient and modern; also that he should have a religion of his own.

Devout people, I must warn you, seldom take this point of view; in my experience most of them fear that their own faith might be shaken or qualified if they knew any other. There is in general a reluctance among religious people even to set foot inside the building which those of a different communion regard as the House of God. But for me it would be very disturbing, since other men do hold a different point of view from mine, to realize that I was afraid to know what they believed. A robust faith, based on the deep convictions of the heart, cannot, I am sure, be damaged by additional information. That information may even enrich our faith by helping us to a more kindly respect, even for those with whom we shall never entirely agree.

2.

Perhaps you will forgive me if I speak of my own experience, to illustrate how, without interfering with our personal beliefs, information about other religions may enrich our charity and broaden our point of view. I was brought up in the Episcopal Church and had my early religious instruction from my parents and from that Church, but all my life I have been indebted for my ideas about religion in general to literature and music and the arts, or to some other source not primarily theological or ecclesiastical. The influence of the arts conditioned my approach to religion long before I was born. My father was a Scot, born in the Methodist Church. My grandfather was Presbyterian, a poor Scottish weaver with a passion for music and history. Love of music led him quite frequently to the liturgy of the English Church, but as the story came down in the family, he felt himself in his comparative poverty unwelcome among the prosperous and socially select. He then turned to the Methodist Church where poverty was not snubbed and where the music, though not so good as in the Church of England, had a measure of excellence and much warmth. In the next generation my father, in the United States, was led by the same love of music into the Episcopal Church, where he met my mother. She came of a Yorkshire family, with some Scottish blood, and from the Reformation downward her ancestors had been members of the Church of England.

Most people, I dare say, have been influenced quite consciously, as I have been, by the history or the experiences of ancestors, immediate or remote. When I first visited the Cathedral at York I thought of the men and women of my mother's line who had stood where I was at the moment standing, and the sense of tradition was stronger in me at that moment than ever before or later. I realized of course that a Roman Catholic might have enjoyed the sense of a far older tradition, and a Jew, the sense of a tradition older still. By a tradition I here mean of course nothing that cramps or confines, rather a continuity which ameliorates the loneliness of this world.

My father was a business man on a larger scale than my grandfather, but he too had a passion for music and history. In addition he had a great love of France, which I note here as part of my inheritance though it affects only slightly my religious experiences. Or perhaps I shouldn't say slightly. During the last war and on later trips abroad, whenever I had a Sunday in Paris, I went to Saint Sulpice. I first went there because Widor was the organist, but I returned because the service gave me a certain aid and certain inspiration which I could find nowhere else. My father's library was excellent, and in youth I explored not only the volumes of fiction and poetry but the historical works. Particularly profitable to me was a handy commentary on the New Testament by Charles John Ellicott, Bishop of Gloucester and Bristol, an old-fashioned work in many volumes and of encyclopedic scope. Many of the references roused my curiosity as to Jewish history, and I soon made the acquaintance of encyclopedias in which I have had occasion to read much ever since. When I wrote the novel *Solomon, My Son!* in 1935, a Jewish scholar was kind enough to express astonishment at the amount of history I had picked up. I had to confess how much of it I had absorbed, decades ago, in a comfortable chair exploring Bishop Ellicott in the vine-shaded window of our library.

My father's love of music and his competence in the art led him to organize, drill, and generally support the music in the church we attended on the Weehawken heights. He let me play the organ as soon as I could, and later I drilled the choir. Church services through boyhood and youth were occasions of sheer delight, but I am not sure the delight wasn't in the music rather than in the religion. The study of church music led me immediately to Palestrina, and through him to a study of the Roman Catholic liturgy. My literary tastes, which grew with my love of music, led me to investigate the history of the English prayer book with its marvelous prayers, many or most of which I soon learned were translations from the Roman Catholic services. Father's library contained a copy of Blunt's *Annotated Prayer Book,* which opened my eyes to much history, and I spent some time studying the so-called First and Second Prayer Books of Edward the Sixth, which are now available for the general reader in *Everyman's Library*.

These prayer books, the work chiefly of Bishop Cranmer, record his shifting theological point of view at different times. For me they threw light of a surprising kind on the whole Reformation. The need to reform the Catholic liturgy by simplifying it and restoring it to its early simplicity was felt almost as strongly by some of those who remained in the Church as by those who left it. In Spain, Cardinal Quignon published a Reform Breviary in 1535, a revision which went through many editions in the following thirty years and must have had the approval of the ecclesiastical authorities. The First Prayer Book of Edward the Sixth was published in 1549 with an eloquent introduction, which to a considerable extent is translated directly from Cardinal Quignon's preface. No credit, however, is given to the original author.

My studies in Catholic Church music and the Catholic liturgy led me of course to Thomas Aquinas, and I made a determined but not at that time a very successful attempt to follow the majestic logic of the *Summa*. But from first acquaintance I learned at least this, that the scholastic philosophers were not attempting to make converts; they were of course addressing an audience who were already believers. The object of their studies was to develop a technique for clarifying their faith by the aid of their intellect. My very bungling study of the *Summa* taught me for the first time that truth can be explored as successfully by reason in the world of the mind as by experiment in the realm of nature, and that many if not all of the discoveries of modern science were made at least in principle by another method, in the Middle Ages. From this point I went on to the only skepticism I have ever profoundly felt. I became, and I remain, skeptical about the kind of science which is cocksure of the experimental method, and indifferent to the method of pure reason.

In my school days the doctrines of Darwin were taught with a certain fanaticism which has since, for the most part, disappeared. At the turn of the century you weren't an intellectual at all if you didn't believe that the great English scientist had not only thrown light on the variation of species, but had solved the mystery of the origin of life. The soul was only a figure of speech. We were the result of an accidental combination of matter and force, which in time, learning to adjust itself to the environment, moved up through higher and higher planes until it reached a happy end in us.

But I never could understand how intelligent men, some of them among my teachers, many others among my friends, could be so credulous and so unobserving. In the field of religion they were skeptics, but they could swallow whole any doctrine if only it were sufficiently materialistic. They would point out the variations, contradictions, and obvious inaccuracies in the Bible, but in order to get their theory of evolution started, they would smuggle the principle of life surreptitiously into an atom when you weren't looking. The discrepancies in the Bible or in other sacred books didn't bother me in the least, since books were the subject of my habitual study and I should have been astonished not to find discrepancies in them. In Samuel Butler's *The Way of All Flesh,* the skeptical tinker embarrassed the young minister by driving home the variations in the account of the Resurrection given by the four evangelists. But I never found two students in my class who could agree in the summary they gave of a book they had all read, or of my own words to them a few minutes before.

Any theory of evolution, I noticed, starts with a vast act of faith. The evolutionist can't function unless he assumes an unlimited amount of time. The Bible in England used to have a chronology printed at the top of the page, on the authority of that good and credulous gentleman, Bishop Usher, who was satisfied that the world was created on Monday, January 1st, 6324 B.C. Evolutionists in my boyhood used to laugh at Bishop Usher, who assumed the date for the convenience of his theories, a late date because his theories needed so little elbow room. The evolutionists thought they were on more scientific ground because for their hypothesis they had to assume several million years. They were hot on the trail of primitive man, the theoretical first improvement on the ape, and now and then they would turn up a promising skull, but whenever they caught up with primitive man in person he turned out to be a disappointingly sophisticated fellow, who drew wonderful pictures on cave walls and showed considerable engineering skill in moving massive rocks around, or otherwise was entirely over-educated to serve the evolutionary hypothesis. Was materialistic science discouraged? Of course not!

Science immediately assumed a few more million years and went on to look for primitive man further back. I can't say accurately how much the earth has aged during my lifetime, but I've grown accustomed to an addition of geologic years, like further extensions on an old house, whenever a larger hypothesis moves in. Primitive man is now chased back, I understand, into the infinite past.

I believe the past is infinite, and the future also. I am skeptical about finite beginnings and finite ends. There are constant changes, but the elements which are moved into new combinations are also, I believe, constant. Perhaps it is only our finite minds which crave a definite beginning and end in order to avoid the weariness and strain of contemplating the infinite. When we teach the children that two and two make four, we are dealing, of course, with a timeless truth, but we conceal the fact by talking of finite things, two apples, perhaps, added to two other apples. We don't disturb either the pupils or ourselves by speculating about the date when two and two first made four, or the date when two and two will make five. In school I studied the geometry of Euclid, and my teachers then were quite positive that parallel lines never meet, never! Our solar system, I was informed, drove through space at terrific speed, and as I understood, in a straight line, and it always would continue so to drive, since there was plenty of space, in fact, an infinite amount of it. There still is, I believe, but the finite mind is not comfortable trying to grasp it. We now favor the geometry of Riemann, which announces, just as positively as Euclidians taught their contrary doctrine, that parallel lines do meet at last. Plane surfaces are now spherical, and lines apparently straight are really curved. The universe as we know it may seem to be moving through space in a straight line, but after a while it will come around again to where it started. The idea is restful. Herbert Spencer said his head ached when he tried to imagine the infinity of space, which could have no origin, no evolution and no end. We get rid of the headache by limiting space and shutting it in, and by refusing to consider what are these enclosing walls which for our convenient ease we assume, and what lies outside of them. A good mathematician will probably tell me that I don't understand all the mathematical

conceptions here involved. I admit I don't. I never heard of a
skeptic in religion who understood the theological conception
which to him seemed nonsense. I am not here trying to be dog-
matic or to settle an argument; I am confessing that when modern
science takes a flier in abstract logic, I lose my breath but I am
not converted.

I wonder if strict believers in Darwinian evolution would have
embraced the hypothesis so seriously had they been familiar with
Greek and Roman literature. The idea that life began in very low
forms and evolved through higher phases, from a low creature
squirming in the mud up to man, was one of the two creation
fables dear to the Greek mind. In his gradual rise from a beast-
like condition to the perfection represented by the Athenian citizen, man was aided by Prometheus, by forethought.

The other Greek creation fable told of a golden age in which
this world, and man in it, were at their best, and from which
both earth and man have deteriorated ever since. These fables,
diametrically opposed, as the nineteenth century Anglo-Saxon
would have said, were the work of poets. The Darwinian scientist
did not invent his theory; he merely accepted as a sound hypothesis one of the two Greek creation stories, and he has been trying
ever since to verify by search and research what was once sheer
poetry.

Don't let me give the impression that I under-value the truth
in poetry. I'm sure the Greeks knew how true this account was
and still is, the account which represents man as beginning far
down and rising. But they recognized also the truth in the account
which represents man as beginning in perfection and constantly
deteriorating. The nineteenth century debated whether man
began in the mud and came up, or started in Paradise and fell.
Most of us still think we must choose between one hypothesis or
the other. The Greeks with their better understanding of poetic
truth believed both hypotheses at the same time. From the point
of view of youth and plans and hopes the world is to be better,
and since preceding generations before us observed the same
tendencies to improve which we see, it is obvious that the world
must have begun in a very low state indeed. On the other hand,
memory and time idealize the good old days; our leaders now are

less heroic than they once were, governments are less satisfactory, even the weather is not what it was. The earliest literature of which we have record complains of the degenerate times. Obviously if the decline has been so constant for so long, the original condition must have been perfect.

Recognizing the validity of these two poetic fables, perhaps the Greeks understood that they state an inner psychological truth rather than an outward fact; perhaps life has changed neither for the better nor for the worse. But observing human nature as they did, with great accuracy, they knew that poetic fables are necessary to express our convictions, and though no writer who left us an account of creation was present in the Garden of Eden, that is, in the perfection of the golden age, or saw with his own eyes the slow evolution from the lowest life to the next higher, nevertheless both fables express the soul.

In the same way the great fables of a Last Judgment, of a future life involving heaven, purgatory, and hell, express spiritual truths, though Vergil and Dante and the other poets who gave the details, never saw with physical eyes what they wrote about. The skeptical scientist and the skeptical layman, picking flaws in the various accounts of a hereafter and denying the possibility of any heaven or any hell, miss the point by a wide margin. I know that I am writing these lines; there are philosophers who would challenge me to prove that I know it, but for the ordinary purposes of sanity the assertion may stand. I do not know in the same sense that the soul survives after death, but I believe it does, and though I cannot substantiate that belief or faith or confidence as I could demonstrate to you, were you in my study just now, that I am writing these lines, yet the undemonstrable is more important to me, a deeper kind of truth than the mere fact of my writing. It expresses more profoundly my experience in this present world and my judgment upon that experience. It is perhaps not too much to say that a belief as to heaven and hell and a hereafter is a record of experience in this world, precisely like my statement that I am at this moment writing—a statement of experience of the same kind but of larger scope.

In the Sixth Book of Vergil's *Aeneid,* the Sybil leads Aeneas to the other world, where he has a glimpse of the rewards and punishments which are earned in this life. Vergil's scheme of eternal justice perhaps inspired Dante's picture of hell, purgatory, and Paradise. So at least the scholars suggest. Yet he might have thought out the scheme for himself, as still earlier poets did, and as so-called primitive peoples have done everywhere on earth. The virtues and vices which Vergil would have rewarded or punished, and the forms of the rewards and punishments, do not correspond entirely to those in Dante, nor to those in other pictures of the next life, but reading Vergil we understand perfectly what ideals of virtue and what conceptions of vice he wished to impose on his fellows in Rome. Dante, in his scheme of the hereafter, was articulating ideals for Florence and Italy.

In a word, when men speak of the next world, it is this world they are describing, this world as they'd like it to be. In the famous description of the Last Judgment reported by St. Mark, Jesus tells what will happen to the good and what to the bad, but he emphasizes chiefly what will be said to the good and to the bad during the process of their trial, and what answer they will make. He names as virtues a number of attitudes and acts which were not Roman, though the Roman world was all around him as he spoke. He was defining goodness and wickedness in terms of practical religion. The good are to inherit everlasting life because they fed the hungry and gave drink to the thirsty and were hospitable to the stranger—because they clothed the naked, visited the sick, and were not afraid to be kind to those in jail. The wicked inherited death because they failed in all these charities.

There is no question that Jesus believed in a future life and preached it. Anyone who knows what poetry is, will I think agree that in his picture of the Last Judgment he was talking of what men should or should not do now. Conduct has infinite and everlasting consequences, he was saying, but the fatal decision is here and now.

3.

My studies in literature, undertaken for purely literary purposes, have more than once helped me to understand religious experience. Life itself, before it gets into literature, has a way of interpreting for us whatever we believe, but the illumination which comes from specific books is easier to recall and to cite.

I owe a great debt to Sir Thomas Browne's *Religio Medici*. Browne lived from 1605 to 1682, and in his day he was a remarkable scientist, not simply a great doctor but an explorer into all fields of knowledge, sometimes investigating old doctrines and superstitions, sometimes anticipating modern doctrines which may seem characteristic exclusively of our day. He belonged to the transition period between scholastic philosophy and modern laboratory experimentation. Francis Bacon had turned his back on the Middle Ages, and for England at least had made himself the advocate of the new method. The reaction against pure logic was exaggerated by Protestant emotions; techniques even of secular usefulness were easily discarded if they had been developed by Catholics, even if they had been developed in the old days when all men were Catholics. Francis Bacon, in his rejection of the past, went pretty far. Only in our own time has a balance of justice been established toward the Middle Ages. The change is in my opinion not yet sufficiently recognized. When Edward Gibbon, at the end of the eighteenth century, wrote his *Decline and Fall of the Roman Empire,* he closed his great work at the point where he believed the classical world had sunk to complete barbarism. He stopped, that is, at the thirteenth century, the century of Chartres and of Saint-Michel, the century which preceded Dante, Boccaccio and Petrarch, the century which many scholars seriously regard as the peak of western civilization.

I mention this to praise Sir Thomas Browne. In the midst of bitter religious controversy and counter-persecution, he remained enlightened and charitable. Though he welcomed the marvelous resources and possibilities of modern science, with its laboratories and its experimental method, he valued no less the medieval art of thinking. He saw clearly then, what we've since needed to rediscover, that unless the experimental scientist knows how to think, he may not always make the happiest interpretation of his own experiments.

My first interest in Browne was, I must confess, purely literary. He wrote in a style all his own, very compact and therefore sometimes difficult, amazingly precise, with such an employment of Latin words and with such an effective mixture of Latin words

with Anglo-Saxon, that he has astonished and influenced writers
from Dr. Samuel Johnson to Lafcadio Hearn. Hearn's study
of Browne, published first in *Interpretations of Literature,* and
reprinted in the more convenient *Talks to Writers,* is, I think,
the last word on the purely literary genius of this many-sided
physician. But growing older I have learned to prize Sir Thomas
Browne for his charity, his humaneness, his intelligence. His most
famous book, I suppose, is *Religio Medici,* "A Doctor's Religion."
I should rank even above it the less popular *Urn Burial.* The
first book is a sort of intellectual and spiritual autobiography; the
second discusses some ancient burial urns discovered in Norfolk,
and from this discussion passes to meditations on death, fame, and
immortality. The first book, therefore, has to do with a complete
life in this world; the second with the ineradicable human desire
to be remembered after we are gone, and with the hope to live
again in other worlds than this. The first book fascinated me by
its good sense and its sly wit, as in the following well-known
passage:

"I have no Genius to disputes in Religion, and have often
thought it wisdom to decline them, especially upon a disadvantage, or when the cause of Truth might suffer in the weakness of
my patronage. Where we desire to be informed, 'tis good to
contest with men above our selves; but to confirm and establish
our opinions, 'tis best to argue with judgments below our own,
that the frequent spoils and Victories over their reasons may settle
in ourselves an esteem and confirmed Opinion of our own. Every
man is not a proper Champion for Truth, nor fit to take up the
Gauntlet in the cause of Verity: many, from the ignorance of
these Maximes, and an inconsiderate Zeal unto Truth, have too
rashly charged the Troops of Error, and remain as Trophies unto
the enemies of Truth. A man may be in as just possession of
Truth as of a City, and yet be forced to surrender; 'tis therefore
far better to enjoy her with peace, than to hazzard her on a battle."

The common sense which I admire in this passage has been
thought skeptical by many readers from the seventeenth century
until now. If skepticism is the word for an unflinching observation
of difficulties, then Sir Thomas Browne is indeed a skeptic. He
was a thorough student of the Bible in a day when to question

the fallibility of the text was dangerous indeed. Yet in the *Urn Burial* he insinuates many a scientific doubt. We are told that the animals went aboard the ark two by two, by which arrangement all living creatures in their various kinds were preserved. What about the fish? Did Noah take aboard two of every kind, including sharks and whales? Or didn't the fish perish? Would a super-abundance of water inconvenience a fish? How about fresh water fish in salt water—and *vice-versa?* All these ideas Sir Thomas slips into a few words at the end of a sentence, when he is about to speak of the burial customs of mankind:

"Though earth has engrossed the name, yet water hath proved the smartest grave; which in forty days swallowed almost mankind and the living creation; fishes not wholly escaping, except the salt ocean were handsomely contempered by a mixture of the fresh element."

Among various methods of disposing of dead bodies, burning to ashes was in ancient times widely favored; Sir Thomas's Norfolk urns contained the ashes of men who once, perhaps, were famous. How large a fire is needed to burn a human body? Many of Sir Thomas's readers had seen with their own eyes what stacks of wood were required to reduce a human being to powder, yet the Bible tells us that the boy Isaac carried on his own shoulder enough wood for the sacrifice. Sir Thomas doesn't contradict the Bible report; he merely calls attention to it. "In the plague of Athens, one private pyre served two or three intruders; and the Saracens burned in large heaps, by the King of Castile, showed how little fuel suffices. Though the funeral pyre of Patroclos took up an hundred foot, a piece of an old boat burned Pompey; and if the burden of Isaac were sufficient for an holocaust, a man may carry his own pyre."

Sometimes Sir Thomas misleads the unwary by the whimsical lightness of his tone. Missing none of the questions which still perplex us, he tucked them into his discourse wherever a convenient nook could be found. There are certain questions, he says, which he is willing to leave untouched—yet he proceeds at once to touch them:

"I can read the History of the Pigeon that was sent out of the Ark and returned no more, yet not question how she found her

Mate that was left behind; that Lazarus was raised from the dead, yet not demand where in the interim his Soul awaited; or raise a Lawcase, whether his Heir might lawfully detain his inheritance bequeathed unto him on his death, and he, though restored to life, have no Plea or Title unto his former possessions. Whether Eve was framed out of the left side of Adam, I dispute not; because I stand not yet assured which is the right side of a man."

The intention here is far from frivolous. We have not yet decided whether right and left should be determined by the person facing an object or by the object faced. We know which is the right arm of a man, but like Sir Thomas we are not sure which is the right side. The dramatist and the actor would say that the right side of a stage is on their right hand when they face the audience. The audience feels that the right side of the stage is on their own right hand as they face the play. Which is the right side of a picture? Which is the right wing of a building?

Provocative though Sir Thomas Browne's observations are, I value more the uplifting eloquence of those pages in *Urn Burial* in which he deals frankly with death and with certain matters connected with death which ordinarily we gloss over. In the preservation of the human body, whether in the form of ashes or otherwise, the hope of immortality mingles with the desire not to be forgotten. Whatever justification there is for faith in another life, we have small reason to suspect that any of us will long be remembered on earth. The burial urns persisted, still containing their ashes, but the names of those dead were lost. Sir Thomas believed, perhaps because he was so close to the Renaissance, that man desires fame on earth almost as much as eternal existence. After many an hour wondering if he were not right, I can recite almost by heart the superb paragraphs in which he holds up this challenging mirror:

"What song the Syrens sang, or what name Achilles assumed when he hid himself among women, though puzzling questions, are not beyond all conjecture. What time the persons of these ossuaries entered the famous nations of the dead, and slept with princes and counsellors, might admit a wide solution. But who were the proprietaries of these bones, or what bodies these ashes made up, were a question above antiquarism; not to be resolved

by man, nor easily perhaps by spirits, except we consult the pro-
vincial guardians, or tutelary observators. Had they made as good
provision for their names, as they have done for their relicks, they
had not so grossly erred in the art of perpetuation. But to subsist
in bones, and be but pyramidally extant, is a fallacy in duration."

"Who cared to subsist like Hippocrates' patients, or Achilles'
horses in Homer, under naked nominations, without deserts and
noble acts, which are the balsam of our memories, the *entelechia*
and soul of our subsistences? To be nameless in worthy deeds,
exceeds an infamous history. The Canaanitish woman lives more
happily without a name, than Herodias with one. And who had
not rather been the good thief than Pilate?

"But the iniquity of oblivion blindly scattereth her poppy, and
deals with the memory of men without distinction to merit of
perpetuity. Who can but pity the founder of the pyramids?
Herostratus lives that burnt the temple of Diana, he is almost
lost that built it. Time hath spared the epitaph of Adrian's horse,
confounded that of himself. In vain we compute our felicities
by the advantage of our good names, since bad have equal durations, and Thersites is like to live as long as Agamemnon. Who
knows whether the best of men be known, or whether there be
not more remarkable persons forgot, than any that stand remembered in the known account of them?

"Darkness and light divide the course of time, and oblivion
shares with memory a great part even of our living beings; we
slightly remember our felicities, and the smartest strokes of afflic-
tion leave but short smart upon us. Sense endureth no extrem-
ities, and sorrows destroy us or themselves. To weep into stones
are fables. Afflictions induce callosities; miseries are slippery, or
fall like snow upon us, which notwithstanding is no unhappy
stupidity. To be ignorant of evils to come, and forgetful of evils
past, is a merciful provision in nature, whereby we digest the
mixture of our few and evil days, and, our delivered senses not
relapsing into cutting remembrances, our sorrows are not kept
raw by the edge of repetitions. A great part of antiquity contented
their hopes of subsistency with a transmigration of their souls,—
a good way to continue their memories, while having the advan-

tage of plural successions, they could not but act something remarkable in such variety of beings, and enjoying the fame of their passed selves, make accumulation of glory unto their last durations. Others, rather than be lost in the uncomfortable night of nothing, were content to recede into the common being, and make one particle of the public soul of all things, which was no more than to return into their unknown and divine original again. Egyptian ingenuity was more unsatisfied, contriving their bodies in sweet consistencies, to attend the return of their souls. But all was vanity, feeding the wind, and folly. The Egyptian mummies, which Cambyses or time hath spared, avarice now consumeth. Mummy is become merchandise, Mizraim cures wounds, and Pharaoh is sold for balsams."

One quotation more. Light, which divides with darkness the course of time, is for Sir Thomas Browne a theme inevitably inspiring. In his little book, *The Garden of Cyrus,* he discusses the best way to plant trees so that they may have most light with the greatest economy of space. He would set them out in a pattern of five, one at each corner of a square and one in the middle. The pattern of five starts him off on the countless appearances of this number in nature, in practical experience, in fable; he mentions the five wise virgins and the five foolish, the five fingers and the five toes, the five torches carried at Roman weddings, the five-leaf blossom common in trees and flowers, the ancient rule to eat the fruit of newly planted trees no earlier than the fifth year, the five acts of a play. Why should five recur frequently, and seldom four or six? From this seductive investigation he rises suddenly, in a marvelous paragraph, one of the supreme glories of English prose, to the praise of light, the mystery of mysteries:

"Light that makes all things seen, makes some things invisible; were it not for darkness and the shadow of the earth, the noblest part of creation had remained unseen, and the stars in heaven as invisible as on the fourth day, when they were created above the horizon with the sun, or there was not an eye to behold them. The greatest mystery of religion is expressed by adumbration, and in the noblest part of Jewish types we find the cherubims shadowing the mercy-seat. Life itself is but the shadow of death, and souls departed but the shadows of the living. All things fall under this name. The sun itself is but the dark *simulacrum,* and light but the shadow of God."

I know no writer who compels us to a more alert attention or who forces us to do more thinking. Even in this rhapsody he reminds us that if sun and stars were created together on the fourth day, the stars must have remained invisible until they were properly segregated; and if creation began with the command, Let there be light, by what preliminary and supernatural illumination was the work of the first three days accomplished, before the sun, the moon and the stars were made?

4.

Perhaps in no field more than in religious philosophy can a great book help us even though we don't entirely grasp it, even though we are not equipped to evaluate the grounds usually assigned for its fame. In middle life I owed much to René Descartes and his *Discourse on Method.* It would have been impertinent for me then, as it still would be, to comment on the famous seventeenth century mathematician in his own realm; he was a pioneer in science, he advanced the study of optics and of light, he earned the name of father of analytical geometry, grave subjects in the presence of which I walk as a child. As you have doubtless observed, there is no chapter in this book on the major sciences, for the plain reason that my knowledge of chemistry, physics, mathematics, botany, geology, astronomy, biology, zoology and whatever else should go in the list, is but a poor smattering. But the logic which any scientist employs always fascinates me; I presume to believe that I do know something about the art of thinking. If my presumption is at all justified, I must acknowledge here a large debt to René Descartes.

It is easy to see why mathematicians of the first rank often, perhaps usually, esteem him above Francis Bacon, whom in many ways he resembles. Both men were leaders in the movement which took science out of medieval channels and set it on modern roads in new directions. Bacon, in his *De Dignitate et Augmentis Scientarum,* 1623, later translated as *The Advancement of Learning,* discarded the syllogism of traditional logic, on the ground that instead of aiding the discovery of new truth, it merely proved or clarified what was already known. For the exercise of logic, from syllogism to syllogism, Bacon would substitute experiments in research laboratories. Our eyesight and our other senses, he held, were poor instruments for the observation of nature; mechanical means would in time be devised to do our investigations for us without error. If you have ever breathed into that little tank which reports on your metabolism, or if you have watched the mercury and the rubber tube which pry into your blood pressure, you can imagine the numberless directions in which the Baconian influence still unfolds.

Descartes likewise discarded the syllogism, and he welcomed the experimental method, but he resembled Sir Thomas Browne in this, that he believed the art of thinking was still important; however ingenious the Baconian machine in the laboratory, its performance would still need interpreting. If he were here today he would duly admire the ease and the accuracy with which the doctor finds out whether our blood pressure is 140 or 160, but what would really interest him is the fact that the doctor is none too sure what those figures mean. Descartes asked what was—and still is—wrong, not so much with our method of observation or of producing new phenomena, as with our method of thinking. In particular he wanted to know the defects in his own mental processes. When he had, as he believed, located the fault and found the remedy, he wrote his great book, published in 1637, fourteen years after *The Advancement of Learning*.

The *Discourse of Method* is an autobiography, perhaps it would be more accurate to say the biography, of a mind—a very French mind, given to ideas of the most general or universal kind, yet lovingly occupied with the realistic details of life. What attracted me to the book was its revelation of the man rather than its scientific content. René Descartes was, like most of us, a divided character. By training and temperament he was a Catholic; his faith was natural and untroubled, he had to an extraordinary degree the virtue of humility, he was unconcerned with the new currents in religion, he hoped that his Method, by increasing knowledge, would only confirm truths already revealed. But that Method of his, as the theologians at once saw, made every man's private judgment the ultimate authority, both in scientific truth, as he intended, and also by implication in matters of faith. By his Method he could prove, he thought, the existence of God, an achievement which the orthodox would not frown on, but if the success of his demonstration should be complete, the significance of the apostolic Church would be diminished. This result was no more pleasing to him than to the clergy, but he was caught between loyalty to what was already known and curiosity to know more, and though it would have been comfortable to stop, it would have been cowardly not to press on.

Whether he did indeed follow his ideas to their full conclusion, his critics, whether friendly or severe, do not agree. He withheld some of his bolder writings; they appeared only after his death. Perhaps he found in mathematics and optics an application of his theories which would involve less outer controversy and less inner conflict. In our honest moments who of us cannot sympathize with him? Terrible are the collisions of heart and mind. To be loyal is admirable; to be loyal and nothing more, is easy; what is difficult, also, is to be both loyal and intelligent—to keep faith with our past and at the same time not to fall out of step with our own time.

Descartes did not presume, he said, to improve the thinking of others, but merely to describe the method which had helped him. His education was of the best, he was an ardent student, a great reader of books, but at the end of his studies he had acquired no certain knowledge of any subject, aside from the technique necessary to speak or write foreign tongues; and what was more discouraging, the learned men who had been his teachers stood, as he now realized, on no surer ground than he. The result of study, then, was confusion and doubt. Yet the world about him was a good world, and the ordinary men in it were successful and happy to an extent obviously impossible had they been as stupid as his professors and he. He resolved to learn, therefore, not from teachers and books but from life.

Some books he continued to read, old books which enjoyed the approval of many generations; to consult such pages, he says, is almost equivalent to talking with the best of the human race, almost equivalent also to travel. "It is useful," he says, "to know something of the manners of different nations, that we may form a more correct opinion of our own, thus escaping the prejudice that whatever is contrary to our ways is unreasonable or ridiculous—an opinion too often held by those who visit no country but their own. Yet if too much time is spent in travel, we become strangers to the place where we were born, and if we study too exclusively the ancient world, we shall know little of the world in which we live."

Since universities, books, and travel had for him these limitations, Descartes came to a somewhat startling resolution; he would first study himself, a subject which couldn't easily get away from him, and having mastered that primary lesson, he would proceed to study the universe, not in its parts but as a whole. To study himself, a correct method must be found; but any method by which one man could learn all there was to know about himself, would serve as well to solve larger mysteries, even the largest.

He was convinced, first of all, that a man must study himself without aid from others. The customary failure to arrive at truth should be blamed, he thought, on the number who simultaneously engage in the quest, getting in each other's way, blocking each other's vision. Though one man might not know as much as twenty, he would end by knowing more than all put together—if he traveled alone. Descartes would have been better educated, or so he believed, had he not studied under so many teachers.

His method of procedure he describes under four rules.

1. Accept nothing for true unless we know it is true. Know, that is, by experience or by instinctive conviction. The first obligation of the truth-seeker is to be skeptical, to believe only under compulsion, to challenge every theory.

2. Divide the problem into as many parts as possible, and probe skeptically into every part.

3. Take the problem, or its parts, in such an order that the simplest question comes first and the most complicated, last. Seek for each question the complete answer, so that no amount of learning could meet that particular question more fully. Be like the child who does correctly its sum in addition. No mathematician, adding the same figures, could get a different answer.

4. Review the problem, from time to time, to be sure no aspect of it has been omitted.

Along with this intellectual method, Descartes laid out for himself a few rules of conduct, moral and practical. Here we observe the other side of this divided soul. The two systems are set forth within a page of each other, with no sign that Descartes was aware of a contradiction. He resolved to obey the laws and adhere to the religion in which he had been brought up. He would conform to the customs of those among whom he lived, but he would imitate what they did rather than attend to what they said. This, in order to get at their sincere opinions. In all disputes he would take middle ground. When he decided on a course, he would act at once. He would try to conquer himself rather than fate, since it is easier to change our desires than to rearrange the world. He believed we should accept this at least for true, that we control nothing but our thoughts.

Neither the intellectual method nor the ethical system of Descartes attract me greatly. I read him for delight in his clearness, his wit, his homely observation of the world about him; even more, I value the complete frankness, whether it was intended or not, with which he exposes the rift between the two wings of his appealing soul.

5.

I'm conceited enough to think that few men love life more than I do, yet I've very little fear of any kind—least of all, fear of death. In my younger years, when most of my life was still to be lived, I should have rebelled against an interruption, but on two fairly recent occasions I've had the strongest reasons to expect my end within the next thirty seconds, and though I found the prospect startling, in neither case was it frightening. I really doubt if I've ever been much afraid of anything. If I seem to boast, bear with me for a moment. There are reasons for being afraid, and for not being.

I cannot understand a religion which has in it an element of fear. The idea of hell, philosophically or theologically considered, is logical—relentlessly so, and I should dislike extremely to go to hell. But if I understand the theory, those who go to hell make that journey because of their own character and because of the behavior which expressed that character. Perhaps I'm going to hell at this moment without knowing it; in the same tremendous sincerity, and in the same unawareness, good people are on their way toward Paradise. The sheep and the goats, in the great parable, didn't know they were sheep or goats until they were authoritatively informed. Hell has been well advertised, but it doesn't seem to frighten the wicked much. We are told that the way of the transgressor is hard, but we are also told that strait is the road and narrow the gate that leads to salvation. To be very bad, a technique is needed, difficult in either case; we choose one or the other because that's what we want. The blessed go to Paradise because Paradise is the kind of existence they crave and yearn for and work toward; where there is no Paradise they try, within the measure of their powers, to build one. Could Paradise tolerate a soul which was backed into it by a bad scare?

There is something often called fear which is an aid to the good life, but I doubt if it has much to do with being frightened, or even with the impulse to save our skins. It is rather akin to a sense of honor, to self-respect. In the first World War, when the transports carried our armies abroad, one of my students was asked what his motives were in going so far to get into a fight. "I'm going," he said, "chiefly because I'd rather not consider what my motives might be if I stayed out of it."

The integrity of this man comes to mind now as I write. He enjoys today, I believe, a full and complete life, something which the timid and the cowardly are not likely to achieve. We may state their case just as accurately, perhaps the other way 'round; *because* they have not lived to the full, they are afraid of life and they are afraid to die. If we have exhausted the possibilities of our days we pass out of them with no regret; consuming our own smoke as we move on, we come fresh to the next horizon. If a man remembers his childhood wistfully, we may suspect that he outgrew his childhood before he had fully explored it. If he pines for his youth, it perhaps is not youth he pines for, but opportunities unseized. If he is afraid to die, it's because he has not finished the task for which he was born, he has not developed his talents to the utmost, he never put forth his last ounce of strength, he has avoided the depths but he has missed the heights, he has not lived. Of the men and women who really live, I never knew one who was afraid. They finish each stage of life, remember it with pleasure, and are satisfied not to repeat it. In old age, in their last hour, they are ready, I believe, to go forward, even into the dark.

When I say that those who live most completely have least fear, I state a truth which experience has forced upon man from the beginning of time, the truth that we can afford to be afraid only if we don't know how much danger there is. If one place and one moment of the day held all the peril, we'd be fools not to avoid it. Those who live narrowly imagine they have located the danger spots, the dangerous moments, but those who venture far, discover that danger lurks everywhere at all times. The attempt to keep ourselves safe in such a world as this, is a form of suicide. Why make the attempt if it cannot succeed? Those who live completely exercise, of course, as much prudence as is consistent with living at all, illustrating the spirit of Walt Whitman's lines,

"He is wisest who has the most caution,
He only wins who goes far enough."

In one form or another every great religion teaches this wisdom —to accept the dangerous conditions of existence, but also to put on the armor against danger, which is fearlessness. You may call yourself a fatalist or you may say you have faith; you may believe that your hour will come when your number is turned up, no later and no sooner, or you may believe that the souls of the righteous are in the hands of God. However these two philosophies may differ, they have this one effect in common, that they liberate from fear. If I define the righteous as those who try to learn and to obey the eternal laws, and if I have sincerely sought that knowledge and that obedience, then I am permitted to believe that I am in God's hands and that no harm can touch me. If I believe on the other hand that harm can indeed touch me, but not until the appointed time, then I am probably less comfortable, yet equally free. Suppose an intruder enters my home in the middle of the night, and suppose I believe in free will; how difficult in such a predicament to know whether to grapple with

the burglar at the risk of my life, or whether to lock the door of
my bedroom and let him prowl, trusting to the insurance company
to make up my loss. A true fatalist, however, would go straight at
him and lead for his chin. If my hour is not yet come, he can't
possibly injure me; if he is the instrument of fate, I can't possibly
avoid him, not even behind strong barriers.

The doctrine of courage rooted in faith is, I think, the essence
and the most precious gift of true religion, since its incalculable
profit is for this immediate world. I believe that life was and is
eternal, that our existence did not begin when we were born or
begotten, nor does it end when we die; but I believe also that
the world most important for us is the one in which we find ourselves—this world now, some other world later. I suspect that my
emphasis on the present life, an emphasis which some of my
friends think pagan, is a matter of temperament, and I recognize
that my temperament comes from my mother. Both my parents
were sincerely religious, entirely sane and without fanaticism. I
am everlastingly grateful to them for a childhood not shadowed,
as childhood sometimes is, but made happy, by churchgoing and
by familiarity with theological doctrine. But temperamentally my
parents differed. My father was the wistful kind of Scot, not the
practical; he was a dreamer, an idealist, a thoughtful student,
much given to speculation about the unknown. I recall vividly
an evening in my youth when some new scientific discovery had
been mentioned in the newspaper. How wonderful it would be,
he said, if communication were indeed established beyond reasonable doubt with the other world, so that those who have gone
before could tell us what that world is like. My mother in the
next room, overhearing, came to the doorway with her dear alertness. "I think it would *not* be wonderful, James. It would be dis-
concerting. For me, one world at a time."

6.

Sir Thomas Browne spoke for more than himself when he discussed in *Urn Burial* the human desire to be remembered. Though
I have little fear of death, yet I cannot contemplate with equanim-
ity the fact that on this earth I shall some day be altogether forgotten, and my place shall know me no more. This sentiment is

not peculiar to me. Every man and woman who thinks at all, recoils from the prospect of mortal oblivion, even though confident of continued existence elsewhere. We combat the thought of a total expunging with what we call none too aptly the desire for fame. The wish to live on men's tongues or on perpetual tombstones is indeed, as Sir Thomas said, ignoble and futile, but to contribute to the inheritance of mankind and in our works to continue even after our names are lost, is a kind of survival neither futile nor unworthy. The hope to gain it spurs us on. Let me correct myself—not the hope to gain, but to deserve it.

Long ago I came on a sentence or two in Sénancour's *Obermann,* a book which, as you recall, Matthew Arnold constantly read and frequently quoted. Sénancour was a resident of Switzerland, a French émigré not conspicuous for boldness in living. He was, in fact, afraid of life, and his book, an autobiography in the form of letters, analyzes and tries to justify his abnormal timidity. But along with the fear he had genius, and these words of his were written by a great soul:

"It may be that after this life we shall perish utterly, but if that is our fate, let us so live that annihilation will be unjust."

CHAPTER X

Politics

1.

"POLITICS" IS A WORD which has richer meanings in life than in the dictionary. It derives from the Greek word for "city." A politician is therefore a citizen, a citizen who governs or helps to govern a city, a citizen who governs the city for his personal advantage, a citizen whose profession is holding office. So the dictionary says, recognizing the shabby decline of a noble idea. To recover somewhat of that nobleness the dictionary advises the use of "statesman."

But when Aristotle made his famous remark, that man is a political animal, he spoke as a scientist, recording essential and permanent characteristics. In his time as in ours well-meaning but stupid folk thought better of themselves for having no traffic with politicians, or for keeping out of politics. In his encyclopedic inventory of Nature's miscellaneous products, Aristotle must have classed these fastidious sniffers or nose-holders, not among the pure, rather among the congenitally blind and the incurably unsocial. Politics cannot be escaped. Every one of us, unless he is Robinson Crusoe, is a politician.

As soon as we are born life defines politics for us in the organization of the family. Here is our first city. The elder generation argue that the Governor or Mayor should be the father, or at least the mother. Nature, which tolerates nonsense so long as her plans are undisturbed, smiles at our slowness to see what daily she spreads before our eyes. In every family there is one character stronger than the others, recognized by them, however unconsciously, as their leader. The primary law of politics, in the family as in larger cities, is that the strongest governs. The strongest may be the father or the mother or a brother or a sister or an uncle or an aunt. A distant relative may guide us, though our parents are nominally in charge. The strong man runs the city, whether or not he holds office.

But the dominant relative heads the family only so long as he leads in the direction the family, as a whole, wish to take. They turn to him by instinct, but by another instinct they would join to get rid of him. He for his part may accept leadership unwillingly, having talents and ambitions which they cannot or would not share, but unless he takes control, a weak sister may take control of him, in which event his only remedy would be separation from his flesh and blood. So he takes command, forestalling revolt by allowing for individual quirks. The rest of the household, recognizing his services and the credit he sheds on them all, humor *his* peculiarities, partly out of gratitude and partly to keep him on the job.

This is politics. The picture would be no truer, however it might be enlarged. The apparent contradiction persists in all human groups, that the strongest rules, yet the majority, the weaker individuals, decide ultimately who shall rule them. Office carries no authority with it, merely the presumption of authority. We expect the father to take charge of his family, but we can do no more than expect; the rest lies with him. We can elect to a title, but not to influence. The strong man brings his strength with him.

The strong man cannot rule unless he understands his fellows, and he will hardly understand them if he doesn't like them. To win their loyalty he must first, on one ground or another, deserve it. Political power does not rest chiefly on self-interest, nor upon ideas; it rests chiefly on affection, even on love. Underestimate this truth, and you'll stub your reforming toe. The ward politician is an open book to his neighbors; they know how the gold got into his pocket but they know also—they have plentiful reason to know—the gold in his heart. You, on your higher plane, they don't know at all; not really caring for them, you give them no occasion to make your acquaintance; your life doesn't meet theirs, you don't know where or how they live, you don't know their names. Last winter during the freezing spell the ward boss sent them a bucket of coal. Now it's freezing again, and here you are, bringing instead of heat a summons to cleaner politics. You're not doing so well, brother. "The hell with it!" say they.

Awkward though it is to press home this truth, yet even the absolute ruler, the despot, the dictator, draws his power from loyal affection. If he is our enemy we tell ourselves his people would throw him out if they could; he rules, we say, by force rather than by willing consent. We deceive ourselves. The affection and the loyalty may be misplaced, but when they come to an end, out he'll go, and not before. Dictators rise on a tide of approval; at first they are in every sense spokesmen and representatives of their people, coming as they usually do from humble conditions. So long as they lead where their people wish to go, they cannot be unhorsed, but when once the opinion spreads that they now drive instead of lead, the devil himself can't keep them in the saddle.

2.

Do you think of justice, of law-making and law-enforcing, as an aspect of politics? If the idea is unpalatable, the reason probably is that the terms need defining. If by politics we mean the influence of office-holders exerted for the benefit of themselves or their party, it will not be surprising if we wish to keep legislation and the courts as far as possible from politics. But if by politics we mean the organizing principle of society and if the processes of justice have for their end the social good, then justice and politics can hardly be kept apart. The wise citizen will not think meanly of politics, even though some politicians are scalawags.

Yet we may still hesitate to identify politics with justice. The reason probably is that we attribute to justice an abstract quality, absolute and enduring; what is just is just, what is unjust is unjust, and the business of the courts is to say which is which, without fear or favor. Justice in that sense is our ideal, certainly, but ideal justice can be defined once for all and enforced without modification only in an ideal world. In life as we know it justice must deal with individual cases, no two of them alike, and laws which seem reasonable, so long as they are not tested by use, have a way, when enforced, of astonishing us by their injustice. We do not doubt that there is an eternal difference between right and wrong, but to make an adequate statement of that difference—at least to make it on the first attempt—is sometimes beyond our power. The best we can do is to recast the law as quickly as we learn its imperfections, and we learn the imperfections, not from the lips of an absolute authority on justice, since no such person exists, but from experience—that is, from contact or conflict with other members of the family or the city, in our efforts to perfect the organization in which we must live.

The difference between justice as ideally conceived and justice in practical application, has troubled the wisest for centuries. It is the theme, you may recall, of Plato's book, the *Republic*. Most of us find significance in the details of the perfect city which it describes—in the startling marriage regulations, for example, the processes by which the most distinguished men and women were to be mated and re-mated and shifted around, to produce the most remarkable children—or in the contrivances by which the most competent citizens would invariably be elected to office. But the Utopia in the *Republic* is offered as a large-scale example of justice, and the example is offered because Socrates and his friends, as Plato tells us in the early pages of the book, cannot agree on a definition. At the end of the *Republic* the reader sees that this ideal example of ideal justice is nothing more nor less than a despotism, benevolent if you choose but still a despotism. Justice, then, is as hard to illustrate as to define. Yet throughout the famous story Socrates is present, one of the justest men who ever lived. Did Plato intend us to conclude that justice, difficult to capture in a definition or in an institution, can easily—or only—be achieved in daily living? Did he mean to say that justice, if it is vital, must be looked for in continuous growth? If that was his intention, it has taken us some time to acquire his view, but we are coming to it at last. Few would now deny that law-making and law-enforcing are among the most human and personal activities of the body politic.

In those early pages of the *Republic* in which the friends of

Socrates try to define abstract justice, one man shocked the others
by saying that justice is the interest of the strongest. They did
their best to refute him, but to their astonishment they made no
headway. Who is the strongest? In a tyranny, the tyrant; in a
democracy, the majority of the people. The friends of Socrates
were bothered by the idea that the interest of the majority, rather
than abstract justice, determined the laws. They were unwilling
to agree that the people as a whole, rather than the legislators,
make the laws. Yet this is the fact, however it may be obscured.
It would be more precise, perhaps, to say that life makes the laws,
our common life, the needs and wants of our common life, some
of which neither the people nor the legislators may entirely realize.
The passing of a statute is an experimental process. The legislature acts in good faith, sincerely hoping the new law is sound, but
we must wait and see. If the law articulates the needs and aspirations of the city, it will be respected. If it has missed the point,
it will be ignored.

As in other aspects of politics, a citizen learns the elements of
justice, even of legislation and law-enforcement, in his earliest
city, the home. The head of the family makes with the other
members certain agreements, which are in essence laws. To fill
the household pocketbook, he will contribute so much a month;
a younger brother, earning less, will contribute a smaller sum;
mother and one sister, perhaps, will market and cook; father,
perhaps, will tend to the rent and the furnace. This arrangement
is flexible, not more flexible than the provisions for justice made
by larger groups, but more obviously so. If brother's earnings
increase, he contributes more to the common purse; if mother is
ill, someone must relieve her at the kitchen stove. The changing
condition of the group, the unequal changes in the condition of
each individual, call for new agreements, if equity is to be maintained.

The problem of justice, of law-making and law-enforcement, is
acute in education, where I have chiefly encountered it. The
school board, the Regents or the college trustees make rules. The
faculty of school or college makes rules. The individual teacher in
his classroom makes rules. All this legislation has a single purpose,
to facilitate the process of education, to guard against abuses, to

set standards of conduct and of intellectual accomplishment. And all this legislation has a single fate; the rules are soon revised, or if not revised, they are soon out of date, and if left on the books they are soon forgotten. If the rules, being true laws, are obeyed, the statute on the books becomes, as Emerson told us, only a memorandum, a rather thin description of an order which is self-enforcing.

I began my teaching at Amherst College. My first class of freshmen stared at me on my twenty-fourth birthday. I had much to learn. Freshman English on that campus had been taught by a great and lovable scholar, himself an accomplished writer, but too much occupied in his researches to correct student themes. Lucky for me he didn't enjoy that fearsome exercise! Because themes were not corrected and with time ceased even to be written, he was asked to give more advanced courses and I, callow and inexpert, was offered a job. The President of the college explained that the boys must be taught to write. He didn't care how I went about it, so long as I produced practical results.

Believing that writing is learned only by writing, I called for two themes a week. There were a hundred and twenty students in the class. The more work I got out of them, the deeper I was submerged. I read themes till my eyes ached, till I recognized a kind of immoral merit in the compositions of the lazy who usually skimped on the number of pages.

My first freshmen class included a generous number of the worst spellers I ever met. After deciphering their orthography for a fortnight or two, I announced a leeway of three misspellings to a six-page theme, but if I came on a fourth I would mark the theme zero and read no more of it. This rule seemed to the boys fair enough. They submitted without protest, though the resulting havoc in their grades was terrible. Perhaps they tried to spell, but the effort was vain. My law, though enforced, was not producing the intended result. Had I been wise, I should have repealed it.

The repealing came from the students, most unexpectedly. One of them, a terrific speller, was also a born writer, and my instruction, I am glad to say, did not stunt his talent. Perhaps he would have come on faster without my help, but the fact is that each

of his themes was more brilliant than the preceding—the villainous quality of the spelling remaining constant. One evening,
under the lamp, wading through the week's crop, I came to his
manuscript. The first page contained a dozen misspellings, the
second page even more. I ought to have marked a zero and
stopped reading, but I couldn't; the theme was too interesting.
It held me from the first word to the last. For a minute or two I
stared at the logs burning in my fireplace. I and my legislation
needed sorting out. After all, the college when it engaged me had
said nothing about spelling; my business was to teach writing.
Here was a boy who *could* write; it was I, God grant, who had
developed in him this ability; how then could I flunk him? I
marked the theme A—, explaining in a note that though the spelling couldn't be worse, there were extenuating qualities in the
writing, as writing.

Next day I returned the themes, and my promising author must
have passed his around. By nightfall most of the other hundred
and nineteen had called at my study, each bringing his bundle
of goose eggs.

"Professor, when you marked this essay, could you by chance
have overlooked some extenuating circumstances?"

I replied, of course, that the literary quality of the manuscript
had made no lasting impression on me.

"But Professor, didn't you tell us that you always stopped reading when you came to the fourth misspelling? I misspelled five
times on the first page. May it not be that the literary virtues of
my composition lie in the following pages which you never read?
May I ask you to look the themes over again to be quite sure?"

Their position was flawless, but I had no intention of rereading
five or six hundred themes. I revised the rule. I said four misspellings would produce a flunk *unless* the literary quality stunned
me so completely that I couldn't see the misspellings. I can't say
I saved my face. The class laughed. They knew as well as I that
my well-intended legislation was on the scrap heap.

The law-making of school or college faculties runs, as I've
noticed, through a well-defined cycle. Teachers agree, as citizens
do everywhere, that the fewer rules, the better. School and college
faculties would gladly rely for discipline on the common sense

and the sound heart of the students and on the influence of their own good example. Sooner or later, however, some student does something of which they don't approve. To protect the school's name they must notice the offense, but when they have the culprit on the carpet they can't punish him for doing what they never told him not to do, so they pass a rule at once telling him not to do it. Crisis of this kind follows crisis, until the book of rules is so jammed that no one remembers clearly what has been forbidden. The time is now ripe for some student, accused of transgression, to make the sincere-sounding plea that though he meant to read the code entire, he was too busy with his studies and therefore never got as far as this particular rule. Overcome by obvious good sense, the faculty then votes to abolish all rules and to rely on the intelligence and honor of the students, and on the influence of their own good example.

When I came back to Columbia to teach, Fred Keppel was the young Dean of the College, an intelligent and humane citizen if there ever was one! He stimulated in us all a watchfulness for the students' needs, and a lively attention to their complaints. In principle he was right. Though we don't always admit it, the development of a school is ultimately determined by the community which it serves—let's complete the picture, by the community which pays for it. The development is determined by the whole community, of which the students are only a part, but they are at least the spearhead of influence.

The boys in Columbia College at that time felt that contact with their teachers was not sufficiently personal. Dean Keppel therefore proposed, and his faculty most cordially agreed, that he should assign to each of us, on their request or his own initiative, ten students who should have the privilege of calling upon us as their advisor on any subject at any time. We on our part were expected to cultivate our advisees, to consider them, academically speaking, our nearest relatives.

No question but the Dean had proposed, and we had established, an excellent institution, but at the end of two years we all testified that not a single student had asked advice on any subject but this—how to break a college rule. Just before each new term one of my boys would come to my office, a catalog in his hand.

"Professor, I want to take this course in Sociology, and it says here that History A is a prerequisite. I didn't take History A. What shall I do?"

I might have told him to take History A. But he didn't come for that advice, and had he expected it from me, he wouldn't have given me the pleasure of conversing with him at that moment. I helped him, of course, to beat the rule. Naturally, I spoke to the Dean and secured his hearty cooperation.

In a college which I know well and greatly admire, recent legislation by the trustees, enacted for excellent reasons, has produced undesirable results. I describe the case to complete the illustration of the law-maker's problems even in a comparatively small field. The college of which I speak owns most of the houses in which its teachers live, and in these difficult times additional building is impossible. The trustees felt compelled to rule that all professors, when retired on their pensions, should move out, to make room for their successors. The expectation was, I suppose, that they would find other homes further from the campus but still in the same town. But since moving was obligatory, most of them have gone far, attracted by a gentler climate or by lower costs of living. The loss to the college is great. A widely known and well-loved teacher strengthens a school by his presence, by his continued association with new students, by his inspiration to the new faculty. The trustees are not happy in the result of their action. Yet what else, in the circumstances, could they have done? They wished to be just. How just were they? And how flexible is their law? Could they make an exception in favor of one faculty veteran without affront and injury to the others?

3.

Someone in every body politic, in a group no larger than the family or no smaller than the state, must act as head or leader. But the organization of human society is far from simple; most of us belong to several groups at the same time, and in each group we probably occupy a different position. Though not the head of our family, we may be the head of our class in school; though not the head of the class, we may be captain of the football team. Only the rarest of personalities will be the leader in all groups, only an exceptional weakling will lead in no group. Man, the political animal, aspires to a society which shall resemble the corps at West Point, where even those who for the moment drill in the ranks, are training to be leaders. No individual life is complete without the experience of leadership, and though some men and women lead by instinct, the principles of the art might as well occupy our attention before they are driven into us by hard knocks.

In the simplest terms, a leader is one who knows where he wants to go, and gets up and goes. Decision of any kind is attractive; he will have a following at once, even though—or because—his destination is not known. In time, however, feet are sure to weary, and the owners of the feet will ask the leader where he is leading them to, and if they don't like the answer they'll go home, whereupon the leader automatically is a leader no more. He probably will say he is just as glad; he didn't ask them to come; they forced leadership on him, by following. This, as I say, is leadership in its simplest form. From your experience you can supply many illustrations of it; from public life you will recall how this man or that appeared temporarily above the heroism, had a large following, then disappeared. I do not here refer to would-be leaders who fail, but rather to those who, doubtless to their own surprise, are hailed as leaders simply because they go somewhere, and who are deserted because their direction doesn't interest the community as a whole. I assume also in this example of leadership in its most elementary form that the temporary leader does not try to gather followers nor to retain their loyalty.

Decision is the first mark of a leader. Any human being of course should be able to decide, but most of us lack the courage; timidity is confused in our self-flattering thought with judicial reservation of judgment. Instead of a frontal attack upon life, we wait to see what life will do to us. That this philosophy is wrong is proved by our admiration of the men who don't follow it. Viewed in the large, human experience is much the same from age to age, but to each of us individually it unfolds in a process of change, so that our affairs six months from now will present a problem other than that we face today. If it seems otherwise, if we think there is no change, we are deceived. He who knows how to live keeps up with the changes; he who knows how to use his imagination keeps ahead of the changes; he who has the principle of leadership in him, helps to bring the changes about.

Unless you agree with me here, you may class me among the ultra-liberals or the ultra-radicals, or whatever is your pet name for subversive folk. There are destructive spirits in the world, of course there are! But it is hard to see how anyone can lead a complete life or even a mildly satisfying one without accepting the condition of ceaseless change. It is a saying among educators that any school which for five years teaches exactly the same courses in exactly the same way, had better look to itself; it will soon be out of date. As a matter of fact, it is already out of date if for one year it has no new ideas. If your business satisfies you, and if you hope to continue it just as it is, you are heading toward failure. If your private life repeats itself comfortably in one channel, it must contain too large an element of mortality. We either go on or we die. By instinct we hail a leader as a bringer of salvation.

But if the leader is content with his salvation-bringing, he too plans his downfall. He owed his rise to his ability to make decisions; he can perpetuate his influence only by fostering the same ability in his followers. It is not difficult to recognize this truth in the merely famous, a fairly large number, who led their country for a comparatively short time, and in the immortal, the very few, whose leadership outlasted their day. The short career is his who is jealous of others, who wants no strong men around him. The permanent influence rewards him who calls to his aid his outstanding rivals. In our country popular judgment pronounces Washington and Lincoln supreme leaders, for this reason, more than any other, that they gathered greatness around them. Neither was afraid to include in his cabinet personalities hostile or discordant, but also powerful. Though Lincoln touches us by his warmth of heart and his personal charm, by his humble birth and his poverty, by the pathos of his death, yet Washington was probably our noblest politician and our ablest; he attracted

to himself men qualified to succeed him in office, and he retired
from office so that by their succession democracy as he conceived
it might endure. Whether Lincoln would have attained this
grandeur of vision, we do not know, since he died early, but
affection persuades us he would.

You and I face the problem on an infinitely more modest scale,
but we do face it. In business, in education, in the local parish
church, in the club, in the family, it is not enough to have behind
us what we call a strong organization; we must raise up those
who will carry on, and when they are ready, we must step back,
to give them room.

In my university life I had the privilege of working for many
years under a great leader, Nicholas Murray Butler, my University's President. Though he may read these lines, and though he
has no need of commendation, I would here pay tribute to his
extraordinary quality. With many of his ideas I did not in my
student days agree; some of the directions in which he led Columbia while I was teaching there, I would not myself have chosen;
some of his dearest hopes for the world I do not, in detail, share;
but his unique position in our body politic results from incomparable leadership. I once heard him say, quoting an English
statesman, that we can get almost anything accomplished in this
world if we do not ask for the credit. The anonymous English
statesman may have said this, but the idea must have been in
Doctor Butler's bones. So far as I could see, it made no difference
to him as President of the University whether or not a teacher
agreed with him, so long as the teacher in his field was competent,
and competence was understood to include imagination, initiative, the ability to produce new ideas, the ability to lead. He
not only backed us up, he pushed us forward. Some of my colleagues opposed me, with sincerity and firmness, when I first
suggested the so-called Honors Course in the reading of great
books. Doctor Butler's prompt and unequivocal support, when
the proposal came before him, saved me from defeat. When I
was asked to take charge of the Juilliard School of Music, I went
to him for advice, half hoping he would tell me not to accept;
much as I loved music, I thought my path lay in teaching and in
writing. But he told me to go, though I cherish the notion that

he didn't wish to get rid of me. As I remember his words, they were something like this: "In this life you can't say no to a call for help, not if it's genuine. These people think they need you or they wouldn't ask you. They believe you can do for them what they want. If you too believe you can, you have no choice; do it!" He said other things too which amounted to a counsel of faith: Accept for the guidance of your career the leadership of life itself, by responding, so far as you can, to every serious call.

From his practice I learned this rule of leadership, that our colleagues old or young, so long as they are our colleagues, are the best of men, deserving the last ounce of loyalty. It isn't probable that he admired us all with the same degree of enthusiasm, but no difference showed in his frequent public mention of us. He played us up as masters in our field, and though we sometimes doubted if he really knew us well, we were of course willing to be convinced that he was right, and we tried more nearly to justify him. In his ripe years he may now contemplate the rich result of his humane labors, not only in the University which he built but in the students and teachers who have gone out to build elsewhere.

The true leader knows well the principle I mentioned before, that his authority comes not from his position but from himself. We can persuade by personality, by example, and by ideas, but not by commands. The good sense of Doctor Butler's remark about getting things done without asking credit, lies in this, that in order to turn a weak follower into a strong leader you must help him to outgrow his weakness, which usually is nothing but lack of self-confidence. How can young people gain confidence except by a series of successes which they know they have earned? A true leader, anxious for their progress in maturity, gives them all the credit they deserve, or even a little more. It's an investment of faith. When baby son or daughter is learning to walk, we help by ecstatic applause, which to say truth the wobbly performance doesn't yet warrant, but in a few days it will. We might of course leave the child to its unencouraged tottering, and in due time, no doubt, it would without us use its legs, but not necessarily with boldness. Swiftness of locomotion may be found in scared rabbits. Some among us will protest that the best education is grim experience, that the young, or those of any age who have not yet found themselves, should be tossed into life to sink or swim. If there is a philosophy more brutal or more stupid, I don't know it. Were we all dropped into this maelstrom, most of us would sink and the survivors would be permanently scarred by terror. Where, meanwhile, would the person be standing who gave the cruel advice? Would he be looking on, collecting statistics of the struggle, adding up the score?

We sometimes speak as though the apprentice system had gone entirely from our modern life, as though the duty of the elder generation to train up its successors were fulfilled by proxy, through persons or institutions which do nothing but teach; but wherever there is leadership we may be sure that in some form and to some degree the apprentice system survives. We don't invite our youngest employee to jump into our private business and see what he can do with it, sink or swim; even if he survived, the business might not.

4.

A true leader in any field—science, statecraft, religion, sport— is consciously or unconsciously an educator. He shows the way. He explains why one direction is taken rather than another. He puts heart into the travel-worn. Like other good teachers he ought to be, if he succeeds he must be, a keen psychologist. Causes operate to produce effects in human character, as elsewhere, but since personalities differ, each particular kind must be recognized promptly and furnished with the special inspiration he needs. The ward politician who knows how to handle men or "situations," relies on no rigid formula.

To observe accurately the present condition of a person is, for a leader, not enough. He must have the rare kind of imagination which foresees what, in the process of time, the person will become. If I am only a moderately capable teacher, I probably can measure the knowledge or the ignorance of my student, and impart to him what momentarily he lacks. But this is a short-sighted kind of education. A great teacher, foreseeing growth and providing for it, will put the student in the way of acquiring later whatever he later may need. I speak here of teachers—let me remind the reader again—because all leadership has the quality of education. The problem, here described, I have met in the classroom and in the administrator's office. It would not be difficult to administer the affairs of an organization if nothing more were wanted than mere housekeeping from day to day; but to select assistants who will grow with their work, to start them toward posts more and more responsible, to impart to them the wish and the ability to train others, is difficult indeed.

When I was Chairman of the Army Educational Commission in the A.E.F., the military commander of the A.E.F. University at Beaune was Colonel Ira L. Reeves, a professional soldier, as true a leader as I have ever met. Having the gift of leadership, he was temperamentally an educator. I recall his delight in the fact that our art school offered courses, not only in portrait or landscape painting, but also in sign painting. I recall almost his exact words—"That's *my* idea of it—see what a man knows and give him a send-off toward knowing more." One of the soldier students had earned his living—a poor living—painting signs. After an excellent course in lettering he came home to a job which brought him three times his former wage, and he had acquired not only this one technique, but also an insight into the general principles of design.

Until the Mexican incident took Colonel Reeves into the army again, he had served as President of Norwich University, the well-known military school. One of his faculty was an engineer of promise whom the Colonel wished to advance in his profession. As I heard the story, he asked the engineer to make a study of the roads in the neighborhood, with suggestions as to their improvement. Though this invitation must have seemed rather blind, the engineer did what he was asked to do, and did it well. Colonel Reeves had the report printed and widely distributed, with the immediate result that the engineer was asked by neighboring counties—if I am not mistaken, by neighboring states—to tell them what to do with their roads. In no time at all he was recognized as an expert in the field.

The Colonel wore many decorations, among them some notable insignia for marksmanship. When I asked him about this skill with rifle and pistol, he said he wouldn't care to lead any regiment in which there were better marksmen than himself. "An officer, to be worth his salt, must be one jump ahead of his men."

The true leader's ability to estimate the latent talents of his followers was illustrated at the Juilliard School by Paul Kochanski, the violinist. He was a great player, a great teacher, and a guiding spirit in whatever group he found himself. His colleagues still speak with respectful envy of his almost unerring skill in judging candidates for entrance to the school. It happened more than once that they were of a mind to reject a candidate, but he would protest, insisting on some sign of promise which they had overlooked. Seldom indeed was he mistaken. On the other hand, they occasionally admired a candidate in whom he foresaw no further growth. Since he was kind and modest, he would not insist on barring the youngster from an opportunity, but few showed talent later if he had found in advance no reason for expecting them to do so.

The citizen who is called upon to govern the state, or otherwise to serve the body politic in a post of leadership, must foresee the development not only of individuals but also of situations. With practice and with a modest share of this prophetic wisdom, those engaged in public affairs acquire a sense of cause and effect, at least over a brief arc of time. The man whose vision extends only a short distance ahead of him is what we usually call, in the derogatory sense, a politician. If he is very short-ranged, we call him an opportunist. If, however, he looks far ahead, even beyond his own lifetime, we call him a statesman. The difference is significant, as we correctly feel. The far-sighted politician, whose eye is on benefits which he himself may never enjoy, is likely to be less selfish than he who sees only from month to month or from year to year. Yet the difference between the short-sighted and the far-sighted politician remains relative; the statesman cannot look so far ahead as he would.

Even the partial recognition of cause and effect in life is made possible for us, we believe, by the existence of universal and eternal laws. We perhaps occupy too small a corner of the universe to grasp entirely any one law, but great politicians in the right sense of the word—great citizens, governors, teachers, leaders —know that whenever they succeed, even for a short time, their strength comes from harmony with an order larger and more lasting than themselves. When we chop wood, we don't hang the log on the ceiling and raise the axe against it; we lay the log on the ground and let gravitation do most of the work. When a leader of a country finds himself, as we say, in an irresistible current of history, he goes far; when he fights against it he is lost, no matter what the merits of his personal character. What I remind you of here, has nothing at all to do with the time-serving which steers by popularity. If ever a man had the universal tide with him, it was Abraham Lincoln, yet until after his assassination he was not a popular leader, not even in the North. He was a minority candidate, in a sense a minority President. Robert E. Lee, on the other hand, enjoyed and deserved a personal prestige which went far beyond ordinary hero-worship, yet the cause for which he fought was lost before the fight began.

There is a paradox here which I almost hesitate to mention for fear we may confuse ourselves. Where does the great politician, the great statesman, seek the universal laws? In his own instincts undoubtedly, but also in the will of all his followers. I have just reminded you that he does not rely on popularity; I now say that he finds the universal laws in the will of the people. The paradox is more apparent than real. The universal order which takes the race of human beings aeon after aeon down the appointed path, can be studied now in the race of human beings, not in a few individuals but in all humanity. When a man appears in touch with humanity, it is easy to believe that he is in touch also with the larger will. Emerson said that Lincoln was himself the history of the American people in his time. "Step by step he walked before them; slow with their slowness, quickening his march by theirs, the true representative of this continent; an entirely public man; father of his country, the pulse of twenty millions throbbing in his heart, the thought of their minds articulated by his tongue."

The conviction that there is indeed a universal order which reveals itself most clearly in the general will of mankind, accounts for the gradual adoption of the representative principle in government. Since it would be impractical for all of us to manage our public interests, we delegate certain of our rights to a few fellow citizens, who exercise them for us. The right of self-defense, for example, belongs to us all; if we chose to do so we could all sit up every night watching for a possible burglar, but it's more practical to engage one of our number to do the watching for us. This is the principle of democratic government. Theoretically our representatives may exercise only the rights which we delegate. If government, instead of carrying out our will, uses its delegated powers to coerce us, a reform of some kind is necessary— and inevitable. Dictators, by substituting their own will for the will of the people, guarantee that their rule, however protracted, will not be permanent.

When the American colonies obtained their freedom, and when the Constitutional Convention devised the form of government which with some amendments the colonies adopted, the theories which I have here summarized were already well known, but they were not widely nor completely held. To the makers of our Constitution, the will of the people was something to guard against. The delegates to the Convention showed in their discussions a reluctance to elect the President or any other officer by direct popular vote. Their point of view can be understood. In the various colonies the poorer citizens were known to favor the printing of paper money and other wild financial or economic schemes. In the Convention it was proposed at one time, by way of caution, that no one should be elected to Congress who was not a land owner. There was a strong sentiment for the protection of property as well as of human rights. It is not surprising after such debate that passionate advocates of human rights often describe the Founding Fathers as property-minded. Yet the Constitution, as it was finally adopted, did give the ballot to all free males over twenty-one, and underlying other arguments for this step was the belief, held with varying degrees of conviction, that right political courses can be determined by the will of the whole people.

This conviction grows, though even today we do not hold it absolutely. Women now vote as well as men. Theoretically the colored race now votes. But where the white man still lacks faith in democracy, by extra legal pressures he deprives the colored race of the right which the Constitution guarantees. If the country as a whole tolerates this defiance, it is probably because we believe the injustice wears itself out and will in time disappear—perhaps also because we believe that the universal laws operate to the disadvantage of those who defy them. Where the will of the people is not fully trusted and therefore not ascertained, the body politic is less strong than it should be. Of two states side by side, in one of which all men and women vote, and in the other only a privileged minority, the undemocratic state is backward, however careful we are not to say so out loud.

It may be that the torment of the world, in the midst of which these pages are written, will compel us to advance more rapidly toward the democratic ideal. It may be that the confusion produced by the will of dictators may force us to seek more earnestly the will of God, as he discloses it to the heart of men. The universal order has its own way of punishing the transgressor; it may be that we ourselves are among the transgressors. The prospect is not very bright for special privilege. Since the white race apparently could by no other discipline be taught to respect the equal rights of the black, the brown, the red, and the yellow, it may be that the eternal justice has placed us in dire need of their fellowship and aid. The course in politics is compulsory.

A friend of mine, a shrewd student of politics, told me long ago that every human being should cast a vote, and that those of us who feared the result are little short of fools. All classes of men, he said, will divide on most questions, but they will divide always in the same proportions. I told my friend he sounded rather cynical; he would give the ballot to the ignorant as a sop to their wish to have a place in the body politic, but he was willing to do this only because he believed their votes would cancel out, so that he, or men like him, would still control the state. He replied with some warmth that though differences of opinion would probably occur in the same proportion, no matter how many people voted, yet the effect on the voters would be not at all the same. Each individual, having articulated his choice, would be more aware of that choice. We might come a little nearer to thinking of ourselves not as dispossessed souls carried along by the class which is in possession, but as integral members of society.

5.

It is often said that the purest example of democracy in the United States is the New England town meeting. Perhaps this legend does injustice to other examples, but it appeals to me because, though not by birth a New Englander, I have lived in two places where the town meeting still functions. During the six years I taught at Amherst no citizen stayed away from those almost painfully public sessions in which the township's expenditures, and therefore next year's tax rate, would be fixed. Since I then owned no property, the tax was not for me a matter of great concern, but I was fascinated nonetheless by the demonstration of government in the open. Certain charges on the town—for water supply, for electricity, for police and fire protection, for education, for health services—were fairly constant, yet even these items provoked annual challenges from the floor; a surprising number of voters, having kept lynx eyes on the yearly financial statement of the public utility companies, were ready with suggestions as to how the electricity could be produced and the water furnished at lower cost. If a new street was proposed, or if you wished the sidewalk repaired in front of your house, the street or the repairs became an item on the agenda, which was printed and circulated among the citizenry. You were then asked in public what repairs your sidewalk needed and how much you thought it would cost. If you put the figure too high, some neighbor would protest that he could make the repairs for twenty-five cents less; in that case he'd probably be asked by the moderator to take the job—unless some other citizen offered to do it for a smaller sum. When all proposals and requests had been considered and voted, the total amount would be the budget for the following year. Knowing the assessed property values and the amount received from poll taxes, each citizen could figure for himself the new tax rate, and we all did figure it before we left the Town Hall.

Since the appropriations covered every side of the community life, you couldn't attend the town meeting without becoming a fairly well-rounded citizen. You would think of the public school as one of your essential enterprises, along with the police department, the fire department, and the hospital. You acquired the conviction, perhaps after that incident of the repairs to your sidewalk, that the complete citizen must be in every good sense a politician—that is, he must not only be familiar with municipal business, but he must know how to get on with his fellow citizens. Life is a very personal matter; it never seemed to me more personal than in the Amherst town meeting. I intend a tribute. It was to the interest of every man there to see that no more money was spent than was strictly needed. For that reason the men were there in force, and the women too, although in those days women didn't vote. They were difficult to persuade. If you wished their support, you had to win it.

Many years later I attended the town meetings of Wilton, Connecticut, a smaller place but of the same democratic tradition. One episode in particular stays in my memory. Wilton is a fairly large township, at that time sparsely settled. In each district there was a small one-room schoolhouse where children of different ages and grades were instructed by a single teacher. The older families had been rooted on the Wilton soil for generations. Their children now had their education in the same modest buildings which their fathers, perhaps their grandfathers, formerly attended. More recently, however, newer families had moved in from larger towns. It was proposed to the Wilton meeting that a central school should be built, spacious and modern, and that the children from the districts should be brought in buses to enjoy the advantage of graded instruction in the most fortunate environment. The proposal, after heated discussion through many meetings, was at last adopted.

The resistance to it surprised me, yet before the debate concluded, my respect had risen for the resisters. I doubt if they had put their heads together to organize any opposition; each followed his impulse. They were not sure that the new facilities would be necessarily more adequate; they thought the instruction in a small schoolroom would be good if the teacher was competent, and that instruction in a modern building would be poor if the teacher wasn't competent; they thought a small schoolhouse crowded would perhaps be no worse than a large schoolhouse crowded. I can't say they were mistaken. Their schoolhouse was built at last, the news of it attracted many residents who wished better opportunities for their children, and as a result the new building was inadequate from the day of its opening. Evidently the old residents felt by instinct what the modern theorists overlooked, that the advisability of putting up a new schoolhouse could not be determined by educational arguments. The question was whether the town wanted a larger school or a larger population.

Here I hasten to say that I am not arguing for the ungraded school as against modern buildings and modern teaching; I merely point out that unless all the laws of life are reckoned with, our best intentions may produce astonishing results.

6.

In small places democracy may be direct; in large cities it must be representative. We may be good citizens in our immediate neighborhood, friends of all with whom we come in contact, sympathetic with their good and bad fortune, as they are sympathetic with ours, but to maintain any such relation with millions of people is impossible. Large cities, therefore, break up into small units which may or may not correspond with the wards or districts into which the map is officially divided. We tend to associate with others of our profession or trade, no matter in what part of the city they live. So in the vast body politic which is our country; cross-sections of it we may partly know, but we cannot live in all of it at once, and direct citizenship is found only where political life begins, at home. We can be active in neighborhood politics; through our representatives we take part in city politics, and through other representatives in state and national politics. It is important, as we are often reminded, to choose able men to represent us, but it is still more important to keep them informed as to our wishes. In us, not taken singly but listened to as a total group, our representative finds whatever inkling he has of the people's will.

Yet if the New England town meeting is called the purest form of democracy which still exists among us, we should remind ourselves that definitions of democracy vary and change. No two countries have entirely agreed as to whether a democratic state is one in which there is representative government or one in which all men are actually as well as theoretically free and equal. The democracy of England was never quite like that of France, nor the democracy of France exactly like that of the United States, nor our democracy quite like the democracy of contemporary Russia. All these countries I have no doubt are democratic. If we wish, we can make them all seem to resemble each other, or we can make them seem headed in different directions.

I believe the essence of democracy lies in an attitude toward our fellows rather than in any particular political or economic system. For nearly two hundred years the democratic spirit has been working like yeast throughout the western world and in large sections of the Orient. For a complete grasp of politics today, understanding and sympathy with that ferment is essential. In my youth I read Montesquieu's *Spirit of the Laws,* and was fascinated by his contrast of different modes of government, but as an American I marveled at his distrust of the common people. Knowing the influence he exerted on early American political thought, I assumed that he would have approved of our Constitution in the form in which it was adopted—would have approved, that is, of a government based upon the popular vote, with certain checks and balances. It was disturbing to learn that he approved of no such thing, and still more disturbing to learn that our Founders, when they met to frame the Constitution, shared in large measure his dread of what the people, with power in their hands, might do. But I now find encouragement in the fact that the ancient distrust was displaced in the new world by faith in the ultimate soundness of man's common instincts and common judgment. The political animal must trust his brothers. Heaven knows how far we are from satisfactory demonstration of that confidence, but it is our goal and we move toward it.

Admirable though the town meeting is as a democratic mechanism, it is still possible for some who speak on the floor of those sessions to regard their fellow citizens with snobbishness, with prejudice, or with fear. To know the procedure by which we govern ourselves and to play our part in it, is an obligation we cannot escape. I wouldn't call education complete unless the schools teach our children the fabric of our political society, and the processes by which that society is maintained. But our private lives are not complete unless our hearts as well as our minds accord to every member in the family the rights and privileges which we ask for ourselves. I wish I could suggest exercises in humanity, as in other chapters I have suggested exercises in music or in writing, but perhaps the titanic convulsions through which our civilization now passes will prove to be the discipline we need.

In my student days much emphasis was laid on economics. History, even personal biography, was interpreted by sordid motives. Only yesterday the new era in Russia was attacked or defended as a conflict between Communism and Capitalism; Karl Marx was a name to bandy about, and the Communist Manifesto was praised or damned, whether or not in either case it had been carefully read. But I never was persuaded that man is chiefly an economic appetite, and the developments in Russia have confirmed rather than shaken my faith that every one of us is first of all a spirit, a soul. Russia today is an illustration, not of prosperity, but of the human family organized to advance and defend an ideal. I doubt very much if that ideal has much connection with economics; I believe the astounding unity of the Russian people results from the practice at last of that human democracy which we have long professed, the abolition of race, religious, or color prejudice, the granting of equal opportunity to all, and of honor to every man and woman, according to the use made of opportunity.

Twenty years ago we still could hold the primitive doctrine that superior races should control the inferior, ourselves of course being by definition very superior, and rather permanently so. But only the thick-skinned unteachables advocate that doctrine now. The mills of the gods do grind.

CHAPTER XI

Love

1.

WHEN I WAS a student in the University, and later during my teaching years, I heard often the name of George Santayana, the exquisite New England-Spanish scholar who lectured on philosophy at Harvard and wrote—and still writes—some of the most beautiful prose in the English language. His judgment of books was, and is, illuminating, but of literary critics we have, even without him, a formidable supply, and I am indebted to him rather for insights into daily life, a service which is the more striking since he is one of the last surviving inhabitants of the Ivory Tower. His philosophical masterpiece, I suppose, is the *Life of Reason,* which in its five volumes expounds, for various departments of experience, the philosophy of naturalism which at the turn of the century he held. More recently he has modified his account of the universe, or so, at least, I understand from those who should know.

Fine books fade too quickly. I doubt if many of us are now familiar with the *Life of Reason.* We nudge ourselves to recall *The Last Puritan,* that magnificent novel of Santayana's which only yesterday took us by storm. But I am faithful to books once admired, and some words of his I know by heart. One passage provides a springboard for this chapter. I quote it from *Reason in Society,* the second volume of the *Life of Reason.*

"Love is a brilliant illustration of a principle everywhere discoverable: namely, that human reason lives by turning the friction of material forces into the light of ideal goods. There can be no philosophic interest in disguising the animal bases of love, or in denying its spiritual sublimations, since all life is animal in its origin and all spiritual in its possible fruits."

I quote these sentences with admiration, but as you will see, not with unreserved approval. They present a striking truth which we cannot afford to overlook, yet they make it too simple and perhaps they emphasize the wrong end of it. That life may be animal in its origin and spiritual in its possible fruits, is illustrated by what was said of table etiquette, in an earlier chapter. It is natural to be hungry, and if we were merely animals the dinner table would be merely a feeding trough, but because we have other than bodily hungers we deliberately convert by our manners the consumption of food into an opportunity for intelligent and spiritual companionship. Shall we say we should never desire that companionship unless we first were hungry? Is the soul a product or "fruit" of nature?

There are many who think it is, but if you have read thus far in my book you know I am not of their number. To understand love we must understand sex, but they are not one and the same thing. Indeed, the problem of love, the most difficult of human problems, is to establish between body and soul a harmony which without the exercise of our will does not exist. At puberty sex unleashes its tremendous force, an energy which may either serve or enslave us. We are conscious of it as an energy of the body. But the soul also has its energies, which possess us long before we feel the urge of sex. From the moment we are aware of life we have our dreams and our ideals. Romance and love do not follow the awakening of sex; they precede it. Life would be simple if sex, when it stirs at last, gave aid and comfort to romance and love, but it does no such thing. Fables like *Daphnis and Chloe* are wishful thinking, written in decadent moments of sophisticated civilization by authors jaded with experience, who seek escape from difficult decisions by inventing a world in which no decision need be made.

I have known men and women who delighted in *Daphnis and Chloe* but derided the *Vita Nuova*, Dante's account of his love for Beatrice. The old Greek pastoral, they said, expresses an ideal and in that sense is profoundly true, but what sensible person

believes that a boy fell in love, once for all, at the age of nine?
Or that the unexpected sight of his beloved made him faint? Yet
children do fall in love even though their elders do not take them
seriously. To say that a child's romance is not serious, is to pronounce a permanent judgment on character. The deep heart is
always deep. Dante's fainting would now be peculiar, I admit,
but in his time it did not seem so. The sensitive, both men and
women, fainted easily then, just as in the nineteenth century
sensitive women blushed. They blush no longer. Fainting and
blushing are acquired fashions. It's as easy to learn to faint and
blush as to learn not to.

But love, with or without fainting, is as inevitable as sex, and
it comes to us earlier. Why speak of it as the "fruit" of a natural
impulse which comes later? Why aren't the motions of the quick
soul as "natural" as those of the sluggish body? Why should not
our own experience correct a lopsided account of life?

I first read the *Vita Nuova* in my graduate years at the University. The professor of Italian was Carlo Leonardo Speranza, a
man of singular nobility, who treated his students as his equals,
which we by no means were. One of us challenged Dante's
precocity.

"You really don't believe, Professor, do you, that a boy of nine
was bowled over this way by a girl he hadn't even spoken to?"

Professor Speranza smiled amiably, leaned back in his chair,
took out his handkerchief, took off his glasses, began polishing
the lenses.

"When I was somewhat older than Dante, perhaps ten or
eleven, I walked past a house which had a balcony, two or three
stories up, and on the balcony was a little girl. I did not see her
face, but she had beautiful curls and I fell in love with her—
desperately, I assure you. Every day for a week I walked past, had
my glimpse of the curly head, and lived on the memory until I
walked again. At the end of the week, just as I was straining my
neck in bliss, a woman came out and carried off the curly head.
It was a flower pot. Only on the first day had it been a little girl."

We laughed with him, and the skeptical student said, "I suppose
you never saw her again, Professor?"

The spectacles were put into place, the handkerchief went back into his pocket, the text of the *Vita Nuova* was lifted from the desk, the face lost its smile.

"Until God took her from me, she was my dear wife."

Very few of us can be faithful all our days to a romance begun in childhood. What usually happens is that the child's first love leaves its mark on later romances. Or it may be nearer truth to say that child-love discloses the pattern of all the love to follow. Time makes less difference to the spirit than to the body. With no intention of matching myself against Dante, nor even of setting up a parallel with Professor Speranza, I recall vividly the day I was first conscious of having lost my heart. I was somewhere around eight years old, younger than the Florentine poet and otherwise distinguishable from him. I describe the incident, not because I think it extraordinary, but on the contrary, because I believe it very common.

It occurred in church on the afternoon of a sunny Easter day. I mention the church, not to suggest here a religious influence but to explain a tendency I have had ever since to associate love with music. The singing of the choir impressed me deeply, and I listened to it with my eyes on a little girl, very little indeed, who sat with her elders in a near-by pew. She wore a white dress with a pink sash, a pink bow at her neck, and a broad, white hat trimmed with pink ribbon. Her hair was brownish, and her face, as the story books of the time would have said, was demure and sweet. I don't know who she was, and I never saw her again, but she made an impression which is vivid to this day—a spiritual impact, awakening my imagination to the beauty of this world. I remember clearly in what a daze I walked home with my parents, how urgently I needed solitude to think over what had happened, in what a surge of beatitude I paced the narrow hall which led to our library, feeling with a kind of triumph the new pulse of my soul.

The ecstasy which I then felt was self-sufficient; I don't recall that I wished to meet the child or to see her again. I had no further need of her. She had given me something which would be mine always. Do you say, therefore, that what I fell in love with was not the girl, but myself, or some ideal which supplemented myself? I agree with you. If love began with an animal impulse, we should proceed immediately to possess one of the opposite sex, but childhood experience before sex is awakened is the key to mature experience and to its problems. Grown men and women, like children, fall in love with themselves, with the ideals which are the energizing part of themselves, the difference between the children and the mature being this, that until sex is roused we are content with our ideal, but later we insist on imposing that ideal upon a specific person. To multiply difficulties for ourselves we cherish the flattering notion that this person was destined to be ours, that we and our affinity have met at last. Do you recall the wistful laughter which George Meredith, in *The Ordeal of Richard Feverel,* expends upon this pathetic illusion?

" 'You for me: I for you!'

" 'We are born for each other!'

"They believe that the angels have been busy about them from their cradles. The celestial hosts have worthily striven to bring them together. And, O victory! O wonder! after toil and pain, and difficulties exceeding, the celestial hosts have succeeded!"

If the relatives and friends at a wedding ceremony looked on with clear eyes, they would see two ideals, two preconceptions, plighting their troth and promising to live happily together. The wildest of promises, the least predictable of experiments! They would foresee for bride and groom an inevitable surprise as they gradually make each other's acquaintance, and thereafter a possible disappointment, a possible surrender of the ideal, a possible compromise and adjustment, or in the happiest event, a creative miracle achieved by both lovers, each discerning what ideal the other fell in love with, each for love's sake striving to make the ideal come true.

Here in outline is the problem of love, inescapable for any of us whether we marry or not, whether we remain celibate or whether we yield to nature's hungers. The tide of sex breaks upon us all, the power of ideals will not let us go; we must either be torn apart by a war between body and soul, or we must take command of all our energies and unite them.

2.

Because the soul speaks first in us and because the hungers of the body, when at last they make themselves known, are not identical with our spiritual ideals, some of us treat sex as though it were ignoble, and some of us still more tragically turn our eyes away, as though sex were indecent. We might as well hope to ignore gravitation. Nature may be unwelcome, but in spite of many invitations she refuses to go out of existence, and so long as we live the body as well as the soul, each in its sphere, insists on being respected. Love is the most personal of experiences. Sex is the most impersonal of forces. Our inescapable task is to take command of the natural force without diminishing it. It was not by accident that Greek sculptors, poets and philosophers used the horse as the image or symbol of natural impulse. The rider tames the horse, but not by weakening it. The soul on its heavenly ride must control the steeds of its chariot, but the more fiery the steeds, the more heavenly is the ride.

If we try to simplify the problem of control by pretending that sex is a disreputable nuisance, nature takes her revenge by tying us into psychological tangles and knots. To represent nature as evil is cowardly, and to destroy or atrophy a natural force would be a form of suicide. Nature is neither evil nor good; it furnishes the energies which we control for good ends or for bad. The moral choice is ours, and it is unavoidable. If we try to weaken a natural impulse so that it will be less effective for evil, we thereby render it less effective for good.

The fact which men and women might as well admit, is that nature stirs in youth, whenever sex meets opposite sex, a desire and an answering desire. Not all boys and girls are conscious of this call and answer; they merely think they are falling in love, and a few days later they think they are falling in love with someone else. So far as nature is concerned, any one of these combinations would be as good as another; nature, having no regard for social consequences, would be content if all the combinations were tried out. Our intelligence guides us toward self-restraint and selection, and our ultimate choice, we hope, will be decided by spiritual affinity, yet if I choose one woman rather than another, it's rather shabby of me to say I do so because the other is desperately unattractive. The explanation is no compliment to my choice. The spiritual love which we admire is shabbily praised if we insist that the desire of the body is ignoble or sinful or even diabolical.

Perhaps we don't think ignobly of sex; perhaps we are merely convinced that for respectability's sake we ought to think so. Respectability so timid will make the whole field of sex, for ourselves and for our children, furtive and surreptitious. Neither books nor plays nor motion pictures are permitted the frankness about love and sex which prevails in private life. Many of us think it atrocious taste to say plainly that a woman is pregnant. We adore children, we pour upon them streams of sentiment and solitude, but we will not mention the disgraceful fact that children are conceived and born. In churches at Christmas time we listen with decorously downcast eyes to the story of Bethlehem.

This cowardice in the presence of nature leads to exaggerated indecency. Natural impulses, when repressed, explode. The reaction to prudishness is obscenity. The facts of life, when learned in secret behind the barn, turn out to be strictly barnyard facts, with no hint of majestic truth, of that universal love which brings on the seasons in their order, which kindles a divine spark in human creatures, and moves the sun and the other stars.

How sex, properly respected, can minister to true love, more than one wise man has told us, and millions of noble people have furnished examples. But another doctrine and another practice are only too common, and their tragic importance is that they derive encouragement from the timidity of those good people who wish sex suppressed. It is only too common for men, accepting the fact of sex, to keep physical impulses apart from their spiritual ideals. With this bifurcated philosophy they hope to enjoy the lifelong satisfaction of spiritual companionship, yet satisfy intermittent bodily hungers on the side. They won't admit they lead a double life, since the phrase implies deception, but double is the right word, and the deception is practiced upon themselves. Some remnant of sex, perhaps a small remnant, they use to express their official loyalty, but the division of ideals, illogical and absurd, produces hesitancy in their character and uncertainty of direction in their conduct. If they pretend to be sophisticated, perhaps they are simply embarrassed; they turn away from love, having too long contradicted themselves on the subject. They probably suspect too that the contradiction is indefensible. In the region of experience called natural, they seek pleasure exclusively physical. In a higher region they try to unite the sex impulse with ideals. Yet if this harmony can be achieved in part, there is no excuse for not achieving it altogether. Man can live comfortably as an animal, and with a quite different kind of satisfaction as a soul, but with little peace on the two levels simultaneously.

Some day when we really tell children the facts of life, we'll include the mind and the spirit. Morality in sex is far less widely practiced than we pretend, but if man has risen at all above the beasts, it is for two reasons—something in his human endowment makes him wish to rise, and experience is slowly teaching him that if he doesn't rise he suffers for it. Some advocates of the good life will translate my words into a warning against venereal disease, but if moral consequences were felt only in the body, then scientific precautions and strict hygiene would eliminate moral consequences. The suffering which follows betrayal of our best selves is deep and obvious. Those who accept the philosophy of a double life pay for animalism by a corresponding distortion of spirit. The commonest illustration is the exaggerated sentimentality of the promiscuous woman-appropriator. He will defend his conduct by telling you that's what life is, and that's what men and women are, but when he decides to step up into his own higher regions, choose a good woman for a wife, and establish a home, he discovers, or his friends promptly observe, that he has become unable to recognize a good woman when he sees her; either he falls into the hands of a schemer, or he deliberately chooses a brainless doll. In either case indiscriminately he addresses his mate in sappy terms; she's the "little woman," or "girlie," or "rosebud," or "blossom."

There have been notorious illustrations of this truth; the self-punishment of a bifurcated life is as clear in history as in our private acquaintance. Byron, for example, pursued women all his life, and the more experiments he made, the less able he was to choose. His biographers, like his friends at the time, are glad he settled down more or less with the Countess Guiccioli, toward the close of his short life, but the Countess wasn't much to give thanks for, except by comparison with her predecessors. The men who know least about women and least about themselves are the Don Juans. Casanova, who furnished us with voluminous data about his own spiritual and physical careers, told us really only this, that he was a psychological case, a puzzle to himself.

Not only do the immoralists pay heavily for their misunderstanding of sex, but even those men and women who believe their morals are of the soundest often follow a mistaken theory of sex with unfortunate consequences. It is still commonly believed that young lovers are, and should be, drawn to each other by passion, and that afterwards, as they live together, the passion will cool off and affectionate companionship will take its place. In this theory the facts of life are not faced. Sex is an energy, and if passion cools off, the weakened life that remains may be harmless, but it won't be good. Sex is not a temporary thing. As we have already said, it is impersonal. Unless it becomes incorporated in a deliberately chosen fidelity, it will flare up again in new directions. Companionship should be a prelude to love, not a sequel. Since the impulses of the body and the ideals of the soul are both creative, the companionship which prepares for love is a partnership in some form of work, even of toil or danger. A man and woman "thrown together," as we say, on a desert island are more than likely to fall in love with each other. The love is the climax and the expression of a companionship which life has previously enforced. The desert island is the metaphor of most companionships and of most loves. Brief and casual meetings are enough to stimulate sex hungers, but enduring passion is kindled by a joint effort to solve an emergency, such as results from shipwreck on a desert island—life itself being an emergency and in some sort a shipwreck.

3.

I have been using words here which need definition, or at least comment. Foreseeing that many readers might object to such terms, I have none the less spoken of love, of spirit, and of soul, to make a contrast with sex. The passage from Santayana quoted at the beginning of this chapter expresses a philosophy more widely current among us. Those who agree that spiritual fruits develop by natural growth out of animal origins, will therefore think me very old-fashioned indeed to oppose the soul to the body; only an out-worn theology, they will say, would introduce the fiction of soul into what should be a scientific discussion.

It is true that some ideas about the human soul I derive from the Bible or from other religious sources. I don't believe those ideas are so much out of fashion as materialists say, but even if they were, I should still hold them, since they are supported by experience. If our ideas and ideals were the fruit exclusively of animal impulses, small children ought to be complete animals, but the contrary is true; they are complete idealists. Experience may disillusion them; I don't see how it could have taught them their trust in their elders and their generous expectations of the world in which they must grow up. If love between the sexes had an exclusively animal basis, human youth should be distinguished, as in animals, by promiscuous and unconsidered mating. The fact is, however, that youth, instead of being animal, is romantic, and the first stirrings of sex arouse not only curiosity but resentment. The problem of love—perhaps we should say the art of love—is not to deny physical sex, but to employ it in the service of that romantic ideal which I believe is born in us, and comes from the soul.

In our time much has been said and written about the art of love, but the subject has not been properly named. The discussion usually deals with the art of love-making, a theme on which the Don Juans and the Casanovas are the authorities. The art of love is a different matter. It is a total ordering of our lives so that the body will be the aid and the companion of the soul, rather than an enemy for the soul to war against—so that we can advance our ideals by the use of all the energies which sex puts forth. The exclusively physical or materialistic philosophers amaze by their narrow observation of life. To hear them talk about sex, you'd think its influence was felt only in those moments and moods when men and women make love. The truth is that in a society of men and women sex exerts many different kinds of influence, all of them constant. Very different influences, yet none the less sex influences, are exerted in a society exclusively masculine or

in a society exclusively feminine. The Don Juans and the Casanovas, and I presume to add the physical or materialistic philosophers, attach small importance to these secondary influences, but
we begin to suspect that if mankind is to pursue any ideals at all—
if we are to be more, that is, than passive victims of animal or
mechanical forces—all the influences of sex must be understood.
If you and I are in a company, public or private, among strangers
or friends, and if one more person joins the group, it makes a
difference to the group whether that person is a woman or a man.
Here is a sex influence which probably has nothing whatever to
do with love. How many times in your life have you ridden on a
bus and a street car; how many times has a passenger got on; out
of all these instances, how many times has the sex influence stirred
in you intimate cravings, whether of body or of soul, or of both?

To say that sex is a constant condition of life is to describe that
companionship in which are found the preliminary conditions of
love. The influence of sex as a condition of life is, I repeat, mental
and spiritual rather than physical. When men and women associate with each other, all the values of even humdrum experience
become more colorful. Say if you will that the difference between
the sexes is first of all physical, and only as a consequence emotional or intellectual, but it is this so-called consequence which
we notice and are chiefly interested in. Women and men feel and
think in different ways on practically every subject, most of all,
perhaps, when they seem to agree, and whether or not they are
aware of it, the difference of approach sharpens for each sex all its
perceptions and judgments. The benefits of companionship are of
course not automatic; women and men working side by side will
be less efficient if their attention is on sex, but if their minds are
on their work, the association makes them far more efficient than
if they worked alone.

The psychological stimulus which one sex gives the other is explained by the differences between them, differences which certainly exist though they are hard to describe. To say that women
are emotional and that men are rational, is convenient, but in
some respects it is also absurd, since all of us are at times swayed
by emotion, and when we are, our rational processes may be suspended. Perhaps it is truer to say that women excel in a sense of

reality; their minds or their instincts fasten on the immediate problems, and they like to settle one problem at a time. Hence their reputation among male critics for lack of logic or for indifference to abstract ideas; men, by contrast, approach experience through ideas or logic, and theory often blinds them to facts. Yet whole nations, decidedly masculine in character, are noted for the feminine disposition to see facts as at any given moment they are, and to deal with each moment separately. This disposition or habit has sometimes been called "muddling through." It is far removed from the long vision of statesmanship, it produces the effect of inconsistency, yet it has elements of great strength. The feminine instinct is to secure all possible aid, whether from natural forces which can be counted on permanently, or from temporary circumstances. Yet though the moment-to-moment method is as natural for men as for women, in the practice of it a difference between the sexes is revealed. The man who takes life strictly as it comes, attending always to the immediate fact or situation, seems to other men, perhaps to himself, sophisticated or hardboiled. If he once had far-reaching theories or ideals he has discarded them as useless in a practical world. A woman, on the other hand, treating each separate problem on its own merits and answering one question after another in contradictory ways, will be faithful to her ideals, even to extremely romantic ideals, without the slightest embarrassment.

She has at least this advantage, that being unfettered by theories, she can make her decisions once for all. Men are firm in their choices before the choice is made, but afterwards, thinking it over and comparing it with other possibilities, they may regret the choice. A woman does her worrying beforehand, but her decision is final; what she does, after she has done it, is right. In this difference between the masculine temperament and the feminine I believe we have a clue to the aid and inspiration they give each other. Men are encouraged and fortified by women's ability to deal with the moment; women are impressed by men's ability to take the long-range view, though they may not take that view themselves.

Some of us believe the sexes are so utterly different that any attempt to compare them is futile. Some of us deny that between the sexes there is any difference at all. A famous book, *Sex and Character*, by Otto Weininger, advanced the theory forty years ago that the sexes differ not in qualities but in the proportion of qualities which they share. If there are some characteristics which you are willing to call masculine, and others feminine, then perhaps it's true that the average man has eighty-five per cent of the masculine qualities and fifteen per cent of the feminine. Those percentages reversed would be true of the average woman. But from this decidedly theoretical average we all vary; an exceptional man may have almost no feminine characteristics, or he may be eighty or ninety per cent feminine. He would make a satisfactory companion for a woman who is eighty or ninety per cent masculine. Who hasn't seen friendships or matings in which the woman dominates? In the chances of life, however, the perfect complements rarely meet, and in most companionships between the sexes there is a duplication or overlapping of characteristics, therefore rivalry and antagonism. The art of love begins when we are willing to recognize those overlappings and consequent rivalries. I speak here not of marriage but of love, and not necessarily of conscious love, revealed in preliminary companionship, but of that companionship itself. Sex harmony or sex antagonism is present in any association of men and women, and intelligence would try to reduce the irritations and increase the genuine satisfactions. To get on with our fellows at all, adjustment and re-education is necessary, even though love is not involved and marriage is unthought of. To postpone the art of companionship until we are married, is to go to school after taking our degree.

When the sex characteristics overlap, should we compromise by suppressing any part of those characteristics? It would be wiser to make the masculine qualities more masculine and the feminine more feminine, to increase the differences rather than to suppress the resemblances. It's a fair question today whether in the progress of political and economic equality we are not pulling up by the roots the very differences which make men and women important to each other. A frank recognition of physical differences ought to be accompanied by an equally frank recognition of psychological differences—by more than recognition, by deep appreciation of their value. Women are the equals of men, most of those I have met seem the superiors, but I think they are different from men, and if they aren't, they should make themselves so. The same principle holds for the men. One of the worst threats to the human race is the development in European and American society of a neutral sex, neither strongly feminine nor strongly masculine. It's a conviction of mine that in the United States we achieve this undesirable result so far as boys are concerned by giving them female schoolteachers during childhood. I'd let women teach boys later on, but if a male child until his twelfth year is introduced to life chiefly by women, it is only by a miracle that he afterwards makes up for lost time and learns to play a manly part in the world. With so bad a start he may not be prepared to contribute masculine characteristics to companionship. Physical sex will not be impaired in him; he will marry and have children. But by inevitable reaction from the anaemic atmosphere of the school-room, he will become an animal, therefore not likely to know much about the art of love. That art for men is a masculine art, a feminine art for women.

4.

That physical desire should serve as the expression of ideal love is not a moral program invented by the experienced and the aging; it is a conviction of romantic youth. Men and women on the threshold of life find no hope more attractive than to possess the one they love and to be faithful forever. That this hope is so often disappointed seems to the young, and should seem to all of us, a tragedy, the sadder because in most cases a clearer understanding of love might have prevented the disaster. We lose our hearts, as we think, to another person, but actually to an image which we have created out of ourselves, an ideal which supplements what we are. There is always a good chance that the person we say we love and the self-ideal which we really love, may not be far apart; if Weininger's theory is sound, the person as well as the ideal will be the complement of us. There is probably little to criticize, therefore, in our falling in love; the danger is that we shan't be able to keep it up.

You may have noticed the type of person who changes mates frequently, but is always careful to obey the rules; perhaps you

are among the caustic lookers-on who ask why alliances so temporary need any legal endorsement or any legal dissolution. These
cases are examples of prolonged adolescence in love, of love which
refuses to grow up. The undiscouraged faith that this time the
inoculation will take, is pathetic, it may even be ridiculous, but
we should not dismiss it until we understand its cause. Certain
famous men, in other respects mature, have remained all their
days adolescent lovers, utterly faithful so long as the passion lasts
but incapable of making it last long. To such temperaments it
seems nonsense to suggest that love by any wisdom can be
stretched out beyond what they consider its inevitable end.

The adolescent lover can recognize authentic passion only in
its first stage. The sex impulse, of course, he can't ignore, and the
spiritual ideal of the moment he recognizes as imperative. The
two forces take hold of him together in fortunate harmony. From
that moment on, however, the adolescent is literal-minded, he
lacks imagination. Because his mate represents to him the ideals
of the moment, and because his ideals will progress in spite of
him, he is only too liable to conclude that his mate has changed.
It is very unimaginative not to foresee inevitable and constant
change, and still more unimaginative not to realize that we change
as much as other people. When the adolescent abandons one mate
for another, he is almost sure to fix on a companion who differs
from her predecessor in only a slight degree, which is approximately the measure of his own development.

If love were nothing but the spiritual fruit of an animal impulse, perhaps these perplexities would not attend it; perhaps
falling in love would be a straightforward adventure, as adolescent
lovers try to make it, relying on frankness and decisive courage to
get into it, and on ruthlessness to get out. But nature is not simple,
neither is the soul, and to love wisely or continuously or completely calls for imagination, a quality less available to most of
us than decision and courage. In any lasting companionship each
lover creates the ideal loved; each lover contemplates in advance
the ideal which will be loved tomorrow; by sympathetic exchange
of aspiration and dream each helps each to make the ideal become
real. To ask of an ideal that it should stop growing is a little
insane and very youthful. To say that someone has fallen short

of our ideal or has disappointed it or has destroyed it, is adolescent nonsense. The only possible disappointment in companionship is a failure of one companion to go along with the other, and the adolescent lover is precisely that kind of failure. His stunted little heart refuses to go along with anybody, it wants to stand still.

If the adolescent lover is not disposed to foresee his own intellectual or spiritual growth or that of his companion, it is idle to lay before him any of the methods by which that progress is encouraged. Without imagination the lover will not be interested in the future, and without a certain delicacy of spirit he can do little to aid the development either of his own character or of his companion's. Physical desire creates merely a hunger; spiritual love creates an illusion, the self-ideal of the lover being imposed upon the loved. Those who are intelligent in the art of love realize that the illusion exists, but they understand also its function and they are careful not to destroy it. The illusion is precious even though it looks backward toward the past in gallant loyalty to a mistaken ideal. I think of Sir Leicester Dedlock in the Dickens novel, *Bleak House*. His love for his wife was complete and his estimation of her character noble. When she went to her death in despair over the dangerous secret of her past, Sir Leicester ignored completely the scandalous rumors, and continued to worship her dead as he had worshiped her living. He had loved an ideal; the ideal was still his. But the illusion in this instance, since it merely preserves the past, is not in the full sense creative. The service of illusion is chiefly to the future. The consciousness that someone thinks well of us helps us to justify that good opinion. If we value companionship, we are bound to justify a good opinion so far as we possibly can, and the obligation lies equally upon our companion to maintain faith in us. Much faith will be needed, much imagination, much tact.

I call to mind an illustration which may not seem entirely appropriate, since my own mother furnishes it, and mother love is not the kind of love we are here considering. But in all companionship affection creates illusions. My mother exerted strong control over our conduct by her unshakable confidence that it would be what she thought it ought to be; never by any tactless slip did she let us know there were moments when she worried about us. I first became aware of this peculiarity of hers—few parents command such art—in early school days, when partly by luck, as I was honest enough to see, I brought home some good marks and a prize. I overheard a visitor tell my mother she ought to be proud of me. My mother, doubtless aware that I was listening, asked why. Because he has done so well, said the visitor. Of course he has done well, said Mother, but I should have been disappointed had he done less.

Young though I was, I knew that most people would say my mother's attitude was a little cold, that she might have permitted herself some warm congratulations, that she should have patted her child on the back; but since I happened to be the child, I can testify to the effect of her rare and difficult policy. She made all her children feel downright shame if they did less than their best. We were far from being little angels, but we did grow up eager for her good opinion and conscious that we could have it, not for special successes but for a constant attitude.

When I returned after many months abroad in the first World War, I had the good fortune to bring back with me some decorations. She was then in her last illness, but when she knew the boat was docking she had herself dressed and sitting up in the living room to greet me. I placed my medals in her lap—they really belonged to her. But the old philosophy persisted. Though her eyes lighted, she gave the baubles only a casual glance, remarked how pretty they were, and turned the conversation promptly to other matters. Her children found in this self-control the expression of a passionate love which all their lives had understood the art of creating and developing companionship.

We knew also that she and my father, having married very young, were lovers to the end. The strongest resemblance between them was their faith in each other. It was amazing to see how accurately each understood the other's character. At moments which memory treasures my father would confide in me, almost diffidently as though the subject were too intimate, his enormous admiration for my mother and the reasons for it. In equal confidence she would tell me how unique he was among all men she had ever heard of. They praised each other for the virtues which each admired. "Your father," Mother once said in deep and tender seriousness, "thinks far better of me than I deserve." She treated him as she treated her children, with the same assumption that he was precisely what love would have him be, and that her confidence in him was the highest tribute she could offer.

I intrude my personal memories upon you because I am sure you can match them out of your own childhood. I take an illustration from old age to set over against what has been said about adolescent love. Only the hopelessly adolescent, the permanently immature, think that love belongs exclusively or chiefly to youth. The young man Tobit knew better when he prayed on his wedding night, "Mercifully ordain that we may become aged together."

5.

It has been the fashion in modern times for women to say they'd rather not be put on a pedestal; an unidealizing companionship is what they want. In some moods, however, they must doubt the soundness of this philosophy. All higher progress comes through the imagining and the pursuit of an ideal. To create romantic illusions is one of the most natural occupations of the human mind. From childhood we imitate those whom we admire, and probably they wouldn't seem worth imitating if our admiration were not somewhat exaggerated. Lucky for your children if they create a paragon out of a schoolmate or teacher; tragically sad if they discover nobody worth making a paragon out of. Those who in mature life, in politics or business or in any other human relation, insist on seeing things literally, untouched by emotion, are not so wise as they believe, they are not even quite sane. The healthy in body and mind progress by pursuing generous illusions, and the literal find no ideal to pursue.

The girl who falls in love will naturally overestimate her hero, and he will exaggerate her merits. Both will be put on pedestals. Why should they ever wish to come down? The descent, when it occurs, will be a signal that love has died for want of the art to sustain it, and the companionship is ended. I grant you that in previous epochs society made a cult of false delicacy, of a prudishness which verged on indecency; the concealment of the body, the forbidding of all reference to physical birth and passion, I can say no good word for. Yet the very fact that we are honest about life ought to teach us the value of that pedestal which some women would dispense with—ought to teach us the necessity of maintaining in our conduct, not prudishness, but illusion—nourishing delicacy.

Years ago one summer day, swimming in a mountain lake, I sunned myself on the diving raft. Two youngsters came ploughing through the water toward the diving raft. They both wore rubber caps; they swam equally well; I couldn't tell their sex. When they got to the raft they heaved themselves up promptly, superb acrobats that they were, and I saw with a start that one was a boy and the other a girl, both slightly under twenty. Their swimming suits were scant and thin. As they stood for a moment talking, letting the water drip off them, they might just as well have been naked. Every curve of their bodies was revealed. I noticed that their talk was happy and unembarrassed; their companionship was ideal. For a moment I admired them without reservation —envied them a little, perhaps, since in my own youth comradeship so frank had been unknown. Let me say clearly that my admiration for this frankness remains undiminished; I would no more ask swimmers to conceal the body than I would ask lovers to ignore sex.

But in the midst of their cheerful conversation the girl wanted to get the water out of her head, particularly out of her nose, and her frankness of conduct shocked me. She achieved the desired result in the most primitive manner, by putting her thumb first to one nostril then to the other, and blowing like a trumpet. Reticence is not the opposite of frankness; it may be a form of frankness. Without imaginative delicacy the illusion which love builds up can be shaken out of existence. No one has a right to destroy the pedestal which he or she has not built up and cannot restore. A woman would do well to remember that the pedestal which she objects to may be entirely inappropriate for her. She needn't destroy it; she can get out of the way and leave it for the rightful occupant.

6.

When I was young I pitied any human being who didn't marry. Two maiden aunts lived in our home; even as a child I was sorry for them, as having missed life. Growing older I extended the scope of my sympathy; I was sorry for those who, even though unmarried, missed all the experiences of love. The implications of the idea troubled me and I tried to persuade myself that there are compensations which enabled the unmated to achieve what by some definition is a complete life, but I have observed small evidence that such a belief is sound. It is not good that man or woman should be alone. Here let me clear myself of any suspicion that I would revert to a conventional disparagement of sex. The cause of morality is served, I believe, by recognizing the sex force in all nature and by wishing for ourselves and for others more vitality rather than less. When we feel sorry for the unmarried we are regretting that they have missed, among other things, their full share of sex life. They are harmed by missing it. But the harm which loneliness does to the body may easily be exaggerated if we give it our exclusive attention; the loss of companionship is a loss to the soul. In the spiritual realm as in the physical we aspire to greater vitality. No one is more deeply convinced than I that marriage is the desirable condition for adults, but conventional marriage too often is merely a respectable satisfaction of sex. Marriage without love is horrible, and love is a spiritual art too seldom studied or taught and too seldom illustrated. We should reserve our deepest sympathy for those who have missed the marriage of true minds.

Those who attach importance exclusively to sex are individualists. Married or not, they live alone, in that selfish isolation which is not good for mankind. The essence of love is creative companionship, the fulfillment of one life by another. It would be comforting to believe that such companionship begins automatically when vows are ceremonially exchanged and blessed, but the fact is otherwise. True marriage is the result of true love, not the cause of it.

In every page of this book I have spoken to those who like myself wish to make the most of all our talents and to live as

richly as our opportunities and our best efforts permit. Who of
us does not hope for a complete life—from our strictly personal
point of view? When we contemplate matrimony, it is our marriage we contemplate, the benefits to us, as though no one else
were a partner in the experiment. Yet our mate has an equal right
to the complete life, and we from that other angle serve to fill out
our companion's destiny. Neither in poetry nor in morals is this
truth often or adequately mentioned, yet without an understanding of it there can be no understanding of love. The adolescent
will continue to proclaim that they are made for each other, that
their meeting was arranged by kindly fate before they were born,
but in spite of these co-operative words the adolescents will remain
hopeless individuals, each intent on going it alone. Love is grown-
up when the two companions think of themselves as one, neither
dominating, each personality making the other more complete.

It is a defect in our education that we are encouraged to take
seriously what the poets in the English language say about love.
English novelists, especially the contemporary novelists, not infrequently see this subject clearly and discuss it honestly, but
the poets, even the great ones, stick at the adolescent stage. From
Romeo or from Juliet, from Antony or from Cleopatra, we
can learn about falling in love, but how much can we learn about
companionship? The two characters in all the Shakespearean plays
who in my opinion illustrate a mature and complete companionship, are Macbeth and his wife. It is unfortunate that the validity
of their contribution to the theory and practice of love is impaired
by the perhaps irrelevant circumstance that they are murderers.
A better textbook is Somerset Maugham's *Of Human Bondage,*
where the noble companionship of Philip and Sally, at the close
of the story, gains by contrast with the other companionships, false
and abortive, which fill the preceding pages. Yet the Sally episode,
evasively romantic, presents ideal companionship as a miracle; it
rather discourages the hope that the secret of the miracle can ever
be learned and imparted. Moreover, the miracle of companionship is seen through Philip's eyes, egotistically; for him Sally is
God's gift, and we see why. What kind of gift he will be to Sally is
less clear.

If you will read again the speech of Pietro Bembo, quoted in an earlier page from Castiglione's *Book of the Courtier,* perhaps you will find new meaning in the doctrine that the purpose of education is to teach men and women to love. Other educational theories prevail today, but I for one am willing still to sit at Bembo's feet, and at the feet of his master, Plato. If love is, as I believe it must be, an experience in which two lives have an equal stake, and if the companionship of love must broaden out to include all the interests which two distinct and growing souls may find vital, then lovers need imagination and sympathy and tact and humility and an unflagging willingness to learn. The expansiveness of the prospect is somewhat terrifying but we have no choice. Through love we may take possession of life. Without love we may measure time from birth to death, but the doors of life are barred to us. We may be skilled in the arts and crafts, we may exercise ourselves in all the tongues of men, but without love we shall have nothing to say.

7.

In all times and in all grades of society men and women must have experienced the fortunate union of physical desires with spiritual aspirations. Illustrations of love at its noblest can be cited from all ancient literatures. But the art of love as a conscious philosophy was developed and preached magnificently by the troubadours in France and Italy at the moment when the Middle Ages were passing into the Renaissance. The importance of the *Vita Nuova* for us now lies in its statement of this philosophy perhaps even more than in its record of Dante's personal romance. The troubadours and their better-remembered disciples formulated the doctrine that love is the great educator, that only sensitive and creative natures are capable of love, that whatever the circumstances of birth, a heart in which love can dwell is a gentle heart, that lovers in whom passion is spiritual as well as physical are the only gentlefolk, the only gentlemen, the only ladies. Both the Middle Ages and the Renaissance were fully aware of the advantages which even a gentle heart derives from fortunate parentage, yet the troubadour doctrine of love was in this respect remarkably democratic, that it conceded gentleness of nature to all true lovers, even though they were lowly born.

Perhaps this democratic broad-mindedness was induced by the fact that the twelfth, thirteenth and fourteenth centuries were rich in genius; an extraordinary proportion of the men and women still remembered from those times as founders of distinguished houses, were by temperament pioneers, ancestors rather than descendants. It was not difficult to conclude that genius, otherwise inexplicable, rose out of some favorable condition of spirit. Doubtless this favorable condition was related to the religious faith of the late Middle Ages, but the poets rather than the Church articulated the art of love. The physical impulses of sex never were stronger than in their day, and not one of them gave much encouragement to the dread or contempt of sex which in an earlier period had driven men and women out of life into the desert or the hermit's cell. The troubadours and their disciples sang the praise of energy and vital power, but they celebrated even more the divine force which, in those gentlefolk who were capable of receiving it, gave to sex a disciplined direction. In the ungentle, the base, sex also operated, but without the guidance of the soul, and sex without soul these poets called lust. The 129th Sonnet of Shakespeare agrees with them.

> "The expense of spirit in a waste of shame
> Is lust in action."

Even the base must at least have heard of a spiritual love and by experience they know their lives are not complete; the pleasures of sex, when enjoyed merely for their own sake, have the bitter aftertaste of shame.

A famous sonnet in the *Vita Nuova* states the troubadour faith that love for those who are not base is an education. Few readers are unfamiliar with the much-quoted first line, *Amore e 'l cor gentil sono una cosa.* English readers probably know the poem in Dante Gabriel Rossetti's translation.

> "Love and the gentle heart are one same thing,
> Even as the wise man in his ditty saith.
> Each, of itself, would be such life in death
> As rational soul bereft of reasoning.

> 'Tis Nature makes them when she loves: a king
> 　　Love is, whose palace where he sojourneth
> 　　Is call'd the Heart; there draws he quiet breath
> At first, with brief or longer slumbering.
> Then beauty seen in virtuous womankind
> 　　Will make the eyes desire, and through the heart
> 　　　　Send the desiring of the eyes again;
> Where often it abides so long enshrined
> 　　That Love at length out of his sleep will start.
> 　　　　And women feel the same for worthy men."

Almost as famous is Guido Guinicelli's canzone, *"Al cor gentil ripara sempre amore."* Rossetti again translates for us the first quatrain.

> "Within the gentle heart Love shelters him,
> 　　As birds within the green shade of the grove.
> Before the gentle heart, in Nature's scheme,
> 　　Love was not, nor the gentle heart ere Love."

The early Renaissance spread the troubadour doctrine in fiction as well as in lyrical poetry. Boccaccio, for example, whom some of us prize for his less philosophical moments, told the story of *Cymon and Iphigenia* which Dryden translated in verse. Though we may not have read it, at least we are acquainted with one line, which has become a familiar quotation. Cymon was a loutish fellow who looked "like Nature's error," who spent his time near the soil, finding his congenial companions among cows and pigs and his most subtle entertainment at country fairs. On holidays, having no work to do, he would take a long walk, going nowhere in particular. Dryden's description of him at one such vacant moment concludes with the line which we still quote:

> "His quarter-staff, which he could ne'er forsake,
> Hung half before and half behind his back.
> He trudged along, unknowing what he sought,
> And whistled as he went, for want of thought."

But on his aimless stroll Cymon chanced to see Iphigenia, a beautiful girl. He fell in love—truly fell in love according to the troubadour doctrine; not only his body but his spirit desired her,

and the hitherto unsuspected gentleness latent in him, awoke. The
sequel of the story traces the course of this awakening.

> "So reason in this brutal soul began:
> Love made him first suspect he was a man;
> Love made him doubt his broad barbarian sound;
> By love his want of words and wit he found;
> That sense of want prepared the future way
> To knowledge, and disclosed the promise of a day.
>
> . . . .
>
> Love taught him shame, and shame with love at strife
> Soon taught the sweet civilities of life."

Tennyson restated the troubadour doctrine for the nineteenth
century in *The Idylls of the King,* making the Arthurian story a
parable, as he told us, of the war between sense and soul, and,
in many a passage, pleading for the old faith that love can educate
sense into harmony with the spirit.

> "I made them lay their hands in mine and swear
>
> . . . .
>
> To love one maiden only, cleave to her,
> And worship her by years of noble deeds,
> Until they won her; for indeed I knew
> Of no more subtle master under heaven
> Than is the maiden passion for a maid,
> Not only to keep down the base in man,
> But teach high thought, and amiable words
> And courtliness, and the desire of fame,
> And love of truth, and all that makes a man."

Neither in theory nor in practice are men yet agreed as to what
love should be. Sex is the one unquestioned factor in it, and sex
alone satisfies very few of us; indeed, one danger at present, as
I've tried to stress, is perhaps the tendency to consider sex an
enemy and to see something diabolical in it. Some philosophers
like Santayana want us to believe that out of sex may grow a
spiritual love. Others whom I prefer to follow believe with the
troubadours and with Dante that the sex energy is not in itself a

potential spiritual force, but that creative love can bring into harmony the desires of the body and the yearnings of the soul.

8.

To study an ideal in the statements of it which old poets have made, is well enough if history is what we are after, but in our search to know more of love we want the testimony of our contemporaries, and we want it as nearly as possible directly from them. Of all human experiences love excites the widest general interest, but in the lover it begets reticence—which may be the reason why we all understand little about it.

Reading over what I have said, I am disturbed to see how much I have left out, yet I am perplexed to complete the account. On every page, in almost every paragraph, I have had to use words which to each reader may suggest different connotations, some of them far from my intention. To say, as I've tried to do, that either the physical or the psychological aspects of love may be harmful if the two aspects are separated, lays me open to the charge, or at least to the suspicion, that I don't set much value on sex after all, or that I am posing as a goody-goody who would uplift my fellows by preaching at them. My frequent use of the word soul may throw some readers off entirely. Let me make a final attempt to clear myself.

I have friends, in most cases men, no more highly sexed than I, who early in life made between sex and love that bifurcation which I believe is suicidal. They are married and have children, yet in this chapter I have described them as lonely individualists. In most cases the wife understands that her husband is not faithful and she resents this fact, but sometimes she comforts herself by saying that nothing better can be expected of men. That in any of these cases husband and wife are companions, that they give each other entire confidence, I do not believe. The man's relation to the other women who have crossed his path and satisfied a temporary desire, is even more superficial. Between him and them too there is not companionship but antagonism.

The conventional moralist would call these irregular sex satisfactions sin. When my neighbors apply that severe word to any conduct, I want to know whether they are judging by a purely conventional standard or whether they refer to a violation of some principle which man didn't invent and can't change. I am willing to say it's a sin to go walking on thin ice expecting not to fall through, but that it was a sin for Isolde to love Tristan, I cannot believe. There was bad luck, but if there was any sin, I'd see it in her marriage to Mark. What I am concerned about is that transgression of natural law for which all of us have to pay. Natural laws prevail in the mind as well as in the body. If your habit is to use materialistic terms, translate me into whatever terms you prefer. You will still have to distinguish between what Santayana calls animal origins and what he calls spiritual fruits. It's those spiritual fruits which you and I may wish to call by different names. I shy off from the word sin unless I know what is meant. I speak of the soul, but if you think you're on firmer ground by translating soul into psyche, go ahead and make the substitution. I'm sure that I can love with my body and also with my psyche, but to love naturally and sanely, I'm sure I must not separate body and psyche, but must love with both of them at once. If I love with the body alone I fail of a complete life. I fail equally if I try to love with only the soul or psyche. If sex love without the spirit is sin, then psyche love without sex is sin. Both these partial loves, being partial, are obviously incomplete, and the tragic consequences of their incompleteness seem as plain in one case as in the other.

To offset those friends of mine, chiefly men, who specialize in sex love, I happen to have other friends, chiefly women, who, as I judge from their frankly avowed prejudices, hate to admit the existence of sex. If I understand them, they'd be glad to love exclusively in their psyche. They are to my way of thinking extremely tragic folk. Some of them have never married, which is misfortune enough; those who have married are in worse luck, or their husbands are. Or were. Psyche mates are soon divorced. To be chained to a person who feels repugnance at the sexual act, or who pretends she feels it, is an unbearable indignity.

We seek completeness of life in order to be happy. The problem which sex and love present is so inescapable and to every life so momentous, that discussion of it must be serious. Perhaps we may temporarily forget how happy love can be—tragic too at moments, but when we are fortunate, happy beyond any other experience. There is joy in it, and fun. The bodily caress which succeeds at all in expressing what the heart would say, will awaken the full range of laughter and delight, of poetry and devotion. "With my body I thee worship," said the old phrase in the marriage vow. The "I" which does the worshipping is the psyche—am I using the right word now? For the ritual of that worship how wonderful the body is! How many times I've been thankful that I'm not yet a disembodied spirit!

CHAPTER XII

Marriage

1.

THOUGH WE DO not agree in our accounts of love and though we fall short of what the noblest love by any definition might be, yet it is a mistake to conclude that we are deteriorating. With all allowance for brilliant exceptions it is fair to say that the ancient world did not imagine the high-minded love which in recent centuries has been our ideal. Though society still fails to reach that ideal, the percentage of failure is not, as we hastily judge, on the increase. Only a century ago the ideal was frequently challenged, even as theory. If only in theory it has wide acceptance today, yet the general advance of decency is remarkable, boys and girls enjoy a civilized companionship not even approached before our time, and women can without loss of self-respect or public credit earn their living side by side with men. These may seem but small indications of progress, but at least they suggest a forward motion. We might have moved faster but we have not fallen back.

In the ideal of marriage also there is progress. Confronted with a rising divorce rate and a falling birth rate, we worry about the future of the home and cast about for devices to protect it, yet marriage in our day sets itself a higher standard than ever before. In the pre-Christian world it was a social institution, a provision for the family, for the family line, for the clan. Divorce was frowned on because it involved the rearrangement of dowries and property rights and caused a break in the solid front of household tradition. But when marriage is defined as chiefly a social institution, a bulwark of the state, love has but a secondary place in it. Affection, yes, but not the kind of love the troubadours revealed to us. Where the interests of the clan are put first, neither bride nor groom is quite free to choose a mate; they must make the best of what has been chosen for them. Since the purpose of such marriages is to perpetuate the family line, there must be children whether or not there is love, and if the marriage proves sterile it can be dissolved. These theories underlay the marriage customs of imperial Rome and of ancient Israel. To some extent they persist in modern society, conflicting with other theories more personal and as we believe more spiritual. To hold that children rather than companionship should be the object of marriage and to make sterility the ground of divorce, is to emphasize sex and physical desire. We need not be surprised that where marriages are arranged without consulting the heart, society must shut its eyes to love affairs on the side.

But you may say that the social customs of the ancient world do not concern us, that love is now an essential part of marriage, that spiritual love is once for all placed above sexual desire, since the Church regards marriage as a sacrament. I reply that each of these statements contains truth but needs qualification, simply because we live in a changing world and the Church as well as secular society did not always perceive its ideals so clearly as it does now, and rudimentary survivals of some outgrown ideals remain to perplex and embarrass. If marriage is in an unsettled state, it is not necessarily because men and women are faithless to a beautiful institution; it may be because they try to bring that institution into harmony with some ideals which religion has taught and which modern society accepts. Any doctrine of marriage will now be under attack which pays more attention to sex than to love and deals with the body before the soul.

Christianity adopted in its early years a view somewhat resembling St. Paul's; since marriage was a compromise with the flesh, those who had the spiritual gift would stay out of it. Marriage was an institution of honor, but not of the highest honor. Grace could be fully attained only in celibacy; the blessing of heaven, therefore, was reserved for virgins of both sexes who had taken Christ for bride. It was a long while, several centuries, before

the Church declared unhesitatingly that marriage was a sacrament, and even then the family and the home enjoyed somewhat
less than the high place assigned to them now. Celibacy is still,
in the opinion of many Christians, almost or quite obligatory
upon those who would lead the best life. In the late Middle Ages
the evidence of this point of view is plentiful in quaint sermons,
for one of which I have had a liking since my university days,
when I studied the text for its language. The priest who composed the "Sawles Warde," or the "Soul's Ward," is unknown.
His long-winded but imaginative discourse dates approximately
from the year 1210. It was translated into more modern English
in 1340 by Dan Michel of Northgate, who if he hadn't been a
good man might have been thought a plagiarist, for he passed off
the word-for-word translation as a sermon of his own. The passage
which I shall once more translate, but with no intention of lifting
it, is the climax of a scene in heaven, a court reception such as
the preacher may have witnessed in London. God from his throne
hears the addresses and petitions of his subjects. The prophets
and the patriarchs step forward in turn, the saints, the heroes,
the martyrs, good men and women all, but in most cases married.

"At last I beheld the fellowship of virgins, of such bliss and
beauty, such raiment and sweetness of voice, as no human speech
can tell. The song they sang, no others may sing, and the sweet
smell in their region is so sweet that it surpasses every sweet smell.
To their petitions Our Lord arises; to all others he listens seated."

The old priest, having seen etiquette at work, makes God a
gentleman who knows enough to get to his feet when folks of
consequence enter the room. If God has not changed his opinion
since the fourteenth century, we may be permitted to wonder
why the Church doesn't make celibacy rather than marriage a
sacrament.

We have enough contradictions here to keep wise and good
men busy for some time. Marriage is a sacrament, but celibacy is
a condition of virtue. Adam asked not for children, but for a
companion, a helpmeet. Doubtless the children would come by
inevitable consequence, but the original purpose of marriage was
companionship of spirit. Yet divorces are granted far more readily
to those whose bodies are ill-mated than to those whose minds

fail to meet. Though children are created by the sexual act, and though the begetting of children is encouraged for the sake of the immortal souls who by that act are launched on an earthly career, sex itself still carries an inconsistent burden of shame.

Children or companionship are not the only objects of marriage. Some people have always married to avoid earning a living. In the United States forty years ago a family in comfortable circumstances felt ashamed if one of the girls went to work. The affectionate hope was that she would make a good match, find a husband who was a good provider, bear the children and direct the housekeeping, enjoy his faithful and adequate support as long as he lived, and after his death continue in comfort on his investments and his life insurance. To say that women marry for money sounds brutal, but that was just what most of them in our country used to marry for, and some still do. If hard times come and husband loses his money, the wife will no doubt play the game and so far as she is able put her shoulder to the wheel, but she and her friends may think that misfortune has overtaken her, and that in facing it she makes a heroic sacrifice.

But men also marry for money. It happens frequently in the United States, and in Europe it is or used to be the established rule. The wife was supposed to bring a dowry, which was included with the bride in the sum total of what the husband espoused. That is why many American girls have married European husbands, have even married titles. From the money end of it the European male knows where to look for a good wife. Most American girls, however, have no dowries; from the money end of it they know where to look for a good husband.

Whatever else is the meaning of these inconsistencies and paradoxes, they indicate that the institution of marriage has not yet caught up with our ideals. Conventional marriage becomes steadily more civilized, but our ideals are well ahead of it. My belief is that the apparently precarious state of the institution at present is caused by the fact that when we now think of marriage we think of love, and we'd like to put love above all other considerations. Love is precisely what marriage has not always included and never has put first. Normal people want children, but they no longer marry for children when there is no love. They want money, but they'd rather not accept in place of love what is called "a good arrangement." Unless we love, we see no reason for marrying at all, and unless our love proves companionable and permanent, we find no excuse for remaining married.

There is a conflict here between the philosophy of our day and traditional doctrines of marriage which had their roots in the philosophy of days long past. Unless history misleads us we may expect the institution to modify itself in the direction of the ideals which are shared by humanity in general, but no institution ever catches up with an ideal. The conventional doctrine of marriage at any one moment may be subject to criticism, but marriage, for those who love, will always be a sacrament. The lovers stranded on the desert island would invent some kind of ritual to proclaim the sacredness of their vows.

2.

If traditional ideals of marriage trail inevitable inconsistencies and contradictions, the ideals which at present our world seems to cherish have in them elements of reaction and of exaggeration. To understand the life which we would make complete, we must compare the traditional ideals with the new. What is temporary, time will take care of; our concern should be with the enduring aspirations of human nature.

Whatever disposition society makes of the divorce problem, man and woman are not likely to abandon the self-respecting conviction that vows should be kept. To be sure, divorce seems to be on the increase and no matter how deeply we regret that fact, most of us feel that little is gained by protracting a union which has unquestionably failed. Even the argument that a divided home should be held together precariously for the sake of the children is less compelling than it was; children are hardly benefited by a loveless atmosphere. Yet there are few persons today who do not wish for themselves and for others a continuous and happy companionship. The spread of divorce indicates willingness to recognize a mistake, but with this frankness goes a conviction that the mistake ought not in the first place to be made. We dare not hope that mistake-making will cease to be a large human industry, yet there might easily be more serious preparation for matrimony than society or even the Church has provided.

The youngest of the young generation agree with their elders that marriage should be prepared for intelligently, but they believe that youth rather than age should take charge of the preparation. They also believe that they rather than their relatives should take charge of their marriage. This, of course, is a sharp break with tradition. The new ideal of marriage holds first of all that it should be based on love. This too is a startling advance. The end of marriage used to be, as we have just reminded ourselves, not companionship but children, and not children for their own sake but for the continuance and strengthening of clan or state. Modern marriage puts the companionship of two bodies, two hearts, two minds above every other consideration—certainly far above that economic prudence which has induced some women and some men to marry for money.

In former days the elders did not object to passionate love between the two contracting parties, provided that more broadly social and public aspects of marriage were already cared for, and provided that the contracting parties accepted advice as to whether or not they were genuinely in love. The reaction against control by the elders is so violent that we may doubt whether it will continue without modification. The modern bride and groom identify marriage with love, and their love is their own business, but when their children some day marry they'll discover that parents have an interest in the wedding and expect at the very least an invitation to the ceremony. They don't always get it today. Youngsters in their zeal to be uncontrolled sometimes neglect to count the relatives in. Runaway or impromptu marriages are not ideal. The companionship of the young husband and wife and their right to choose each other will be respected, but so also will be those charities of father, son, and brother which, though less intimate than married love, have their own sanctity. Elder generations are of course a nuisance, but apparently they cannot be abolished, and though we try our hand at it we hardly get started before another generation appears, younger than we, with a healthy ambition to abolish us.

Even if you are the most progressive and understanding of parents, you may be shocked by the readiness of your children to marry on almost nothing at all. This recklessness is not modern, it is youth; perhaps it is not recklessness but courage. If the youngsters are unprepared to earn their living and to get along on a small budget, then marriage for them is indeed reckless, but parents should hesitate to say their children are unprepared to live; whose business was it to prepare the children? It has long been a complaint of youth that conventional society makes a reasonably early marriage impossible. Those who complain belong in general to the more fortunate economic levels; having had considerable schooling and enjoyed a comfortable home, they are expected by their elders to set up housekeeping in the same degree of comfort and affluence. But the young folks today refuse to postpone marriage until they can afford to carry on from where their parents leave off. The children of the poor marry young because they are accustomed to work and because they are not asked to start off on a high economic level. Today the children of the well-to-do envy in this respect the children of the poor; why not enter at once upon a complete life if that life is possible in two rooms, or only in one?

Early marriage based on love will hardly recommend itself to parents if they are called upon to finance the idealistic experiment. It is a misfortune to be inadequate, whether we are young or old. But one characteristic of modern marriage is that the woman as well as the man usually likes to work, either to help out the family budget or for the consciousness of being self-supporting. Self-support as an ideal shows itself in boys as well as girls and at an early age, before matrimony is contemplated; it is not unusual for school children, even though their parents take good care of them, to serve in the school cafeteria or to seek through other employment the satisfaction of having in their pocket something they have earned. The space is lacking here to suggest all the reasons for this development even if I knew them all, which I don't. One explanation may be mentioned. We elders have reason to know that the future of private investments is doubtful. Some of us find it difficult to make a satisfactory defense of capital which is used not to facilitate our own work, but to buy a share in the work of others. Since these doubts are abroad, and since few of us are untouched by them whether our economic philosophy is extremely conservative or extremely liberal, it may be we unconsciously stir up in our children the ambition to be independent. Yet I'm not at all sure that this ambition can be explained by our philosophic theories or philosophic doubts. It's a satisfaction to stand on one's own feet, and the younger generation is finding it out. The fact that we elders are simultaneously discovering, some of us, the difficulty of standing on our own feet, gives hope for a more sympathetic alliance between the generations, but no hope at all for the restoring of parental prestige. Even if the youngsters are not sure they can manage for themselves, they see no one else who can do it better; they see that time is flying—one of the wisest of youth's perceptions—and when they find love they are unwilling to let it go. In most cases love for them means marriage. We needn't worry about them. We should deplore rather the vestiges of an ignoble philosophy still observable in a few parents, who would rather have the young people enter into a clandestine affair than into a rash but honorable marriage.

If the wife earns her living and contributes to the household upkeep, what will happen to the children? Or will there be any? Perhaps there is more in this question than married folk today are prepared to admit. Our society may be falling too easily into the habit of postponing children, or of having only one, at most two. There may be a return toward the ideal of a larger family, yet whatever reasons are brought forward for more children will be scrutinized and perhaps challenged. An indiscriminate praise of what is called the old-fashioned home will be listened to with skepticism. Our ideal of the home, as of love and marriage, has advanced so far that today an acceptable case for the past can be made out only by sentimentalizing or concealing the facts. Not until well into the nineteenth century did children begin to receive what seems now a minimum of decent care and intelligent upbringing. Poor children in Victorian England endured the wretched existence which Charles Dickens repeatedly describes; rich children were brought up by servants and governesses, and the sons as soon as possible were sent away to school. In the United States there were few educators more progressive than Bronson Alcott, and few children for whom we now feel sorrier than for his famous daughters. It was not considered a disgrace to an American family for an enterprising son to run away to sea, or otherwise to disappear. He was credited with an adventurous spirit; no one whispered what in most cases was the fact, that his home was more than he could put up with. In pioneer families and even in nineteenth-century homes where the income was not large the wife worked like a slave, far harder than the wage-earning wives today, and the children worked too. The children, be it said, frequently turned out very well indeed; the mothers, on the other hand, often broke under the strain and died young. Whether these hard-working households were the best fitted for the upbringing of children, I don't know, but I do know that poverty and hard work are not what the admirers of the old-fashioned home have chiefly in mind.

Some advocates of the old-fashioned home fail to notice an inconsistency in their position. They will tell you that a wife should not earn her living because a regular occupation would prevent her from bringing up a child properly; they will tell you this with a certain accent of self-righteousness which must come from the fact, not that they themselves have children, but that their husbands support them entirely. There are few large households today, whether the wife is a wage-earner or whether she isn't. I am sorry that this is so, since I grew up in a numerous family and my life would have been far less happy without my brother and my sisters, but I know that children in quantity have not always been the ideal of civilized people. Large families seem economically desirable on the soil or in other occupations where the children can be employed instead of mature laborers, who would demand adequate pay for their work. In periods of colonial expansion the advantage of large families seems obvious. In the rivalry of nations or races or religions the group which expands fastest has the best chance of inheriting the earth. The motives which underlie these attitudes toward child-producing are still with us, yet the feeling grows that children should be something more than a means to further the hopes and plans of their elders, that a child, though brought into this world without its consent, is entitled to the best possible preparation for a complete life. The conviction spreads that parents have no right to bring a child into the world unless there is some chance for it to live completely.

On the wall of my study is an old sonnet dating from the sixteenth century and still popular in France, where bookshops sell it in illuminated reproductions neatly framed. Its title is *Le Bonheur de ce Monde,* and it tells what is necessary for happiness in this world—among other things, a small house and few children. I have heard harsh comments on this ideal of the small family, an ideal which before the present war prevailed throughout France, and which probably will continue to prevail after Europe quiets down again, in spite of the plea of French leaders for more children so that there may be more soldiers. France is for the most part an agricultural country and its farms are usually small, adequate for the support of one family and no more. The French farmer and his wife pray for a son and a daughter, the son to inherit the ancestral hearth, the daughter to marry a boy who inherits a hearth of his own. The parents would pray for more children if there were more hearths.

When we idealize the old-fashioned home, perhaps our nostalgia is for the hearth. Only in a settled country can the family hearth be permanent, but every hearth seems permanent to the children who grow up around it. The home of my childhood and youth was built by my father. We began to live in it when I was four years old; the family moved away from it and came back to New York City when I was twenty-one. During the intervening years, however, affection made it the permanent hearth of my family. Until I was nearly twelve my grandmother lived in New York City in what seemed the ancestral home of our clan, since my grandfather had built or bought it before I was born, yet that house too was lived in by only one generation of my people. As I grew up I realized we had remained stationary longer than most Americans. Few people in the United States still occupy at the age of fifty the house in which they were born. Many of us, by the time we are middle-aged, have moved away from the village or town in which our childhood was spent. Until our country fills up and we learn to carve a career wherever we are instead of moving around in search of better opportunities, we shall continue to be a heartless people, somewhat wistful, somewhat disinherited. When an American boy grows up on the farm, leaves the farm for a career in the city and makes his fortune, he shares his good luck with his people but in a very American way; he builds for his parents a finer house than the one in which they brought him up, and he probably presents the local authorities with a more elaborate schoolhouse than the one in which he was educated. This generous way of showing gratitude is peculiarly ours; it would not seem entirely admirable to a people who think of the home as a hearth, a shrine, a family altar. Altars are not lightly replaced. The Frenchman who prospers in the world returns piously to the house which gave him his start; never will he of his own volition abandon it.

When our country is older we may have the same feeling about the hearth, but at present nothing is gained by pretending an attitude which is not ours. A home in the United States contains as much affection as elsewhere in the world, but with us the home is a point of departure; we go out from it, every member of the family, to find a richer life. It would be somewhat insincere to keep on saying that woman's place is in the home if only the mother is supposed to stay there. As a matter of fact, the American mother, seeking her share of a broader life, enters into the society of the neighborhood almost as much as her husband and the children, and few of us see any good reason why she should not do so. That we expect the family to have children in it is sufficiently demonstrated by our characteristic provision of primary and elementary schools. Education in kindergarten and in the early grades includes more than the instruction; to an increasing extent these classes take over the functions of the nursery, for a good part of the day exercising the children, looking after them, encouraging them to amuse and entertain each other. The rich have always employed nurses and governesses; our school system now makes this kind of aid available for all families. The wealthy mother who could afford the nurse and the governess spent her leisure as she pleased; the modern parent uses her freedom from drudgery to piece out the family income and to pursue her own career.

Those who think it would be better for the children to associate all day with their mother are a little blind perhaps to some factors in the question. Many a loving parent lacks entirely the temperament which makes a good teacher or educator. Children derive little benefit from incompetent upbringing, no matter how much good will goes into the incompetence. Furthermore, since every human being likes to associate with others of the same age and the same interests, it is natural for children to seek out other children. In the kindergarten-nursery they are happier than in the isolation of their own family. The larger the family, of course, the better off they are from this point of view, but it's a doubtful advantage, even where it's possible, for each household to produce a total society for its youngest generation; it's far simpler to let the children find companionship in their earliest years as they'll find it later, among members of other families.

It is probably true also that children gain something by growing up in a home where both the parents work. I assume that the parents love each other and that the child therefore enjoys what it is entitled to, an atmosphere of complete affection. If in that atmosphere the child learns early that in this world the work of every human being is needed, so much the better. Children are proud of their father if he makes a contribution to the community and is honored for it; for exactly the same reason they are proud of their mother. In my childhood the tradition still persisted that in households of comfortable circumstances the mother should have her children early, should get through with bringing them up, should then put on a white cap and settle into premature retirement. Old age for mothers began in the forties, or at latest in the fifties—in what we now consider the prime of life. With all respect to the sentiment which dignifies the past, I think the progress indicated by modern ideas of the home is beyond much dispute.

Nowadays we press these ideas even further. Precious as children are, the elders as individuals have their responsibilities and their rights. Old tombstones in our cemeteries preserve a record of other days which in some cases is rather ghastly. The inscriptions which tell us how many children rise up to call their mother blessed frequently tell us also how early the mother died. Not seldom the bereaved husband took himself a second wife to look after him and the progeny of the first. If the first wife hadn't been tragically over-taxed she might have survived to enjoy some of

that affection which is inscribed on her tombstone. Since the ideal
of marriage is lifelong companionship, a program which shortens
that companionship is faulty. If we now inherit less wisdom than
we need for the art of companionship, it may be because our
elders in many cases gave up for the sake of children all opportunity to develop that art. Even where the family was small or
where the children died young, the sacrifice of the wife was too
readily expected and accepted.

The tradition which now is drawn upon for criticism of the
modern home furnishes also exasperating examples of that stubbornness which will not learn from mistakes. One of the most
interesting men I ever met began life in a frontier community in
conditions of extreme hardship. He married very young a girl of
the same background. They had two sons who died early of sick-
nesses which in a more progressive community would not have
been serious. When the second boy died the man had risen as far
as anyone else in his terribly limited world. Having started in the
woods as a lumberman, he had picked up whatever skill was
needed for a job in a canning factory. Between him and his wife
there was loyal companionship, of a dumb, almost brutish, sort.
They were inseparable; each would have given life for the other.
Both craved a more complete existence, but until they were nearly
thirty, their intelligence was latent or inarticulate. They grieved
for the children but rarely spoke of them.

One night some impulse made the man say that even the loss
of the boys seemed easier to bear than lack of education. He told
his astonished wife that he really thought he had a mind, and
with a fair chance he might have got somewhere. Her reply was
simple; if he wanted an education, why not get it? Why shouldn't
they get an education together? Difficult though that feat was,
they accomplished it. It cost terrific toil, but in their forties they
graduated from college together. At that point their companionship came to an end. In order that he might go to a university
and later might study in Europe, she dropped her own studies
and devoted herself entirely to his career. He became a well-
known scholar, and in spite of the initial handicaps he acquired
broad culture, but a wide gap developed between his intellectual
outlook and hers. I knew them both well and I had the whole

story from him. Better than anyone else he was aware of the sacrifice which had helped him to his destiny. He thought it a bleak tragedy and so do I. She was much praised by her own generation as a perfect wife, but I would say that through misguided affection she ceased to be an adequate companion. I wish she had gone further, even though he had gone not quite so far.

3.

The relation of this man and his wife was affectionate and from many points of view admirable, yet it was not the ideal companionship of marriage. The self-effacement with which she met him on his return at the end of the day, the heroic sympathy with which she shared his weariness or discouragement, the strength which she lavished to bolster him up, constitute a one-sided record of goodness. Her mothering instinct made of him a child and his acceptance of her aid has a selfish look, yet I believe she considered it her duty to give him no choice. I'm sure it never occurred to her that a truer kindness would have accepted, even demanded, the same devotion that she gave. He and she both lacked imagination, without which happiness is impossible in love or marriage.

When I was sixteen or seventeen years old some relatives took me to hear a lecture on *Hamlet* delivered by an assertive female who wore her hair extremely short and except for trousers dressed like a man. Who she was, why she lectured on *Hamlet,* why my uncle and aunt took me to hear her, I cannot now say, but midway in her discourse she cast a beam of light on the ideal companionship of husbands and wives. Where she picked up this wisdom was a puzzle even to my youth; if ever her formidable personality lured a mate, Nature surely is beyond discouragement. But she knew what she was talking about, no matter how she had learned. Speaking of Ophelia, she confessed small sympathy with those critics who think Hamlet was cruel to his betrothed. Ophelia, said the lecturer, resembled the wife who always smiled cheerfully when her husband spoke to her. Day after day he returned from his work with good news; his business prospered, his fortune increased, civic dignities descended upon him. The little wife smiled and smiled. Time passed—the wind of fortune shifted. Night after night husband grieved that things weren't going so well, he had lost money, he wouldn't be renominated for alderman. The little wife smiled and smiled—till he brought the ax from the cellar and brained her. According to the lecturer the neighbors sympathized with him.

I mention the French ideal of the home because we Americans, for historical reasons, inherit it side by side with an English ideal. The French word for home is *foyer*, which is derived from the Latin *focus*, a fireplace or hearth. We use this Latin word to describe a vital point upon which rays of light. or heat are cen- tered, or from which they branch out. Our word home comes from the old English *ham*, which we still meet in place-names, such as Nottingham, Hurlingham. *Ham* means a village or town; and it contains no suggestion of a fireplace or hearth. The French *foyer*, therefore, stresses the individualistic conception of the family; the English *home* suggests rather a relation to the com- munity and to the landscape. A Frenchman has, of course, a notable passion for his native soil, and the Englishman, no less than the Frenchman, loves the house which is his castle, yet between their characteristic attitudes there is a distinction which bride and groom in our American world must reckon with. They will either set up a *foyer*, a shrine, or they will make their home in the place where they reside—in the community rather than in any one house. If you ask me where my home is, I answer New York City. In the last ten years I have lived in three different apartments. New York City remains my home, no matter how often my address changes. An address, obviously, is not a *foyer*, though anyone, single or married, can carry his household gods in his heart and set them up even in the desert.

I suppose the sympathy of the neighbors took into account the fact that most marriages derive some companionship from trouble. The wife in the story was stupid not to make the most out of her husband's misfortunes. The ideal basis of companionship is not sorrow, sickness, or disaster, yet marriages may be cemented by anything which husband and wife face together. Companionship developed in defense against trouble may be one-sided; if one of the partners is an invalid and both put their attention on the disease or on recovery from it, they aren't likely to be equally unselfish. Yet the number of homes held together by trouble rather than by positive aspirations is distressingly large, and few things are more discouraging than willingness to accept this sort of companionship as ideal. I have heard it said more often than I like to recall that worry, if it is not unbearable, gives married folk something to unite on. The flaw in such a theory is the implication that when the mortgage on the farm is at last paid off, the farmer and his wife will drift apart.

We are bad philosophers if we attribute happiness to poverty, but there is a sense in which smallness of income may hold the family together. Lack of wealth is not the same thing as poverty; so long as you can pay your bills and save for a rainy day you're not in trouble. I wouldn't say that companionship developed by even this less serious economic pressure is ideal, but there's something to be said for it.

When I was very young I met at a summer resort two most likable people, each interesting as an individual and both doubly attractive in their obviously happy marriage. I digress here to recall my youthful admiration, especially of the wife, who was good-looking. The hotel laundry one week included, along with my things, a woman's cuff—they did wear them in those days! The initials on the cuff-band were hers. It is horrible to recall, but I wrote a poem to her in lead pencil on the inside of the cuff, at least five stanzas of four lines each. What must have been her emotions when she saw that the thing must go back into the wash!

She and her husband were at that time well off in a modest way, and wonderful companions. I have seen them only once again, fifteen years after the cuff episode. They had become extremely wealthy, and since they loved each other they were still happy, but she told me that as their wealth increased, their companionship diminished. "In the old days when he needed a suit, or I a new dress, we put our heads together to see whether we could afford it that week or that month. He would save up for my birthday, and I would do the same for him, planning gifts which more often than not were useful in the home. Now I can buy what dresses I wish and he can order anything at all from his tailor. He still shows me the new suit and asks how I like it; I call his attention to the new gown. But it isn't the same."

Today few marriages will be imperiled by an over-supply of wealth; the danger now is that we'll be satisfied with a companionship based only on compulsory care of the home budget. This negative or defensive ideal of marriage surrenders the control of our own happiness, and accepts what fate sends.

Unintentionally, but with inexorable logic, it gets itself into a false position; it relies upon misfortune, even upon the misfortune of others. It is not unlike the philosophy entertained, however unconsciously, by some reformers or social uplifters who could not look forward to a permanent job if they indulged any hope that the folks they work on will be rescued or set on their feet.

If we say that companionship should be founded on happiness rather than misfortune, we risk misunderstanding; the companionship we speak of may seem exclusively a fair weather ideal, and unless we are idiotic we know that in this world fair weather is rare. Yet we make progress only by aiming beyond the solution of our present difficulties. If I fall ill, I try to get well again—that is, back to where I was before; but merely to hold one's own is not enough for the complete life. To fight off poverty together or to share sorrow is not all that ideal marriage promises. Assume for a moment an absence of trouble and worry, no handicap of any sort, nothing to detain us, no excuse for shirking; what then would we make of our lives?

If we know what we'd do in favorable conditions, we can try for that ideal now. If any married folk interrupt me to say that the best thing to do with favorable conditions is to preserve them unchanged, I fear the prospect of their companionship is not bright. They have no creative aims. But if they can imagine a possible improvement in themselves, and through their efforts a further improvement of conditions which will make possible a further improvement in themselves—then a rich experience is before them.

Self-development is the theme of this book. Our lives will remain incomplete unless we cultivate whatever talent we have, all our talents, and though noble characters have grown in lone-liness we are social creatures and we do best when companionship inspires and challenges us. If marriage is a co-operative progress, it will contain the wholesome element of competition. There must be progress. To compete in standing still is not wholesome.

Can we say offhand what we'd like to be if we had the chance? Perhaps we'd prefer not to raise the question—but we should raise it. If we avoid asking because we think it wouldn't do much good, we are fooling ourselves; our reluctance to face our ideals, to define our aspirations, is caused by human inertia. A body at rest will remain at rest unless some outside force moves it; a body in motion will continue in motion until some outside force stops it. Most of us find something agreeable in the idea of being a body at rest. If in spite of ourselves we are in motion we consent to keep on, but we'd rather not increase the speed.

When I was a teacher every graduation day left me conscience-stricken over the large proportion of my students who acquired a diploma before they knew what sort of life they wanted. To rouse youth from inertia ought to be the first benefit of educa-tion. Fortunately, though we have slept late, it is not impossible, even at high noon, to wake ourselves, and the attempt should be the easier when it is made for love's sake. The marriage vow is "to love and cherish." Cherishing is to mind and heart what nourishment is to the body. The promise to support the woman is made by the man but the vow to cherish is made by them both. Each will rouse the other to grow in spirit.

When we welcome the possibility of lifelong continuous devel-opment, marriage becomes a sacrament in a most vital and majestic sense as a dedication to the future. We can then under-stand also why an unhappy marriage is the most tragic of failures. Nature calls the sexes together, love fashions a dream, religion blesses our hopes and says a prayer for us, a prayer in which our elder relatives join, with our body we worship the beloved—and the law says that a marriage has been consummated. But it will never be complete unless husband and wife accomplish the cre-ative miracle of cherishing, each drawing out from the other's character resources which else would remain undeveloped. There are married folk in plenty who tell their mates where improvement would be welcome, but these are domestic pests, not companions; let them now be far from our thoughts! Wife and husband should each define for themselves the image of that perfection toward which their gifts permit them to aspire, and each respecting the other's dream should aid in its realization.

The creative life, so envisaged, is a happy one, no matter what shadows fall upon it. All the languages which nature provides, all words, all caresses, all silences, fall short of what such companionship has to say. The children whom this happiness calls into being, are well born.

4.

Many of the best novels, poems or plays in English avoid full-length pictures of love and married companionship. We have great stories of thwarted love, charming glimpses of adolescent romance, sentimental portraits of Darby and Joan as they show themselves publicly to the neighbors, but of intimate companionship in all its moods we have few serious studies. I hesitate to suggest that English or American writers are ignorant of married life or indifferent to it; perhaps they veer away from the subject because it involves sex, and some fanatics for the proprieties still pretend that sex is a naughty child, which may behave better if we pay no attention. But if you have cut your eye teeth and if you write for readers who have cut theirs, you feel like a fool describing love or marriage with sex left out.

In my first three novels, *The Private Life of Helen of Troy,* *Galahad,* and *Adam and Eve,* I tried to study marriage from various angles but with no hypocritical blinking of sex, and to make it easier for Mrs. Grundy I laid the scene of these stories far in the past. Distance and time fumigate all things. Of course I wasn't writing of antiquity; I had no information to dispense about Troy or Camelot or the Garden of Eden; I was describing men and women as I know them in the middle twenties of this century. By transposing my contemporaries to ancient times I was able to portray them complete and unabridged. Mrs. Grundy enjoys reading about Helen and Paris, about Lancelot and Guinevere, provided you let her think those full-blooded folk crumbled to dust long ago and their passions are now outlawed.

I once was so rash as to discuss the American woman's attitude toward books, pointing out that those who buy books don't shine as readers and those who read don't buy, books being expensive and lending libraries convenient. This sweeping statement brought protests, many of them clever and all of them illuminating. More than one defender of womankind included a list of the books she herself had read, with her critical comments. Though the majority of the letters came from married women whose reading was accomplished in the midst of household duties, and against the educative background of parenthood, yet their literary opinions were without exception severe on writers like myself who would accord the same recognition to sex as to gravitation. We are no longer surprised by fantastic codes of decorum, but we still wonder how the sacredness and the dignity of marriage can be established by blanketing or misrepresenting what we call, with an implication of shame, the facts of life.

I wish I could illustrate from modern literature in the English language those ideals of love and marriage which I have here tried to set forth, but I must go back to a day less cluttered with humbug and hypocrisy. Two poets already mentioned in these pages, two poets more often praised than read, help me now. Edmund Spenser, author of *The Faerie Queene,* had for wife Elizabeth Boyle, whom he married in the cathedral at Cork, June 11, 1594. When his wedding gifts to her, ordered from London, were delayed by storms on the Irish Sea, he wrote the wonderful *Epithalamion* as a sort of promissory note, as he tells us in an italicized postscript or footnote, spelled for the confusion of printers then as now:

> *Song! made in lieu of many ornaments*
> *With which my love should duly have been dect,*
> *Which cutting off through hasty accidents,*
> *Ye would not stay your dew time to expect,*
> *But promist both to recompens;*
> *Be unto her a goodly ornament,*
> *And for short time an endlesse moniment.*

The poem describes the wedding day, from early morning till midnight, every incident imagined as though it had already oc-

curred—the preparations for the ceremony, taxing the bride-
groom's patience; the dressing of the bride in her gown and veil;
the service at the church; the wedding feast; day's end at last
and the lovers in their bridal chamber. Two phases of the wedding
Spenser elaborates and emphasizes as we should expect of him
after his brave definition of Chastity in the third book of *The
Faerie Queene*. He describes with the same reverence the taking
of the vows before the altar and the bodily sacrament of love.
The church scene is often quoted.

> "Bring her up to th'high altar, that she may
> The sacred ceremonies there partake,
> The which do endlesse matrimony make;
> And let the roring Organs loudly play
> The praises of the Lord in lively notes;
> The whiles, with hollow throates,
> The Choristers the joyous Antheme sing,
> That al the woods may answere, and their eccho ring.

> "Behold, whiles she before the altar stands,
> Hearing the holy priest that to her speakes,
> And blesseth her with his two happy hands,
> How the red roses flush up in her cheekes."

Spenser converts the nuptial scene, by a stroke of imagination,
into a universal statement of what, if true only of one man and
one woman, would indeed be too intimate to talk about. But here
is the ideal of companionship from generation to generation, the
forces of nature wedded to the aspirations of the soul for the
endless bettering of the race. From their marriage bed the lovers
see the rising moon and the glittering stars. The moon is Cinthia
or Diana, goddess of chastity, but Spenser as we know identified
chastity with the creative virtues of marriage; Diana in the ancient
mythology was the goddess not only of maidenhood but of childbirth. The rising moon lifts the mood of the poem, transfiguring
sex.

> "Who is the same, which at my window peepes?
> Or whose is that faire face that shines so bright?
> Is it not Cinthia, she that never sleepes,

But walkes about high heaven al the night?
O! fayrest goddesse, do thou not envy
My love with me to spy!
For thou likewise didst love, though now unthought,
And for a fleece of wooll, which privily
The Latmian shepherd once unto thee brought,
His pleasures with thee wrought:
Therefore to us be favorable now;
And sith of wemens labours thou hast charge,
And generation goodly dost enlarge,
Encline thy will t'effect our wishfull vow,
And the chaste wombe informe with timely seed,
That may our comfort breed:
Till which we cease our hopefull hap to sing;
Ne let the woods us answere, nor our Eccho ring.

"And ye high heavens, the temple of the gods,
In which a thousand torches flaming bright
Doe burne, that to us wretched earthly clods
In dreadful darknesse lend desired light;
And all ye powers which in the same remayne,
More then we men can fayne!
Poure out your blessing on us plentiously,
And happy influence upon us raine,
That we may raise a large posterity,
Which from the earth, which they may long possesse
With lasting happinesse,
Up to your haughty pallaces may mount;
And for the guerdon of theyr glorious merit,
May heavenly tabernacles there inherit,
Of blessed Saints for to increase the count.
So let us rest, sweet love, in hope of this,
And cease till then our tymely joyes to sing;
The woods no more us answer, nor our eccho ring!"

Beautiful though this wedding song is, it gives no complete
picture of companionship in marriage; for that, we must go to
Milton's *Paradise Lost*. The famous epic tells the story of the

fall of man, of man's first disobedience, of the earlier fall of
Lucifer and of the war in Heaven. These were Milton's themes,
and what he says incidentally about husbands and wives was not
intended to monopolize our interest. I am one of those readers,
however, who find his poetry far more important than his theology, and his account of Adam and Eve far more kindling than
what he says of God and the angels. As a religious philosopher
he was no Dante. But the seventeenth century occupied itself with
those ideals of love and marriage which we call modern, and to
poets such as John Milton a companionship based on anything
but mutual love began to seem intolerable. When the argument
moved on to the remedies for loveless marriage, Milton advocated
divorce so eloquently that he was suspected of personal reasons
for taking the liberal side; perhaps he didn't get on well with that
first wife of his. In the divorce pamphlets, however, as in *Paradise
Lost,* I should think he was interested chiefly in the positive ideals
of marriage; for exceptional reasons the Church permitted divorce
or annulment but on the wrong grounds, as he believed. If the
conventional grounds for divorce were wrong, perhaps the conventional theories of marriage were also mistaken.

The purpose of marriage, Milton insisted, was companionship.
God saw that Adam needed a helpmeet; nowhere are we told that
Adam needed children. Childbirth in the Biblical story was part
of the curse pronounced on the woman after the fall. If there
was to be no childbirth in Paradise, devout people who now say
that children are the object of marriage are in logical difficulties.
While man and woman were perfect was there no love, no loving?
Milton refuses to believe any doctrine so depressing. Adam and
Eve must have slept together in Paradise, if it was Paradise. In
the fourth book of *Paradise Lost* he goes to some pains to make
this clear, paying his respects in passing to all sex-prudes, past,
present and future. Only with an effort do we remember that
puritans like Spenser and Milton were once the bold thinkers,
pleading for less fig-leaf and more sincerity.

> "Into their inmost bower
> Handed they went; and, eased the putting-off
> These troublesome disguises which we wear,

> Straight side by side were laid; nor turned, I ween,
> Adam from his fair spouse, nor Eve the rites
> Mysterious of connubial love refused:
> Whatever hypocrites austerely talk
> Of purity, and place, and innocence,
> Defaming as impure what God declares
> Pure, and commands to some, leaves free to all.
> Our Maker bids increase; who bids abstain
> But our destroyer, foe to God and Man?
> Hail, wedded Love!"

It won't escape you that Milton, by saying that our Maker bids increase, is himself getting the logic mixed; if increase of the family is desired even in Paradise, then children are not to be accounted for exclusively as a punishment laid on Eve. But I'm afraid the contradiction is in the creation stories which begin the book of Genesis, and it's too late to straighten them out. Perhaps Milton, in the passage just quoted, was arguing as a modern man, using whatever he could to strengthen his case without regard to inconsistencies in his sources.

But Milton takes liberties with the text otherwise, apparently for the purpose of filling out the picture of married life in Eden and at the same time making it recognizable. The Bible says that Eve, as the other part of her punishment, had to accept inferiority to Adam. Milton says that this inferiority is ideal and therefore it manifested itself in Paradise. Man was the superior, and both he and his wife knew it. Adam came first; Eve was an after-thought.

"He for God only, she for God in him."

Adam lectures Eve about the universe in which he arrived before she did; he lets her praise him to his face, but he is careful not to spoil her with compliments. In short, he's a good deal of a prig, and many readers have thrown down the poem, condemning John Milton for being an incurable male without humor. They should read to the end. The story of Adam and Eve in the Bible is a tragedy; in *Paradise Lost* it is a tragi-comedy, a shrewd portrait of men and women as they are, the man assuming superiority, the woman conceding it when it's her pleasure to do so, but keeping her husband well in hand. How Milton escaped the reputation of wit and humor, is a puzzle. When Raphael, the "affable archangel," visits Paradise, Adam asks for an explanation of the mystery which puzzles every husband; of course he's superior to his wife, but why doesn't he feel so when she's around?

> "For well I understand in the prime end
> Of Nature her the inferior, in the mind
> And inward faculties, which most excel;
> In outward also her resembling less
> His image who made both, and less expressing
> The character of that dominion given
> O'er other creatures. Yet when I approach
> Her loveliness, so absolute she seems
> And in herself complete, so well to know
> Her own, that what she wills to do or say
> Seems wisest, virtuousest, discreetest, best.
> All higher Knowledge in her presence falls
> Degraded; Wisdom in discourse with her
> Loses, discountenanced, and like Folly shows;
> Authority and Reason on her wait,
> Like one intended first, not after made
> Occasionally; and to consummate all,
> Greatness of mind and nobleness their seat
> Build in her loveliest, and create an awe
> About her, as a guard angelic placed."

Raphael's reply is short but delicious; he dodges the awkward question.

> "Accuse not Nature! She hath done her part;
> Do thou but thine!"

When the serpent tempts Eve, she yields for a reason not stated in Genesis. She is so tired of Adam's lectures that she wouldn't mind having the wherewithal to do a little lecturing herself. She won't share the apple with Adam. But when she has eaten the forbidden fruit her first acquired insight is this, that now ˏshe may die, and God who has made one woman can create another. She decides quickly. Adam must eat of the tree! Did Milton understand women? Some critics think not.

Adam is at his best when he learns what she has done. He knows the sin will bring death, but he'd rather not live without her. She is even finer than he at the end; she asks whether it wouldn't be decent to save future mankind from the curse; if he and she did not exist, God could start over again, and perhaps the next pair would have more sense; why shouldn't Adam and she kill themselves before they have children? There's that greatness of mind and nobleness which Adam had observed before. Again, did the old poet understand women?

He has given us an allegory of companionship, human and shadowed yet ideal. When the man and the woman are separated, they are in trouble; when they are happy they go hand in hand. So we first see them:

> "Two of far nobler shape, erect and tall,
>   God-like erect, with native honour clad
>   In naked majesty, seemed lords of all,
>   And worthy seemed; for in their looks divine
>   The image of their glorious Maker shone—
>
>   So passed they naked on, nor shunned the sight
>   Of God or Angel; for they thought no ill:
>   So hand in hand they passed, the loveliest pair
>   That ever since in love's embraces met—
>   Adam the goodliest man of men since born
>   His sons; the fairest of her daughters Eve."

Together hand in hand they leave Paradise—or take it with them. Milton doesn't close the poem on a sad note. He couldn't, being himself fond of travel.

> "Some natural tears they dropped, but wiped them soon;
>   The world was all before them, where to choose

Their place of rest, and Providence their guide.
They, hand in hand, with wandering steps and slow,
Through Eden took their solitary way."

Notice that he calls their way solitary. Husband and wife, not
two persons but one.

CHAPTER XIII

How to Be a Parent

TO BEGET OR to bear a child is no art at all. Some of the greatest fools have excelled at it. Being a parent is quite a different matter.

Parenthood, like love and marriage, is a companionship in which nature and art should collaborate but sometimes fail to do so. Affection for one's offspring is so instinctive that fathers and mothers may be pardoned for believing themselves the best people in the world to bring up their own children. Their confidence ought to be justified but in some cases it isn't. Unless instinctive affection is supplemented with thoughtful skill, with a self-sacrificing philosophy, parental care may overreach itself and become tyranny. From the moment the child is born the art of parenthood should begin, and it should continue until the parent dies. But lifelong companionship between generations involves successive surrenders of authority by the parents and the assumption of more and more responsibility by the children.

Companionship of this evolving kind is difficult for some parents, all the more so if their instinctive affection is strong. They can't learn or they won't admit that children do grow up. They fail perhaps to notice that their child is growing up faster than they did. Or they spoil their children and unwittingly train them to be selfish by setting up for them a special little world in which the privileges are many and responsibilities don't exist. Parents when they are intelligent as well as loving supply childhood with the principles by which life can be lived well—and as soon as possible they encourage the children to master those principles by practice. Fathers and mothers who would prolong the infancy of their sons and daughters are not kind, and they can't have entire confidence in the instruction they themselves have imparted or in the example they have set.

For the first dozen years, more or less, of a child's life the influence of the elder generation is enormous. The art of parenthood is then most needed, since children learn by imitating those whom they admire. If you associate with them at all, you are involved in education whether or not you intend to be. If your temperament is unsympathetic to childhood, children will not imitate you, not even though your example is excellent. If on the other hand there is an instinctive bond between you and them, they will imitate you even though your example is bad. Unless you stay away from them entirely, you are under heavy obligation to win their confidence and to deserve it.

This confidence-winning is an art so intertwined with temperament and character that I doubt if it can be taught or learned. We have it or we haven't. If we haven't, we are sadly deficient. Biologically we can produce children, but their true parents will be the relatives or the nurses who know how to be their companions. I like to believe that comparatively few mothers and fathers lack the aptitude for parenthood and are therefore unable to acquire the art, yet perhaps the number is larger than we admit. In how many households has the true parent been a grandfather or a grandmother, an aunt or an uncle, an elder brother or sister! Whether or not we are likely to be good parents in this larger sense, we can find out as early as we choose; we don't need to produce children in order to discover whether we have talent for bringing them up. True parents understand all children, even those not their own, and all children recognize them promptly as desirable companions. If we expect to acquire an interest in childhood after marriage and not till then, we shall be disappointed. The children will be too.

It would be intelligent, I think, for those who marry to discover in advance whether they have a gift for parenthood. In any case I hope they will have children, but if they don't understand childhood I hope they will entrust the children to those who do. No one should try to bring up the young who is not in sympathy with what goes on in the heart and mind of a growing child. When I hear well-meaning educators or parents discuss child psychology, or juvenile interests, or the adolescent this or that, I groan; I fear they are approaching childhood backwards, trying to get at the condition of infancy again by stripping away all they have learned since. Better to drop all retrospective theories and simply recall our own inner life, which if we were normal had in those early years an unforgettable intensity.

When we were children neither our knowledge nor our dreams were limited to childhood. No child ever feels that it is a child. No one of any age ever feels immature. Or if we do feel so, it is against our will; we wish to be contemporaries. To understand childhood sympathetically, we must remember those aspirations which chiefly fill a child's thoughts, the ambition to do things, to get at life, to imitate its elders. If we have forgotten the romance of these early dreams, we are no fit companion for a child. Since most educators and altogether too many parents have indeed to some extent forgotten, they are in that degree disqualified. We are disqualified when we tell a child not to do this or not to do that; the aspirations of childhood, of humanity at any age, are positive. If the active child gets on our nerves, it's because we have lost our own zest for life, the impulse to be up and doing; we have grown old, and we break the news to the child when we say, "Don't." Companionship would be perfect and education would progress if we urged the child to do something, making the suggestion even before the child thought of it.

On a train not long ago I watched a mother struggling with an extremely active small boy. The boy was full of spirits and the mother, at least in her imagination, was tired. She was at that moment and for that particular child a parental failure. He climbed over her knees to look out the window, and she told him not to do it. He climbed up on the back of the seat to investigate the passenger behind him, and she told him not to do that. He got down on the floor to find out what was under the seat, and his mother slapped him for the dust on his knees. He then said he wanted a drink of water, and she told him to go get it, for heaven's sake. The day was warm and the car hot. He went forward to the ice-water, had his drink, got a fresh Lily cup and brought a drink to his mother. She thanked him affectionately— which was right. She also showed her surprise—which was wrong.

For several minutes he behaved very well indeed, partly because he was cooled off, much more because he had been permitted to do something, and because he himself had thought of something courteous and mature. But after a while he became restless again. A born parent would have suggested a drink for every woman in the car. He would have been busy and happy as long as the water held out.

2.

There fortunately have been so many good parents in the world, and so many recorded memories of them, that the outline of their art is clear. Two of the best of fathers in my opinion were Pierre de Montaigne and John Milton the elder. Our Montaigne, the essayist, never missed an opportunity to express his affection for his father, and what for us is more practically helpful, to say in detail just how that father brought him up. Pierre de Montaigne was youthful at heart and he had ideas of education centuries ahead of his time. Since childhood is naturally active, he made himself his son's ideal by being more active than the boy could possibly be. Michel may have been, as he says, of a lazy temperament, but even if he had been a human whirlwind his father would have outdistanced him. When Pierre was sixty he liked to vault into the saddle without aid from the stirrup, and when he wished to get to the other side of a broad table, he would rest one thumb on the top of it and swing himself over. To keep himself in trim he always went upstairs three or four steps at a time. A good hour each day he spent throwing the bar and putting the shot, and he practiced running and jumping in a pair of leaden-soled shoes. I have an idea these miracles were paraded for the benefit of his small boy, on whom, as the essays proved, they made a lasting impression.

Pierre de Montaigne didn't believe in corporal punishment. He had extraordinary ideas of the proper company for his son to grow up in. There was a tutor for Latin and other subjects, but Michel was encouraged to spend as much time as possible with the farm hands, the stable boys, and others who knew life on its hard terms. These are the very people with whom children always wish to spend their time, because they are the ones who do the world's work. Most parents disapprove of this profound instinct, but Pierre de Montaigne encouraged it, apparently on the principle that members of the human family should know each other, and it's easier for the rich to approach the poor than for the poor to introduce themselves among the rich.

The usual method of studying languages seemed to Pierre de Montaigne an unnecessary hardship. Every child learns his own tongue by hearing and by speaking it, and he is aware of no difficulties. Why shouldn't all languages be acquired the same way? Michel spoke Latin before he spoke French. His tutor lived in the house and in his early years addressed him in no other language. Pierre de Montaigne, the father, was careful in the child's hearing to use such Latin as he knew, but no French or Spanish. The unfortunate mother and the servants were compelled to get up a few necessary Latin phrases. As a result Michel's Latin was magnificent, though, as he says, it became contaminated when he went to college, where they studied it the wrong way. French came to him by association after his fourth and fifth year with the workmen on his father's place. Would you think that his French would be vulgar? It is. It's as racy as William Shakespeare's, with all the power and color of speech used by strong men close to the soil.

Pierre de Montaigne brought up his son to be honest and sincere and to tell the truth. He followed the only recipe known for these virtues; he trained the boy to have no fear. That is one reason why he objected to corporal punishment. Children should not have fear planted in them by their parents; it is to their parents they should turn when they are in trouble or have done wrong. To win this confidence parents must be ready with a sympathetic ear—and never, never must they show surprise. After all, nothing that youth confesses can astonish us; we ourselves have been young. If our boy tells us courageously of a fault or a mistake, why shouldn't we smile in recognition of a recurring plight? We needn't condone the fault, but a child is helped by the discovery that elders too are human. If on the other hand we listen with horror or with grave reproof, a gulf opens between us. We have destroyed the companionship; we have removed ourselves fatally into a separate generation which forgets life or never understood it.

After Pierre de Montaigne's death his son inherited the estate, managed the vineyards and the wine-making from which the family fortune was derived, kept up the household customs which his father loved, imitated all his days the example of a remarkable parent. In many respects his natural gifts differed from his father's, and perhaps his career was not what Pierre de Montaigne intended, but the principles of a good life were instilled in him early, and he enjoyed the privilege of companionship, the freedom to stand on his own feet and consort with other men, even with his father, on his own merits.

John Milton's father was a lawyer and a banker, a combination of professions usual in his time. He was wealthy and he had talent for the fine arts, particularly for music. Some compositions of his still exist and still command respect. He is a notable example of the wise parent who permits a child to develop in its own way, and foreseeing what that way will be, provides from the beginning the best possible training. What the father's problem in this case was, we can see if we keep in mind, at least in outline, the course of the son's youth, and then glance at the son's grateful tributes to the father who would not himself have chosen that course.

From childhood John Milton, the poet, showed extraordinary aptitude for all kinds of learning, and for at least two arts, literature and music. He also showed, if not great aptitude, at least more than usual facility in physical exercises. He would have made a good military commander and he would have succeeded in business. Furthermore, in early youth if not in childhood he disclosed a turn for leadership and an interest in affairs of state. All his life he numbered among his friends notable men in England and on the Continent. His personal magnetism made children and mature folk alike recognize him as a great man.

Naturally his father, fully aware of the difficulties which threatened the English people, thought he was destined to a public career. A boy whose talents were so varied and whose concern for the common welfare was so great, seemed a born statesman, but the boy could think of himself as nothing but a poet. With extraordinary audacity he assured his father he would some day write an epic worthy to rank with the *Aeneid* or with any later masterpiece. Such a work would need long preparation, he explained. He ought to learn all that could be known of the arts and sciences, he ought to visit all the countries of Europe, he ought to interview personally the outstanding men of his age; then at the age of fifty, perhaps, he would set himself to composition. More than one young man has promised the world that he would do something great, but John Milton kept his promise, and he knew how much his father had contributed to this success. The elder Milton has a high place among parents for his willingness to respect his son's peculiar gifts and his son's choice of a way of life. He may have asked himself the question which we ask now—how much the world would have lost if the bold and confident genius had been kept from fulfilling his promise.

John Milton, thanks to his father, had just the training he wanted. He spent seven years at Cambridge in prodigious studies, he traveled widely on the Continent, returning to England only when the civil wars were imminent. When those wars broke out he must have felt as young men in all lands feel today, that the good life they should have had is taken from them. He threw himself into the political quarrel, defending the Puritan cause with extraordinary eloquence in various pamphlets, into some of which he introduced autobiographical passages, precious for their information about his activities and his thoughts. He became foreign secretary under Cromwell, acquitting himself well in that public career for which his father had believed him fitted. In the service of the state he used up his eyesight and became blind. The cause which he served was defeated, the Puritans went out of power, and Charles II came to the throne. Then, in obscurity, a fugitive from Stuart vengeance, permitted to live chiefly perhaps because he had lost his sight and seemed harmless, John Milton kept his delayed promise and wrote *Paradise Lost*.

I remind you of these facts by way of paying a tribute to John Milton's father, who deserves credit, how much no one can say, for his son's magnificent career. The son, of course, will always seem great in his own right for his indomitable character, his full use of all his gifts, his undaunted faith, but the father made the way easy for him in childhood and youth, and inspired him to the end by a noble example.

One of John Milton's Latin poems, written early, is addressed to his father. It is easily accessible in translation. As poetry it is of little importance, though scholars who are qualified to say, assure us that the Latin versification is excellent. We value the poem now for its picture of the relations between father and son. In every line there is evidence of great affection, but also of a difference of opinion. Milton thanks his father for the generosity which provided the education he wished. "You did not force me," he says, "to be a business man. You did not make a lawyer out of me nor ask me to be like yourself a banker. You permitted me to study, as I wished, history, philosophy, science, the great works of antiquity and of later days. When I had learned Latin and Greek, you made it possible for me to acquire French, Italian, and Hebrew. You gave me leisure and music and books, and you gave me the means to travel.

"But I do wish you thought more highly of poetry than you do! Or is it only a playful affectation of yours to warn me constantly against the Muses? Really, you are inconsistent, being yourself a musician, or do you think poetry should be the work of an amateur?"

The elder Milton obviously saw no career for his son in verse-writing. We shouldn't be surprised if he took with a grain of salt all those post-dated pledges of a masterpiece. The Latin tribute suggests that with his generosity to his son went some teasing.

The autobiographical passages of Milton's prose expanded some of the information we gain from the early Latin poem. In the pamphlet called "The Reason of Church Government Urged Against Prelaty," occurs this famous boast, or if boast seems too strong a word, this famous pledge:

"I must say, therefore, that after I had for my first years, by the ceaseless diligence and care of my father, (whom God recompense!) been exercised to the tongues, and some sciences, as my age would suffer, by sundry masters and teachers, both at home and at the schools, it was found that whether aught was imposed me by them that had the overlooking, or betaken to of mine own choice in English, or other tongue, prosing or versing, but chiefly by this latter, the style, by certain vital signs it had, was likely to live. But much latelier in the private academies of Italy, whither I was favoured to resort, perceiving that some trifles which I had in memory, composed at under twenty or thereabout, (for the manner is, that every one must give some proof of his wit and reading there,) met with acceptance above what was looked for; and other things, which I had shifted in scarcity of books and conveniences to patch up amongst them, were received with written encomiums, which the Italian is not forward to bestow on men of this side the Alps; I began thus far to assent both to them and divers of my friends here at home, and not less to an inward prompting which now grew daily upon me, that by labour and intense study, (which I take to be my portion in this life,) joined with the strong propensity of nature, I might perhaps leave something so written to aftertimes, as they should not willingly let it die."

In the same pamphlet a few pages later Milton repeats this pledge, revealing in superb images his conception of a true poet's consecration.

"Neither do I think it shame to covenant with any knowing reader, that for some few years yet I may go on trust with him toward the payment of what I am now indebted, as being a work not to be raised from the heat of youth, or the vapours of wine; like that which flows at waste from the pen of some vulgar amourist, or the trencher fury of a rhyming parasite; nor to be obtained by the invocation of dame memory and her siren daughters, but by devout prayer to that eternal Spirit, who can enrich with all utterance and knowledge, and sends out his seraphim, with the hallowed fire of his altar, to touch and purify the lips of whom he pleases: to this must be added industrious and select reading, steady observation, insight into all seemly and generous arts and affairs; till which in some measure be compassed, at mine own peril and cost, I refuse not to sustain this expectation from as many as are not loth to hazard so much credulity upon the best pledges that I can give them."

These words, we remember, were written when it seemed unlikely to anyone except the poet himself that the great poem would ever come to birth. But he had made his promise or his covenant, as he called it, with heaven. Also with that superb parent, his father.

3.

For most parents discipline is the great problem. They'd like to know how on earth to make the child behave. If you ask for a precise description of the behavior they are looking for, you'll probably get a negative answer; the child may do what it likes so long as it does nothing its parents dislike. But unless the parents know what they want, how can the child guess? Behavior is positive action, therefore to be taught and learned quite as much by example as by precept. Discipline should have in it no taint of punishment or revenge; the word means "the training of a disciple." Own up; when you threaten to discipline your children, aren't you saying, more often than not, that if they continue to annoy you you'll get even with them? Discipline correctly defined is another aspect of that companionship we have harped on. There can be no disciple unless there is first a master. The problem of behavior involves two people, and our children watch our behavior even more closely than we watch theirs. If there's anything wrong with them there's probably something wrong with us.

If I haven't already made it clear, let me say right out that I think any person disqualified as a parent who uses corporal punishment on a child, either by flogging or by the milder slapping. I never saw a mother slap a child who hadn't first to some degree lost her temper. If the mother slaps her child in public she usually looks a bit ashamed of herself. No good companionship can be based on physical assault. A child once slapped will keep a wary eye on the parent in future, no matter how harmless the parent may seem. It's no excuse to say that a child is after all only a young animal, in need of training; after the first slap the child knows that mother is an old animal, who if roused will strike. Even if we believe that our children are animals, we might consider what kind of animal we wish them to be. Wild animals are tamed with the whip and the pistol; thoroughbreds are disciplined by kindness, firmness and intelligence. With blooded animals the whip is out; patience and companionship take its place.

On this point I feel so strongly that I part company with my friends who condone the tradition of flogging which persists in some old-world schools. I believe that any educational system which retains flogging as a punishment falls somewhat short of preparing for a civilized world, in which an individual will be respected as a human being, regardless of his age or station. The teacher who takes a whip to a boy is a bully, and the boy who is trained to submit to floggings will grow up to be another bully. He may inherit or otherwise attain power and he may rule the earth, but the earth will not like him, and when it gets a chance it will turn on him. The whipped animal is a wild animal, and an animal so long as it is wild is not a trustworthy companion. From these liabilities I can extract no ideal for the complete life.

When I saw the motion picture based on the novel *How Green Was My Valley,* I was left limp and angry by the scene in which the schoolmaster flogs the small boy within an inch of his life. Even in so decent a story as *Goodbye Mr. Chips,* the lovable teacher in the picture version switches the backside of a pupil. The caning is far from gory, since the old gentleman's right arm has lost its vigor, but a brutal tradition even in an anaemic form is not a pretty sight. I taught my own son that unless he made himself liable to arrest by the police, no one had a right to lay hands on him, and that the school teacher who tried to whip him should have a swift right to the jaw. But I couldn't have instilled this personal pride if I hadn't myself treated him as an equal. Never in his most annoying moments did I ever lay a finger on him.

Discipline is not punishment, and it should not rest on threats. If we remember that parents and children should be companions, and if we are willing to observe our own behavior at the moment our child is troublesome, perhaps we'll admit without argument that in any company the most active mind gets the attention. If our child is driving us crazy with questions or pranks, his mind is more active than ours, and he's finding us a poor companion. Unless our mind can stir itself, we'd better get someone more wide awake to take care of him. We give our case away when we complain that we never can tell what he'll be up to next. He ought not to be able to tell what *we* shall be up to.

The first illustration that comes to mind is a bit of clowning;

I'll try to furnish more subtle examples later on. But the essence of the matter is here. At Trinity Church, in New York City, Dr. Henry Stephen Cutler was organist and choirmaster from 1858 to 1865. He is remembered now, I believe, chiefly for the tune usually sung to the hymn "The Son of God Goes Forth to War." To his choir boys he was one of those parental geniuses who are always up to something. If you have ever tried to keep a boy choir in order, you know the ultimate in human difficulties. Boys endowed with voices fit for praising the Lord are usually imps, so mysteriously does evil divide the world with good. By keeping his imps in continuous amazement, Dr. Cutler made them forget to misbehave, and since he never repeated his tricks, every rehearsal had its surprise. His technique was described to me more than sixty years later by one of his choir boys, Thomas Prosser Browne, Verger at Trinity Church and later at St. Agnes' Chapel in Trinity Parish. Mr. Browne was himself a noble and distinguished character, affectionately remembered by all my family, and I am glad of an excuse for putting him into this book. He as much as anyone I have known developed his talents to the utmost, and made his life complete. He joined Dr. Cutler's choir at the end of the Civil War, and he told me what happened at the first rehearsal. When Dr. Cutler appeared in the choir room, urbane and misleadingly casual, the boys fell silent and fixed their eyes on him. The Doctor looked over the music to be rehearsed and, apparently lost in thought, took out a cigar, opened his pocketbook, chose a clean new dollar bill, rolled it into a taper, stuck it into the candle flame on the piano, let it burn more than half its length, very deliberately lighted the cigar with what was left, recollected himself with a sudden start, smiled sheepishly at his imps. "Bless my soul, boys, what am I doing? Of course we shouldn't smoke *here*. We'll sing now, if you please." The boys were a bit older before they discovered that the bill was an imitation.

Dr. Cutler's method of getting attention was a bribe, yet all education is a system of rewards. The only fault I see in the cigar-lighting is that the bribe had nothing to do with the art in which Dr. Cutler was training his disciples. Parenthood at its best puts children early in the way of discovering for themselves that the reward of good behavior, of conscientious study, or of any accomplishment, is power. The power may take the form of social credit, or of control over one's environment, or of practical facility in whatever the child wishes to do, but it must be real power and the child must be conscious of it. Unless we wish our children to think meanly of us, we'd better not try to bribe them by threadbare and quite untruthful maxims, like

> "Early to bed and early to rise
> Makes a man healthy, wealthy, and wise."

By the time we have children to bring up, our interest in this world has become somewhat routine and perhaps jaded. This should not be the case but it usually is. To the young, the world is still new and worth observing carefully. I doubt if they have quicker minds or better eyesight than their parents, but they are usually more alert. They know far more about us than we do about them, since they give us close attention. It's a waste of time to read books on child psychology written by adults unless we are willing to check every page by what children know about the psychology of parents. While we are telling a visitor the virtues and perhaps the faults of our offspring, the offspring can probably say what vanity leads us to boast or to pretend not to boast, how correct our statements are, and what the visitor thinks of them.

In this book I have explained from various angles my belief that men and women should take the active attitude toward life, should study in order to practice, should seek truth of all kinds in order to live more completely. The active attitude is natural in children, and parental discipline can do nothing wiser than encourage it. The child wishes to grow up as quickly as possible, to do the things which grown-ups do. We should encourage this ambition. When my children were able to reach the keyboard they naturally enjoyed thumping on the piano, a use of energy which nature prescribes next after learning to walk. I told my two young thumpers they could play the piano all they wished if between any two notes there should always be a space of at least one black note and one white note. By this provision I avoided unbearable discords and without their knowing it started them toward an acquaintance with the intervals of the scale.

If you wish to keep your small daughter quiet while you write a letter, ask her to write a letter too. Give her the same kind of paper, with an envelope; suggest writing to a definite person; be sure to supply a stamp. The child may be unable even to print, but unless there's a stamp and all the other trimmings, she'll think you're bluffing her. The stamp can be salvaged of course, and your purpose is not exclusively to secure quiet; you will arouse her curiosity about letter-writing, she knows that her scribbling is not the genuine thing, and she'll be readier to learn her letters because she already knows one purpose to which writing can be put.

If you live in the suburbs or the country where there is a garden, let the child help you outdoors. Indoors too, of course. I'm not suggesting that you make slaves of your children; I'm saying that it's natural for the young, as it should continue to be for their elders, to do things, to use their hands as well as their mind. They enjoy solving practical problems unaided. Some of the most modern schools, as I needn't remind you, base the education of the very young on this principle, presenting them with a series of life-like obstacles to be surmounted or got around by ingenuity and wit. These schools are patronized by wealthy parents who are glad to secure for their children, even at high cost, some of the educational advantages found in the streets by the children of the poor.

If we must punish our children, we should choose a constructive penalty. It is a mistake to inflict on them something which they dislike, merely because we know they will dislike it; out of this we get nothing but revenge. It is kinder and more helpful to withhold from them something they like, something which they ought to have or ought to do; the temporary deprivation will store up a greater eagerness to get at it. I have known some parents who guided their children by penalties still more refined, asking them to punish themselves. They would say, for example, "After this misbehavior do you think you still deserve to go to the circus? I leave it to you whether you go or not." The child may agree in its heart that some circus merits have been forfeited, yet rather than give up the entertainment it will probably insist on going— only to learn that conscience spoils the afternoon. I think this method errs on the side of severity, but it illustrates the main point that punishment as well as rewards may serve to educate. There is small excuse to punish for any other purpose.

A wise parent will avoid as far as possible a crisis which un- necessarily will bring on penalties. When we say to a child, "Don't do that," we impose a command without first enlisting co-opera- tion; we ask for obedience without appealing to intelligence. If our child wants advice, we *can* select one course of action over another, and without further discussion let the matter rest, but the child then will be under some obligation to follow our advice which will have small educative value unless we have explained the reasons for it. Most parents are intelligent enough to give the reasons along with the advice, but if we were very intelligent indeed we'd see that once the reasons are given the advice is superfluous; the child can draw its own conclusions, and should be encouraged to do so. It is said that Emerson rarely if ever gave his children a command, or told them that one course was right and the other wrong; he preferred to set forth clearly the results which would follow from one choice or another. He wished his children to become moral characters, which they could not be if others chose for them.

Whatever penalties or punishments are used in bringing up children, the child should never be made afraid, either of its parents or of anybody else. Haven't you heard a nerve-worn mother tell her irritating offspring to reform quickly or she'd call the policeman? Even worse, haven't you heard her say, "Just wait till your father gets home!" This kind of discipline makes of father a hangman, an executioner, and trains the child in a criminal's attitude toward the law. When your children go to school you wish them to work hard and do well; you ought to wish also that they will see life in its true proportions. Their education will be a failure if they set more value on the marks than on the knowledge which the marks very inaccurately stand for. It will be a failure if their motive to study is fear of the teacher. It will be a tragic failure if they study because they are afraid of you. Every year some boy or girl runs away from home or even commits suicide after failure in examinations, or in anticipation of failure. Such ghastly shipwrecks of parenthood are far more frequent than we guess. The majority of those who don't commit suicide go to school or face their examinations with fear at their heels.

Fear is a kind of insanity. There are indeed perils in the world, but most people are afraid of dangers which do not exist. We should help our children to be afraid of nothing, not even of danger. Danger should be guarded against as long as possible, and when it is unavoidable it should be faced; all of us, children and adults, face it best when our nerves are steady and our heads clear.

In my own teaching I early learned what miserable cowardice poisons the lives of many young men. More than once I made the unpleasant discovery that a student was cheating, copying his themes or lifting the answers to hard questions from his neighbor's paper. It isn't laziness which prompts this kind of dishonesty; it's fear. The student who cheats usually spends on dishonest schemes more ingenuity and more effort than are needed to master the subject, but conscious that he has neglected his work during the term, he takes the short-cut rather than risk a mark. Who taught him that a mark is worth such a price?

The first day my son went to school I accompanied him. He was then about five. The occasion was to him extremely important, but I went with him because it was still more important to me. He started in at the Riverdale Country School, not only because the Headmaster, Frank S. Hackett, was an old friend of mine since college days, but because the property on which the school stands once belonged to my grandfather, who in 1856 built the house which, somewhat modernized, is now the Headmaster's home. My father spent his childhood in the house and the grounds where my boy would now study and play.

As we came near the school I made him a little speech which I confess I had prepared with much thought. I said he was now entering a life which I knew from a different angle; he would recite in front of the desk and have his ideas about the teacher, but I being a teacher spent my life behind the desk and had my ideas about the boys in front. I couldn't understand why some of them were afraid, nor why anybody feared any person or thing. It broke my heart to see a boy cheat or to hear him tell a lie, dishonesty and fear being much the same thing.

I begged him never to be afraid of me. I proposed this agreement with him, that whenever he made a mistake or did something which he knew was wrong, even something very wrong indeed, he should tell me at once, and I for my part would not scold him nor say a word of reproach; we'd find the right way out together.

That was long ago. He is now a grown man doing his part with other men's sons in the army. We have carried out the agreement made that morning when he first went to school. It's the best piece of education I ever did. But to make this record complete I must confess that his education educated me, that in the carrying out of our agreement it was I who had to learn frankness. When he was about eighteen my own life got into a tangle and for a while I kept my trouble to myself, but at last I realized that I must tell him, if our companionship were to remain genuine. So I made a clean breast of it, and I assure you it was one of the most difficult moments of my life. He listened quietly. "Old man," he said, "d'you remember that day you took me to school? We promised to share our problems, didn't we? What you've just told me I heard three weeks ago." I admitted that I was in the wrong, and good talk with him helped me to patch up my life and go on.

In an earlier chapter I spoke of the fear of death, an adult fear which ought not to cross a child's mind. In the nursery and the school room other dreads threaten the beginnings of life. We adults might teach the family the great words of Henry Thoreau which wise statesmen recall to the nation in times of peril—"Nothing is so much to be feared as fear. Atheism may comparatively be popular with God himself."

4.

How large the ideal family should be, I prefer not to guess, but I'm convinced there should be at least two children, to grow up together. Even if there's only one, the father and mother must include in the scope of their parenthood whatever children their child knows. We can't bring up our young in isolation.

Nor can we choose our child's friends. Not entirely. As soon as they move around in the world at all, at their first parties, they will meet some boys and girls whom they like and some whom they don't like. Though our choice of companions might have been different, there's nothing we can do about it. Children here have the same responsibilities and privileges as their elders; we should be courteous to all our acquaintance but we choose our friends by temperament and taste.

Our treatment of the children who come to our home is determined by our wishes for our own youngsters when they go to other homes. Our standards of discipline should be respected; we must respect the standards of our neighbors. Being a parent is therefore a very broadening experience; we may not understand our child but we accumulate insight into the ideals and shortcomings of our contemporaries. We shall be under some pressure to conform to the ideals of the majority. If we take seriously the art of parenthood the majority will not be eager to imitate us; bringing up children, they feel, is burdensome enough, even when we do it crudely by rule of thumb.

When our children are old enough to entertain their friends— even in their third or fourth year—we may be tempted to take the entertaining out of their hands and do it for them. The impulse which leads to this mistake is in part kind, but partly also we are guarding ourselves against the confusion or the collapse of childish experiments. Yet those who take a longer view of education will make even the youngest child as responsible as possible, especially in all matters of hospitality. Children have their own kind instincts, and if put on their mettle will do the honors with surprising credit to themselves. They have a surer instinct than we have for the kind of entertainment their friends want. We can learn by watching them. I don't mean to suggest that when they have their friends in we should leave the house; I merely would give them the utmost freedom to entertain their contemporaries, always with the understanding that this freedom carries responsibility. After all, they are likely to be measurably the same kind of hosts that we are. They will imitate us, if we have allowed them to watch the entertaining we do. For that reason I think children should be included in informal grown-up parties as soon as they are old enough to be present without creating a disturbance.

I owe much to my own parents for allowing me to overhear fine talk and to meet people of interest and distinction. If my father brought a guest home to lunch, my mother allowed us to come to the table. We were not to talk or in any way interrupt the elders, but we could listen as hard as we liked. Before a formal dinner we were presented to the guests, and for this ceremony we dressed with great care. Afterwards we went off to the sitting room, which adjoined the dining room, and there we had our dinner, with the door open so that we could overhear the talk, silence on our part being obligatory. I suppose my parents brought us up on old-fashioned patriarchal theories, the easier to follow because our house was in the suburbs, in those days the country. But the educational value of meeting interesting men and women and of listening to mature conversation could have no equivalent.

When we we entertained other children my mother arranged for the refreshments but she expected us to act as hosts and hostesses, and to see that our friends had a good time. If she watched us while the party was in progress, I think it was to observe what her own children had still to learn in the practice of hospitality.

Let me state again the principle that children acquire the art of life by imitation. To have something to imitate they must associate with somebody—perhaps with us. In the end their conduct will be a comment upon ours. Many a boy or girl who has difficulty with certain school studies, such as mathematics or chemistry, will display skill at the wheel of a motor car, or at a card table. An automobile is a complicated machine and a bridge game nowadays is a scientific exercise. How can children who fail in school subjects possess these other accomplishments which are far more difficult? The explanation is simple. Father and Mother drive a car and play bridge, and the children have watched them. Father and Mother have not been seen studying mathematics or chemistry.

To be a parent with any success, therefore, we must lead a life more complete than is outlined in this book. We never can foresee the talents or the curiosities of our children, yet when they turn to us we should be ready. Those who bring up children well, find that they have completed their own education.

5.

We should not try to select our children's friends, still less should we choose their career. This last advice most fathers and mothers will accept, yet they are not likely to act on it. Not entirely. It is too natural for us to hope our children will have the kind of life which we enjoyed, or will have the opportunity which we missed. It is natural, that is, to think of the youngsters as merely an extension of ourselves. If our parents thought the same way of us, we no doubt resented the denial of our individuality. Once we grant that the children have a right to their own lives, we must concede also their right to the career which expresses them. That logical concession carries with it many implications.

A man may reasonably wish to take his son into the firm or to bequeath the business to him, yet this pious affection may be in essence unkind. The son, if left free, might prefer a different life. Even if he should choose the same work, there is an advantage in starting off among strangers, who will have no special reason for granting favors and from whom new ideas may be picked up. Continuity and stability are reassuring qualities. For their sake we sometimes forgive too readily an incomplete or one-sided development of character. Since we differ from each other in talents and possibilities, part of ourselves may be stifled before we are a close repetition of anybody else.

I'd be sorry to be misunderstood; where there is integrity there will be continuous and stable elements. What is genuine has a way of persisting, but continuity belongs to a growing, not to a static world, and growth is not repetition or duplication. What should persist is character, even though we express it from generation to generation in different activities. Some families have been great for more than a century, the successive descendants occupying themselves constantly in new directions; other families have preserved a good name by making themselves copies of their fathers, but in them we esteem most highly the first of the line, who was obviously the strongest since he pulled the others after him.

Girls even more than boys should be free to choose their career, and like the boys, they should have a career in addition to marriage. They more than their brothers are likely to be handicapped by the conservatism of affectionate parents. They will be brought up, as we say, "more carefully" than the boys in the decorum of a past age. Why not train them to a decorum contemporary with themselves? We parents know why not; we bring them up in the behavior we were taught. We are a little out of date. We insist all the more on the standards of our youth if, when we were young, we didn't ourselves live up to those standards. As we grow older we are haunted by regrets, however faint, and we would expiate our own errors by translating the regrets into obligations for our children. Many a wild boy becomes an over-strict parent. Juliet, had she survived, would have chaperoned her daughter carefully, and I am sure she would have distrusted all nurses.

It's rather shabby for us to live vicariously in our children, taking away their chance to be themselves, shirking our plain duty to move on with the age to which we belong. It isn't true, not in every respect, that we know more than they about life. Our youth was spent in a society which is gone. The children know more than we do about the society which is here. If a mother says to her daughter, "When I was young, it wasn't correct for a girl to do so-and-so," there is no reason why the daughter shouldn't reply, "But it's correct now." If we feel that daughter should have a better definition of correctness, we should admit that her definition is the same as Mother's. Both are speaking of the manners generally accepted in their youth.

What we can hand on are the truths which are independent of fashion, the truths which all generations must recognize in the physical world, the psychological, the moral, and the spiritual. I wouldn't go so far as to say that each generation must discover those truths afresh or apply them in a new way, but I would remind other parents of the warning which I give myself, that as we grow older we are liable to identify eternal truth with our private opinions.

This question of the child's career should from one point of view be postponed until the child can be fairly sure of what it wants. In extreme youth we all entertain for a season half a dozen incongruous ambitions. As I recall, I intended to be a pianist, a lawyer, a preacher, and somewhat earlier either a policeman or a fire chief. Yet in another sense a parent cannot too soon help the child in developing its talents and following its constructive ambitions. This is the first step toward the discovery of the proper career. The parent cannot learn too soon to distinguish between the development of the child's talents and interference with the child's use of them. All we have the right to insist on is that the talent should really be developed by employment, and that it should be employed for self-development, yet not selfishly. The children, for example, should be good hosts and hostesses at their own parties for the obvious purpose of giving their guests a pleasant time.

6.

It's an old saying that selfish parents have unselfish children, and unselfish parents have selfish children. I doubt if this rule is invariable, yet it seems to be illustrated often enough to impress us. The selfish parent demands much, and in answering that demand the child has little time to think of itself. The unselfish parent makes perhaps fewer demands than may be desirable. Yet the point here, I believe, is that the demands should never be for the benefit of the parent. On some economic levels children are thought of as additions to the earning capacity of the household; from that idea it is only a step to the persuasion that they should contribute, not to the family as a whole, but to the parents. Even where the parents need not ask for financial co-operation, they too easily can persuade themselves that the children owe them something. I doubt if they owe us anything. The love between parents which starts children toward existence is for that one moment the most egotistical and self-centered of passions. What we do then is not chiefly for the child's sake. If later our children are glad they are alive, their delight is probably in existence rather than in us. In bringing them up we should take all the care possible to cure them of selfishness, a fault which is natural in us all, but here, as in other branches of education, we teach best by example. To be thoughtful of those around us, to be interested in the fortunes of brothers and sisters, to be considerate of the neighbors, is a training not only in unselfishness but in decency, and parents should show themselves in all respects decent.

There are intellectual as well as moral disadvantages in selfishness, and unless we help our children to learn this truth they will miss the completeness of life which we wish for them. The selfish person closes his heart, but he also closes his eyes. Lacking interest in others, he does not observe them. He therefore fails to see much that would be for him important or advantageous. The writer or the painter, in order to come at his subject matter, trains himself to be all eyes and all ears; at his best he absorbs experience almost through his pores. But any man and woman who wishes to live fully can afford to do no less. A selfish person is always a little blind and a little deaf, having formed the habit of attending, not to the universe outside, but to himself.

In theology, as you know, there is a dispute as to how evil began. To say that Lucifer, the angel of light, revolted in heaven and made himself the prince of darkness, is a historical answer, not a philosophical one. Why did he revolt in the first place? How could an archangel, standing in the presence of God, have an evil thought? Jakob Boehme, the German mystic of the early seventeenth century, offered a simple and impressive explanation. He said that Lucifer certainly could not, in the presence of God, invent the idea of murder or theft or envy or hatred, but he could and did put his mind on something which might lead to crime and sin. He thought of himself. To stand in the presence of God and to lose interest in God sufficiently to think of one's self instead, is to make the supreme denial of light and life. Whether the old mystic did or did not solve the hard question, he left us a truth about human character. Before we can think of ourselves, as selfish folk do, we must shut out from our attention a large portion of the good which should be our inheritance.

The test of parental unselfishness comes when our children leave us. They probably will marry, but even if they don't, they will take up their own lives and unconsciously but firmly push us back into the elder generation where we belong. After years of trying to be their perfect companion, we may resent this disposal of us. My impression is that we behave better when our children marry and move away from the old home than when they leave us intellectually or spiritually. Yet we have no ground for any complaint. If they assume we will always be there to help them in difficulties, no matter what they do, they are not being selfish, they are paying us a tribute; it is our unfailing love for them which has bred this confidence. If they seem thoughtless in the speed with which they hurry toward a future which is not ours, we have only to ask whether, if we could, we would have them do otherwise. Unless they answer the call promptly, the door will be shut. Do we wish to detain them?

I doubt if there ever have been good parents who weren't a little hurt by the success of their own parenthood. Having taught the fledglings to use their wings, we are human enough to wish they would do their flying, at least for the first month or so, in the neighborhood of the old nest. We'd appreciate that evidence of loyalty and gratitude. Instead, our young birds fly away. They have dreams of the wide sky. Even while they were clamoring for the food we brought them, in their hearts they had already left us.

But this is exactly what they ought to do, and let's hope we taught them to do it. If they are eager to try their wings, they need plenty of room, apart from us, to make the venture. It is pleasant to hover over them, as we did in their babyhood, but until we let them go they cannot fill out their lives, nor, until they leave us, can our success as parents be complete.

CHAPTER XIV

The Self-made Man

BY WAY OF postscript I should like to say a word about the old-fashioned phrase which stands at the head of this chapter. The self-made man or woman was a person who, without the ordinary disciplines of education and without initial advantages of wealth or influence, created a career and established a place. The self-made man, as I first heard of him in my boyhood, was a heroic person, honored for independence and initiative. He was often better educated than those who had gone to school and to college or had enjoyed the other facilities which well-to-do parents could provide. In his mature years he was likely to be a rugged character, realistic, capable and resourceful.

He was likely to have, however, two faults which contradicted each other. He was usually over-assertive and over-modest. Because he had made his own way by pushing ahead against obstacles, he liked to say or imply that he was fortunate in his early poverty, and that those who started less poor were somehow his inferiors. If he had mastered a science by rule-of-thumb experience, he implied contempt for the scientific theorist, for the researcher, for the laboratory man. He would tell you how the schools should be reformed, and you observed from his suggested program that children should be taught exclusively the subjects which he had learned. On the other hand, the thought that he had missed formal opportunities of education gnawed at him. Along with his pride in real achievements, he nourished an inferiority complex. He was either embarrassed or humble in the presence of those who had received conventional training. He was likely to fall completely silent when he met a first-rate scientist or scholar.

I'd be happy indeed if anything said in this book helps to cure this inferiority complex. The self-made do themselves an injustice when they regret their lack of a college education; they are perhaps confessing no more than this, that they would have been glad to go through the social experience of the campus. When they say they taught themselves more than a college boy usually learns, they are probably telling the truth. What they miss is not knowledge but contact with college life, a youthful experience which, like other youthful experiences, becomes in memory sentimental or romantic.

I end this book thinking of my father who, like my grandfather, was a self-made man. He was graduated from high school quite young, and he intended to enter the College of the City of New York, which my Uncle Charles attended, but he first spent a year in my grandfather's business, and enjoying the excitement of acquitting himself well among men older than he, he stayed on. In his nature there was nothing assertive or otherwise ungentle, but all his life he regretted what he called his lack of education, and when I chose the teaching profession, he was glad. He used to visit me at Amherst College, and I'd gather little parties in his honor, groups of my fellow teachers. It broke my heart to see how unduly respectful on such occasions he was to them and to me. I happened to know that he was the best educated man in the room, but he couldn't be persuaded of this fact. In mathematics he was something of a genius. He was a passionate student of history and philosophy. His curiosity in scientific matters was unbounded, and he was an indefatigable traveler. He was athirst for truth, and he never wasted a moment; whatever leisure he could command went to study. He was a great man except for this, that he lacked trust in himself.

In ordinary times it is perhaps inevitable that we should overvalue methods and institutions, courses, diplomas and degrees, and shut our eyes to knowledge, the essential power. But when catastrophe overtakes the world, when institutions are destroyed or turned upside down, diplomas and degrees seem as secondary as they really are, and what counts is the genuine man. We are in that soul-searching condition today. Those who in our country and in all other lands rise up to meet desperate challenges, may or may not have attended schools and universities, but before this episode of history is finished we shall realize that they all are self-made men. At this moment they are educating themselves anew. As the fight progresses, our army and navy are re-educating themselves. Our schools are changing their curriculums. Our homes are adjusting to strange conditions. Under compulsion we look at life without self-delusion and teach ourselves any way we can to counter the blows, to strike back, and to push on to a good end.

What we do in emergency we should do always. Even in peace we should educate ourselves. School and university are opportunities merely; improve them as we may, they will remain no more than opportunities. The teacher does what he can, but in the end boy and girl educate themselves. After we leave the campus and the lecture hall, we still need to learn. In technical matters we find help in what the universities call extension courses, or we are aided by a lecture, or take books from the library. But no matter how few or how many the advantages which come our way, our lives in the end must be self-made, and the responsibility for the completed product will rest on us.

Strange that any human being should be content with less than the fullness of life! I take that back. We are not content to be less than we might be, but at times we do fail in courage, or we become tired and need a hand on our shoulder to hearten us. I need it often. When my spirits are a bit low, I give myself Goethe's advice,

"Remember to live."

Bibliography

SINCE THIS BOOK is addressed to the general reader the references here given do not pretend to constitute a comprehensive bibliography. I assume that it may be useful to know where a quotation comes from, or which is the most convenient edition of an author named. In almost all cases I mention books which I myself have used and which stand on the shelves of my own library. My experience in collecting books through a fairly long life has, I believe, a strong resemblance to the experience of others in my generation, and I doubt if younger readers will have a different story to tell. I have always wished to own more books than I could afford; my respect, therefore, for cheap editions is profound. Books in the United States are too expensive, but authors who have long been famous are accessible at a reasonable cost. It is a great pleasure to own an original edition; to hold in our hands the book as the author first put it out gives us a feeling that we have come nearer to his day and to his personality. But this is a luxury possible only for the rich. The first editions of important writers should be accessible to us all in the libraries of universities or nations or cities. Literature and the arts are our common heritage. It is only good sense to look for great books in editions which come within the range of the average pocketbook.

Even though the book costs little the text should be complete and accurately reproduced. If the book is translated, the translation should be the best available. These conditions have on the whole been better satisfied in Europe than in North America, but we begin to make progress.

The English poets are published in reasonably priced editions by the Oxford University Press; also by the Macmillan Company; also by Houghton Mifflin Company, who include in their Cambridge Edition the New England poets. Houghton Mifflin are also the publishers of the New England prose writers. For complete bibliographies of American writers consult the *Cambridge History of American Literature,* published by G. P. Putnam's Sons. Altogether the most convenient and reasonably priced edition of world literatures is the

Everyman's Library, published by J. M. Dent & Sons, London, and by E. P. Dutton & Company, New York. This large collection of books, well edited and printed, is in its way a monument to British scholarship and publishing, and all English-speaking readers have reason to be grateful for it.

On most of the subjects mentioned in this book there may be occasion to consult an encyclopedia, and the standard work of this kind for English readers is the many-volumed *Encyclopedia Britannica,* found in all public libraries. Recent editions represent the co-operation of American as well as British experts. The one-volume encyclopedia which I find myself consulting most frequently is the *Columbia Encyclopedia,* published by the Columbia University Press.

The Greek and Latin classics are well represented in the *Everyman's Library,* but we ought to be familiar with the *Loeb Classical Library,* founded by James Loeb and published by William Heinemann, London, and by G. P. Putnam's Sons, New York. The *Loeb Library* prints the original Greek or Latin text with the translation on the opposite page. If we have ever studied the ancient languages, even to a slight extent, the comparison of the translation with the original is provocative and enlightening. The beautifully printed books in this series cost more than the volumes of the *Everyman's Library*— in fact, they cost about as much as a popular novel.

There are other good and cheap editions besides those I here mention. Any bookseller will be glad to tell you about them. The best way to encourage good and cheap editions is to buy them. I hope my readers will form the book-owning habit. Book-owning of course includes book-using. It's bad for your soul to pick up a book or even a whole edition and then leave it unread. Buy whatever book you need at the moment. When you have read it—and not till then—buy another. You will probably get more out of your books on a second reading, or a third, or a fourth. I have been rereading my books for many years, and my friends do the same, whether or not they consider themselves scholars.

One final suggestion. Read some pages of every author out loud. Catch a patient friend when he is off his guard and read to him. If you enjoy the author and your friend does not, try to convert him by your reading. In any case you will learn two things at your friend's expense: the quality of the author's style, which can best be judged by the ear—and the degree to which you know how to read. Read as though there were no printed page. Read as though you were the author, talking face to face with a friend.

Chapter I:

In the Renaissance educated men and women held the very optimistic theory that by application it is possible to master the whole range of human knowledge. This theory, and the ideals which grew out of it, are summarized in a famous book, *The Civilization of the Renaissance in Italy*, by Jacob Burckhardt, translated by S. G. C. Middlemore, published by Swan Sonnenschein & Company, Ltd., in London, and in New York by the Macmillan Company.

Matthew Arnold's remark about the waiters in foreign hotels occurs in the second chapter of *Culture and Anarchy*.

Hakluyt's Voyages. *The Principal Navigations, Voyages, Traffiques & Discoveries of the English Nation Made by Sea or Overland to the Remote and Farthest Distant Quarters of the Earth at any time within the compasse of these 1600 Years, by Richard Hakluyt.* In the *Everyman's Library*, eight volumes.

Thomas Jefferson's relations with Patrick Henry can be studied in *Patrick Henry: Life, Correspondence, and Speeches*, by William Wirt Henry, Three Volumes, Charles Scribner's Sons.

"The *Present* onely has a being in Nature; things *Past* have a being in the Memory onely, but things *to come* have no being at all; the *Future* being but a fiction of the mind, applying the sequels of actions Past, to the actions that are Present; which with most certainty is done by him that has most Experience; but not with certainty enough. And though it be called Prudence, when the Event answereth our Expectation; yet in its own nature, it is but Presumption. For the foresight of things to come, which is Providence, belongs onely to him by whose will they are to come. From him onely, and supernaturally, proceeds Prophecy. The best Prophet naturally is the best guesser; and the best guesser, he that is most versed and studied in the matters he guesses at: for he hath most *Signes* to guesse by." Thomas Hobbes, *Leviathan*, Part I, Chapter III, *Everyman's Library*.

In the Gospel according to St. Matthew, Chapter V, there are eight beatitudes. St. Luke, Chapter VI, gives four. "Blessed are the meek" is the third beatitude in St. Matthew.

Walt Whitman's remark about the perfect user of words is quoted from p. 14 of *An American Primer*, by Walt Whitman, edited by Horace Traubel. Boston, Small Maynard and Company.

The Art of Thinking, by Ernest Dimnet, Simon & Schuster.

For an account of the Battle of Bunker Hill, the *Columbia Encyclopedia* suggests that we consult *The Siege of Boston*, by R. Frothingham.

Chapter II:

William Wordsworth, who cultivated simplicity in his poems, was fond of complicated titles. The full title of the Tintern Abbey verses is, *Lines Composed a Few Miles Above Tintern Abbey, on Revisiting the Banks of the Wye During a Tour. July 13, 1798.*

There are many excellent translations of Homer's *Iliad,* but the one which I read in my youth and still prefer is that by Andrew Lang, Walter Leaf, and Ernest Meyers. My favorite translation of *The Odyssey* is by S. H. Butcher and Andrew Lang. Both these translations are in prose and both are published by the Macmillan Company.

Walt Whitman's comment on the location of the city of Washington occurs in a letter from him to the *New York Times,* Sunday, October 4, 1863. The passage can be found on p. 35, Vol. II, of *The Uncollected Poetry and Prose of Walt Whitman,* edited by Emory Holloway. New York, Peter Smith.

The old book of travels was called *Illustrated Travels: A Record of Discovery, Geography, and Adventure,* edited by H. W. Bates, Assistant-Secretary of the Royal Geographical Society, with engravings from original drawings by celebrated artists, London: Cassell, Petter & Galpin; and 596 Broadway, New York.

Montaigne's *Essays* are available in the *Everyman's Library,* three volumes. The translation is that of John Florio. This is the great Elizabethan translation which Shakespeare used. Charles Cotton, seventeenth century poet and friend of Izaak Walton, made a version of the Essays which in many respects is closer to the original but which lacks the energy of Florio. An excellent modern translation is by Jacob Zeitlin, published by Alfred A. Knopf, three volumes.

Plutarch's Lives are published in the *Everyman's Library,* three volumes, in the Dryden translation, revised by the poet Arthur Hugh Clough, Matthew Arnold's friend. The *Everyman's Library* contains in one volume twenty of Plutarch's essays under the title *Moralia,* in the translation of Philemon Holland, contemporary of Edmund Spenser and William Shakespeare.

The edition of Edgar Allan Poe's works which I have always used is that by Edmund Clarence Stedman and George Edward Woodberry, published by Stone and Kimball, Chicago. A more modern edition is *The Complete Works of Edgar Allan Poe,* edited by J. A. Harrison. The *Everyman's Library* contains in one volume the poems and selected prose.

The only complete edition of Milton's works is the Columbia University edition in eighteen volumes. *The Tenure of Kings and Magistrates* is included in Vol. V. Milton's prose works are published also in the Bohn Library, London, George Bell & Sons. *The Tenure of Kings and Magistrates* is included in Vol. II.

For the student, the desirable edition of Shakespeare is that made by William Aldis Wright in nine volumes, published by Macmillan & Company, Ltd., London, and by the Macmillan Company, New York. One-volume editions of Shakespeare are satisfactory if the print is large enough. The Temple edition of Shakespeare's works which gives each play in a separate volume of pocket size, and the Sonnets in a single volume, follows the text of the William Aldis Wright edition. Israel Gollancz edited the Temple volumes. The publisher was J. M. Dent & Company, London. Shakespeare's works are in the *Everyman's Library,* three volumes.

The most famous translation of Plato in modern times is that by Benjamin Jowett. The most beautiful translation of the *Symposium* is that by Percy Bysshe Shelley, published in the *Everyman's Library* in a volume entitled *Ion and Four Other Dialogues.*

Both Herodotus and Thucydides are available in the *Everyman's Library.*

Sydnor Harrison, best known for his novel, *Queed.*

H. A. J. Munro's remarkable translation of *Lucretius* is published in a single volume in the Bohn Library, George Bell & Sons, London. There is an excellent translation by W. E. Leonard in the *Everyman's Library.*

Dante's great poem was published in the Temple Classics by J. M. Dent & Company, London. The original text appears on one page, the prose translation by John Aitken Carlyle, younger brother of Thomas Carlyle, on the page opposite. The Temple Classics contain also in one volume *The Early Italian Poets Together With Dante's Vita Nuova,* translated by D. G. Rossetti. The translations from François Villon appear in *The Poems of Dante Gabriel Rossetti,* two volumes, published by Little, Brown & Company.

An excellent translation by Denis Florence Mac-Carthy of Calderón's *La Vida es Sueño (Life Is a Dream),* is included in *The Chief European Dramatists,* selected and edited by Brander Matthews, Houghton Mifflin Company.

Don Quixote is well translated in the *Everyman's Library,* two volumes.

Anatole France's *Rotisserie de la Reine Pédauque* is translated in the *Everyman's Library*.

An excellent account of South American literature is found in *The Epic of Latin American Literature*, by Arturo Torres-Rioseco, Oxford University Press.

The quotation about the waters of Lethe is from a letter of George Edward Woodberry to me.

The Idea of a University, by John Henry Cardinal Newman, Longmans Green & Company.

The story of Naaman is given in the fifth chapter of the Second Book of Kings.

The Delight of Great Boons, by John Erskine, the Bobbs-Merrill Company.

The Summing Up, by W. Somerset Maugham, Doubleday, Doran & Company.

Chapter III:

The best encyclopedia of music available in English is *Grove's Dictionary of Music and Musicians*, six volumes, now published in this country by Theodore Presser Company, Philadelphia.

An excellent one-volume encyclopedia is *International Encyclopedia of Music and Musicians*, by Oscar Thompson, Published by Dodd, Mead & Company.

For a survey of the nature and history of the art, the following are recommended:

Music in Western Civilization, by Paul Henry Lang, published by W. W. Norton & Company.

The Layman's Music Book, by Olga Samaroff Stokowski, W. W. Norton & Company.

The Gist of Music, by George A. Wedge, G. Schirmer, Inc.

A Musical Companion, edited by John Erskine, Alfred A. Knopf.

Our New Music, Leading Composers in Europe and America, by Aaron Copland, Whittlesey House.

What to Listen for in Music, Aaron Copland, Whittlesey House.

Notation, C. F. Abdy Williams, The Walter Scott Publishing Company, London, and Charles Scribner's Sons, New York.

Two books particularly inspiring to the amateur are, *A Little Night Music*, by Gerald W. Johnson, Harper & Brothers, and *Playing the Piano for Pleasure*, by Charles Cooke, Simon and Schuster.

For an understanding of the orchestral instruments, the most helpful book is *Orchestration,* by Cecil Forsyth, published by the Macmillan Company.

There are many excellent books on harmony. For an understanding of modern music, the reader should consult *Modern Harmony in its Theory and Practice,* by Arthur Foote and Walter R. Spalding, published by Arthur P. Schmidt, Boston and New York.

Since the music dramas of Richard Wagner will be known in some form to practically all the readers of this book, I recommend *A Musical Guide to Richard Wagner's Ring of the Nibelung,* by Ernest Hutcheson, published by Simon and Schuster. This is a serious study for the use of well-grounded musicians, yet it will prove stimulating for any amateur already acquainted with Wagner.

Other volumes recommended:

The State of Music, by Virgil Thomson, William Morrow & Company.

Men of Music, by Wallace Brockway and Herbert Weinstock, Simon and Schuster.

The Book of Modern Composers, edited by David Ewen. Alfred A. Knopf.

The Well Tempered Listener, by Deems Taylor, Simon and Schuster.

Books on the dance are suggested in the text. The titles are here given in full: *Balletomania; The Story of an Obsession,* by Arnold L. Haskell, Simon and Schuster.

Ballet Laughs, by Alex Gard, The Greystone Press.

Nijinsky, by Romola Nijinsky, Simon and Schuster.

Other works suggested:

The Dance of Life, Havelock Ellis, Houghton Mifflin Company, and in the *Modern Library.*

The Dance As Education, by Diana Jordan, Oxford University Press.

The Dance: Its Place in Art and Life, by Troy and Margaret West Kinney, Frederick A. Stokes Company.

How to Become a Good Dancer, by Arthur Murray, Simon and Schuster.

Eurhythmics, Art and Education, by E. Jacques-Dalcroze, translated by Frederick Rothwell, A. S. Barnes & Co.

The American Ballet, Ted Shawn.

A work which covers the whole field of the arts in popular but stimulating fashion is *The Arts,* by Hendrik Willem Van Loon, Simon and Schuster.

Choreographic Music: Music for the Dance, by Verna Arvey, E. P. Dutton and Company.

Modern Dancing and Dancers, J. E. Crawford, J. B. Lippincott Company.

Dancing in All Ages, by Edward Scott.

Chapter IV:

Miss Millay's sonnet, "Euclid alone hath looked on beauty bare," is included in her volume, *The Harp-Weaver and Other Poems,* Harper & Brothers.

The following works will be found helpful:

Making Watercolor Behave, by Eliot O'Hara, published by Minton, Balch & Company.

History of Art, by Elie Faure, four volumes, Harper & Brothers.

American Architecture, by Fiske Kimball, The Bobbs-Merrill Company.

The Enjoyment of Architecture, by Talbot F. Hamlin, Duffield & Co.

Art as Experience, by John Dewey, published by Minton, Balch & Company.

The Sculpture of Boris Lovet-Lorski, by Merle Armitage, published by E. Weyhe.

The Outline of Art, edited by Sir William Orpen, two volumes, G. P. Putnam's Sons.

The Modern House in America, by James Ford, Architectural Book Publishing Company, New York.

Design This Day, by Walter D. Teague, Harcourt, Brace & Company.

Modern Housing, Catherine Bauer, Houghton Mifflin Company.

Art and the Machine, by Sheldon Cheney, Whittlesey House.

Chapter V:

The American Boy's Handy Book, by D. C. Beard, published by Charles Scribner's Sons.

Wake Up and Garden, by Ruth Cross, Prentice-Hall, Inc.

What To Do with Herbs, by Mary Cable Dennis, E. P. Dutton & Co., Inc.

The Escoffier Cook Book and Guide to the Fine Art of Cookery, The Crown Publishers.

Gourmet Dinners, by G. Selmer Fougner, published by M. Barrows & Co., Inc.

The Boston Cooking School Cook Book, by Fannie Merritt Farmer, published by Little, Brown & Company.

World Wide Cook Book, by Pearl V. Metzelthin, published by Julian Messner, Inc.

Madame Prunier's Fish Cookery Book, edited by Ambrose Heath, adapted for America by Crosby Gaige, published by Julian Messner, Inc.

Guide du Maître d'Hôtel et du Restaurateur, by J. Rey, published by Carmona & Baker, London.

For Men Only, by Achmed Abdullah and John Kenny, published by G. P. Putnam's Sons.

Edith Key Haines' Cook Book, published by Farrar & Rinehart.

The Complete Menu Book, by Gladys T. Lang, Houghton Mifflin Company.

Let's Cook, A Cookbook for Beginners of All Ages, by Nancy Hawkins, Alfred A. Knopf.

Chapter VI:

The Poetical Works of Thomas Carew, edited by Joseph Woodfall Ebsworth, Reeves and Turner, London.

Swift's satire on conversation is published in Vol. IX of *The Prose Works of Jonathan Swift, D.D.,* edited by Temple Scott, George Bell & Sons, London.

Chapter VII:

Cranford, by Mrs. Elizabeth Gaskell, *Everyman's Library.*

The Courtier, by Baldesar Castiglione, translated by Leonard Eckstein Opdycke. Charles Scribner's Sons. Also translated by W. H. D. Rouse, *Everyman's Library.*

The Nicomachean Ethics, Aristotle, translated by D. P. Chase, *Everyman's Library.*

Chapter VIII:

Emerson's references to strangers or foreigners are found in Vol. V of his *Journals,* pp. 47 and 49.

Wordsworth's lines occur in his sonnet *On the Extinction of the Venetian Republic.*

Plato's *Republic* and *The Laws* are translated by Benjamin Jowett. The *Republic,* translated by A. D. Lindsay, is included in *Everyman's Library.*

Chapter IX:

For an introduction to Judaism, the following books are suggested by Rabbi Solomon B. Freehof, Rodef Shalom Temple, Pittsburgh:

Jewish Theology, by K. Kohler, the Macmillan Company.

Studies in Judaism, by S. Schechter, Jewish Publication Society. Three volumes.

Judaism as in Creed and Life, by Morris Joseph, Rutledge, London.

What Do Jews Believe? by Enelow, the Cincinnati Union of American Hebrew Congregations Press.

What Is Reform Judaism? by Freehof, Cincinnati Union of American Hebrew Congregations Press.

As an introduction to Catholicism, the following titles are suggested by Dr. George N. Schuster, President of Hunter College. I am deeply in debt to Dr. Freehof and to Dr. Schuster for their aid.

The Faith of Our Fathers, by J. Cardinal Gibbons.

The Question Box, by B. L. Conway.

The Spirit of Catholicism, by K. Adam.

The Catholic Church in Action, by M. Williams and J. Kernan.

The Vatican as a World Power, by J. Bernhart.

The Primacy of the Spiritual, by J. Maritain.

Jesus Christ, by L. de Grandmaison.

The *Summa Theologica* of St. Thomas Aquinas is literally translated by the Fathers of the English Dominican Province, published by Washburn, London.

Probably the best approach to St. Thomas Aquinas is through the selections translated by Joseph Rickaby under the title of *God and His Creatures.* Herder, London.

A standard work dealing with many of the ideas referred to in this chapter is *The Medieval Mind,* Henry Osborn Taylor, the Macmillan Company, New York.

No student of religion should overlook *Mont-Saint-Michel and Chartres,* by Henry Adams, Houghton Mifflin Company.

Least of all should he overlook *The Spirit of Man,* a remarkable anthology from the philosophers and poets, made by Robert Bridges in 1915, and published by Longmans Green & Co.

Verba Christi, The Sayings of Jesus Christ, the Temple Classics, J. M. Dent & Company. In this little book, of convenient pocket size, the sayings of Jesus are given in English and in Greek.

The Annotated Book of Common Prayer, being an Historical, Ritual and Theological Commentary on the Devotional System of the

Church of England, edited by the Rev. John Henry Blunt, E. P. Dutton and Company.

The *Religio Medici* is published in *Everyman's Library*. I have read it most often in the Golden Treasury edition, published by Macmillan and Company, London. In another volume of this series appears the *Urn Burial* and the *Garden of Cyrus*. The best complete edition is *The Works of Sir Thomas Browne,* edited in six volumes by Geoffrey Keynes. London: Faber and Faber, Ltd. New York: William Edwin Rudge.

Gibbon's *Decline and Fall* is published in *Everyman's Library,* 6 vols.

A Discourse of Method, René Descartes, translated by J. Beitch. *Everyman's Library.*

The Advancement of Learning, Francis Bacon, *Everyman's Library.*

The two lines from Walt Whitman begin the poem, *Debris,* one of his finest things, which for some reason he rejected from his later editions.

Sénancour, *Obermann.* Paris, Librairie E. Droz. The words which I have translated freely occur in Letter 90. I give them here in the original: "L'homme est périssable.—Il se peut; mais périssons en résistant, et, si le neant nous est réservé, ne faisons pas que ce soit une justice."

Chapter X:

There are a number of famous books, all available in *Everyman's Library,* which come to mind in any discussion of politics. For example:

The Republic, Plato, translated by A. D. Lindsay; *Politics,* Aristotle, translated by W. Ellis; *Gulliver's Travels,* Jonathan Swift; *Areopagitica,* John Milton; *Two Treatises on Civil Government,* John Locke; *The Federalist,* Alexander Hamilton and others; *The Prince,* Nicolò Machiavelli; *The Governour,* Sir Thomas Elyot; *The Rights of Man,* Thomas Payne; *The Social Contract and Other Essays,* Jean Jacques Rousseau; *Capital,* Karl Marx. *Spirit of the Laws,* Montesquieu, is translated by Thomas Nugent, and published by George Bell, London. *The Communist Manifesto* is included in a volume entitled, *Capital, The Communist Manifesto, and Other Papers,* by Karl Marx, in The Modern Library, Bennett A. Cerf, publisher.

Chapter XI:

Reason in Society, George Santayana; New York, Charles Scribner's Sons. The quotation occurs in the first chapter.

Daphnis and Chloe, Longus, translated by George Thornley. The Loeb Classical Library, G. P. Putnam's Sons.

Vita Nuova, Dante, translated by Dante Gabriel Rossetti, in the Temple Classics, J. M. Dent & Sons.

The Ordeal of Richard Feverel, George Meredith, Charles Scribner's Sons.

Byron, André Maurois, translated by Hamish Miles, D. Appleton and Company.

Sex and Character, by Otto Weininger. G. P. Putnam's Sons.

Bleak House, by Charles Dickens, *Everyman's Library.*

The story of Tobit is told in the Apocryphal book by that name.

Of Human Bondage, by Somerset Maugham, Doubleday, Doran & Co., Inc.

Guinicelli's *Canzone* is contained in the volume of the Temple Classics already referred to, *The Early Italian Poets Together With Dante's Vita Nuova,* translated by D. G. Rossetti.

The quotation from Tennyson occurs in the idyll called *Guinevere.*

Chapter XII:

Excerpts from Dan Michel of Northgate are given in *Specimens of Early English,* Part II, edited by Morris and Skeat; Oxford, the Clarendon Press. The "Sawles Warde" is included in Part I of the same work.

The Epithalamion should be compared with Spenser's *Fowre Hymnes,* included in all complete editions of the poet—the *Hymn in Honor of Love,* the *Hymn in Honor of Beauty,* the *Hymn in Honor of Heavenly Love,* and the *Hymn in Honor of Heavenly Beauty.*

The quotations from Milton are found in the Fourth Book of *Paradise Lost*—all except the final quotation, which concludes the epic.

Chapter XIII:

The reader should consult Milton's letter to Samuel Hartlib, *Of Education,* contained in Vol. IV of the complete works, Columbia University Press.

Also Montaigne's essay on the education of children, addressed in the form of a letter to Diane de Foix, Comtesse de Gurson.

Milton's Latin poems are translated in the Columbia edition, Vol. I; also in the Cambridge edition, Houghton Mifflin Company.

"The Reason of Church Government Urged Against Prelaty" is included in the third volume of the Columbia edition.

Index